James and Thomas Publishing Inc.
Suite #626
105, 150 Crowfoot Crescent NW
Calgary, AB   T3G 3T2
Canada

ISBN 978-0-981-161-0-8
Revised Edition
Copyright 2009 by Brent Stoesz
Printed and bound in Canada

The Gluten-Free Chef
Cooks What You Crave

A comprehensive guide to removing gluten from your diet without removing your favourite foods

Table of Contents

Introduction _____ 8

My Journey _____ 9

Why Gluten-Free _____ 10

Can't Eat It – Says Who_____ 11

Dealing With the Urge to Cheat _____ 12

Finding Hidden Gluten Without Eating It First _____ 14

Being Gluten-Free in a Wheaty Home _____ 15

The Gluten-Free Label_____ 17

Eating Out Gluten Free: A Chef's Perspective_____ 19

The Restaurant Card _____ 23

Travelling Gluten-Free _____ 25

You Are Invited… _____ 28

Baking Gluten-Free _____ 29

Working with Bread Machines _____ 31

Following the Directions_____ 33

Where is the Gluten-Free Flour Mix? _____ 35

The Gluten-Free Pantry_____ 36

Helpful Hints _____ 42

Recipe Conversions _____ 47

Nutritional Information _____ 49

Breakfast and Brunch _____ 50

Lunch Options _____ 70

Easy Hot Lunches _____ 76

Muffins _____ 78

Breads and Flat-Breads _____ 100

Gluten-Free Grains, Pastas and Side Dishes _____ 136

Stocks and Soups _____ 171

    Stocks _____ 171

    Soups _____ 186

Sauces _____ 208

Batters and Coatings _____ 230

Holidays _____ 242

Sweets _____ 266

Index _____ 336

Acknowledgements

First of all I would like to thank my "in house" team of tasters, testers, editors, challengers, critics and motivators for supporting this endeavour, celebrating my discoveries, and not grumbling too much when I discovered the next recipe to never make again. Joan, Jim and Tom, without you this book would not exist.

Heartfelt thanks goes to everyone who shared your experiences with me and have given this book a perspective that would have been lacking without your contributions. Your honesty when confiding your struggles and strategies has been this book's guiding vision. Your encouragement has made this long project a much easier task.

A special thanks to those who tried and tested my recipes and challenged me to make them understood by everyone, even novice cooks.

Finally, I would like to thank everyone who has helped bring this book to print. The seeds of this book have been nurtured and tended throughout the whole of my career as a chef by too many people to name. I wish to share this accomplishment with each of them as they have added a piece of themselves to what is now the persona of, "The Gluten-Free Chef."

Introduction

My first requests for gluten-free meals came almost twenty-five years ago while I was an apprentice, beginning my career as a chef. Although I had completed my formal schooling in professional cooking, it was during my apprenticeship when I received the first really useful information regarding gluten-free cooking. This information was handed to me by a nervous restaurant patron who was fearful of becoming ill, but wanted to enjoy a delicious, safe restaurant meal. This patron's gluten-free information was simply printed on a business card.

Prior to receiving that card my formal schooling in professional cooking had consisted of a few hours of instruction about many special diets including gluten-free, diabetic, low fat, high protein, cross contamination control measures for severe allergies, as well as religious restrictions necessary for Kosher and Halal cooking. Clearly, a few hours was not enough time to address the vast topic of special dietary needs and much more time was needed.

Fortunately, over the last twenty-five years I have learned a great deal about many special diets, including gluten-free. I would like to share my expertise with you, offer you a few 'tricks of the trade', and of course provide you with my version of a 'gluten-free information' business card. After all, it was invaluable to me and is a tool which I still consider to be one of the most important items a person requiring a gluten-free diet can use.

My Journey

As chef of a number of private clubs, I found that several club members had celiac disease. Therefore, they were unable to tolerate any gluten. By catering to their needs I gained their trust, and soon I was cooking for the monthly meetings of the local celiac association. I enjoyed the challenge of creating wonderful meals without gluten, but even more gratifying were the heartfelt expressions of thanks and relief that came from my patrons enjoying their worry-free dining experience.

Having developed a 'gluten-free following' throughout my career I have been sought out by gluten-intolerant patrons in the various establishments I have operated. As my career progressed, many of these patrons followed me, even when I changed establishments. Obviously, these patrons appreciated my desire to cater to their needs, but they also helped fulfill a personal need in me as well.

My personal and professional drive is guided by never saying, "I can't do that." In fact, I feel so strongly about this "can't" is considered a 'bad word' in my home because it's only value is in making excuses for not trying. Therefore, being told that something could not be prepared using only gluten-free ingredients has become a wonderful, welcome challenge in my career.

My interest in gluten-free cooking took on greater vigor when the need for a gluten-free diet became necessary for two members of my family. Almost simultaneously, my sister was diagnosed with celiac disease and a trial of a gluten-free diet was suggested for my son. If you tell a chef he can make a sick member of his family well by cooking, you can be assured you will find him in the kitchen stirring up a batch of tasty medicine.

To avoid the risk of any cross-contamination issues, I chose to make my kitchen completely gluten-free. I know this decision may not work for everyone, but it has been the best for my family. Happily, very shortly after adopting the gluten-free diet my son's health significantly improved. The wonderful, unexpected side effect to my own health was that my chronic headaches disappeared. Now, three of four members within my immediate family benefit from being gluten-free. Hopefully, you will benefit from my recipes as well.

As a chef, my philosophy has always been that food is more about enjoyment than it is about sustenance; and that taste, texture, nutrition and appearance are primary goals. I believe that good food is a basic human right. Special dietary needs should not be allowed to take the joy and fellowship out of eating.

In all cultures the act of gathering around to eat plays a huge role in the social fabric of the family and the society. My personal interest in ethnically diverse cuisines has given me many gluten-free alternatives. I have always had the utmost respect and admiration for the culinary expertise demonstrated by many cultures around the world. Many of these cultures use little or no gluten grains in their daily cooking and by doing so have created a gluten-free diet which I include ideas from within this book.

Why Gluten-Free?

A gluten-free diet will not harm anyone and for that reason it may be suggested as a supplementary therapy for many conditions. It is well documented that gluten can have many different, undesired effects for susceptible persons. The reasons for being on a gluten-free diet are numerous and entirely secondary because all those who need to be gluten-free for health reasons find themselves in the same situation - searching for resources and trying to cope. I wish that all those who must avoid gluten could present a united front to food manufacturers, retailers and the public in general. With greater numbers and a broader diagnosis base we would have much more influence. The diagnosis based resource groups seem to cause a fragmentation of gluten intolerant persons into small and much less effective groups. The information which could be so valuable to everyone isn't being adequately shared and the general public is not getting a true picture of just how many people need to be gluten-free.

The most common reason to give up gluten is a diagnosis of celiac disease, but adopting a gluten-free diet can have positive effects on many other conditions as well. Crohn's disease, colitis, rheumatoid arthritis, multiple sclerosis, attention deficit disorder, autism, eczema, psoriasis, and migraines have all been shown to respond favorably to a gluten-free diet.

Coping with removing gluten from our diet is often a daunting challenge. In North America, the classic foods we all know are based upon bread or gluten grains. Toast, pancakes, bagels and cereals are among the staples of breakfast. Lunch doesn't get any easier with sandwiches, burgers, pasta and pizza being the usual fare. Dinner offers some relief, as meat and potato-style cooking requires minimal changes to make most dishes work. But the ever-present dinner roll sitting beside our plate shows that bread is never far away. We are faced with a shift in thinking to 'get the bread out'.

Whatever has brought you to need a gluten free lifestyle; we are all faced with the same challenges. While we can bake gluten-free bread products that are reasonable replacements to the 'wheaty' breads we have come to rely upon, another option is available to us. We can explore the alternatives used in countries where bread is not the staple. Tortillas, rice wraps, soups and stews, stir fries, cooked gluten-free grains and sushi rolls are only a few of the international solutions. Rather than feeling limited by a need to exclude gluten from our diet, we can enjoy more diversity than ever before.

Can't Eat It – Says Who?

Deprivation is the main reason for 'falling off the wagon' so my aim is to banish deprivation. I do not see it as my role to tell you what to eat, only to enable you to safely eat what you want. This book is a, 'how to still eat what I want' guide, and contains gluten-free versions of many of the most loved and missed dishes.

Experimentation in my own gluten-free test kitchen has resulted in a collection of recipes and techniques that friends and family have encouraged me to publish. This collection has grown as I have met more people living gluten-free and I have willingly taken up the challenge of fulfilling their, "I really wish I could eat..." lists. Those lists, when coupled with my considerable culinary experience and my abundant stubbornness have become the contents of this book.

The recipes within this book have been adapted to make them taste and appear as close to the original gluten containing item as possible. My knowledge of food chemistry has been extremely useful when creating my recipes. Understanding how each ingredient contributes to the final product has allowed for seemingly impossible recipes to work, albeit sometimes with seemingly odd procedures. I strongly urge you to thoroughly read the introductory information provided at the beginning of each section as well as the specific directions for each recipe to ensure the best possible outcome.

A balanced diet is also a desired outcome. Therefore, to help you make informed decisions to achieve this goal nutritional information has been included for each recipe, not including variations. The recipes are all basics to build on. Rather than attempting to create recipes which follow all the latest trends in flavour profiles, I have included basic recipes followed by several variations to add more variety to these basics. Feel free to try the recipes once as written and then customize them as you wish with whatever suits you. I think you will find that your families' favorite treat may well be a variation on one of the basic recipes found here.

I have intentionally focused on dishes that were obviously originally wheat based. Therefore, I have included very few recipes for foods requiring nothing more than a 'double check' of the ingredients to ensure they are gluten-free. I don't want to insult your intelligence by filling a book with recipes that were virtually gluten-free to begin with and require very little modification to make them safely gluten-free. I believe that rather than feeling deprived, we should enjoy indulging our cravings safely with foods that have been reworked to suit our dietary needs.

I would love to write that everything on my, "I really wish I could eat…" list has been achieved, but my refusal to believe that anything is impossible still has me trying to make gluten-free phyllo pastry and… Perhaps in my next book.

Dealing With the Urge to Cheat

Let's face it, when we realize there are foods we can't / shouldn't eat anymore, we feel deprived. For many the next hopeful question is, "A little can't hurt, can it?" Well, it can. Our bodies know this and will remind us of this fact in rather unpleasant ways. So, what do we do now? The only sensible solution to feeling deprived is to fill the void with a suitable substitute. Fortunately, wheat and other gluten containing grains are generally the bland filler in most dishes, not the source of the flavours we tend to crave. As a chef, I have found that the best way to deal with cravings is to create satisfying gluten-free alternatives. That is why this book is filled with delicious recipes for foods commonly missed and frequently requested.

Removing gluten from your diet is a massive change. For some, it means learning to cook from scratch for the first time. For others, it means learning to cook all over again without gluten. Regardless of your previous cooking experience, developing the skills needed to prepare wholesome, tasty gluten-free foods will help you stay on track and not give in to your impulse to cheat. Fine tuning your ability to track down commercially available gluten-free products and scour the labels of packages in your supermarket will also improve your chances of remaining gluten-free.

Unfortunately, high prices for products that don't compare well with their wheaty counterparts may leave you with feelings of deprivation in your wallet as well as your stomach. Companies producing gluten-free products have different considerations than those of us who cook at home. Shelf life, ease of mechanized manufacturing, and profit margin are frequently their priorities. However, the considerations important to consumers; taste, texture and freshness, may suffer.

Another point to consider is that whenever the word "diet" is paired with a medical diagnosis, there can be a tendency to look only at the nutritional analysis of the foods, not at the emotional impact of the dramatic lifestyle change that must occur in order to remain healthy. Recognizing this reality, the recipes within this book will enable you to once again make pizza, perogies, chocolate chip cookies, cheesecake or whatever it is you can't live without. Adopting a gluten free lifestyle is challenging enough without further complicating matters by ignoring the very real emotional aspects that accompany it. The intent of this book is to make your gluten free life a little easier and tastier.

Who doesn't look forward to the comfort food they crave at the end of the day? Overindulgence in those comfort foods has its own risks, but with the recipes in this book at least gluten won't be a problem. Many of my 'indulgent' offerings can be portioned and frozen to enjoy fresh-baked (a few at a time) whenever the urge strikes you. A few delicious gluten-free fresh baked chocolate chip cookies will mollify that craving better than a whole bag of store-bought.

Peer pressure and lack of understanding from those around you can make sticking with a gluten-free diet even more difficult. Remember, it is your health so stand your ground. Without being too graphic, explain that gluten-free food is your medicine and without it you become ill. In conversations try to avoid the word "diet." It seems everyone is on a diet these days and cheating on diets is the norm rather than the exception. In all likelihood when those around you have a greater understanding of your situation they will be supportive and accommodating of your needs. A friend who will not support you isn't much of a friend. Most importantly, do what works for you. Listen to your body because when you cheat you only hurt yourself, and you deserve better than that.

Finding Hidden Gluten
Without Eating It First

The gluten-free diet is not simply a matter of avoiding the visible grains wheat, rye, and barley. There are many products which do not seem to have a risk of containing gluten which frequently can trip us up. In the early phases of going gluten-free I had gluten containing surprises on a fairly regular basis. If gluten was listed in ingredients by name the challenge of avoiding gluten would be much easier. Unfortunately, we must deal with all the pseudonyms that gluten masquerades behind.

The following charts are short lists of foods to seek, to be wary of, and to avoid. These lists are by no means exhaustive, but will give you a starting point for your detective work to find food that is safe to eat. If at all in doubt, check it out! Please keep in mind that even if you have researched a product and found it safe you should recheck its status on a regular basis. "New and improved," can sometimes be a problem.

Safe, gluten-free foods

Amaranth	Dried legumes	Polenta	Soy
Arrowroot	Flax	Potatoes	Tapioca
Buckwheat	Kasha	Quinoa	Teff
Cassava	Millet	Rice	Wild rice
Corn/Maize	Manioc	Sago	
Dahl	Nuts	Sorghum	

Check these ones carefully!

Baking powder	Flavourings	Marinades and sauces	Seasonings
Baked beans	Herbal teas	Oats*	Self basting poultry
Bouillon cubes	Hydrolysed plant/ vegetable protein	Processed food mixes	Soups and broths
Cheese, processed and spreads	Ice cream and yogurt	Processed meats and seafood	Soy sauce

Condiments	Icing/confectioners sugar	Puddings	Worcestershire sauce
Dried fruits	Imitation seafood	Rice and soy beverages	
Dry roasted nuts	Candies and confections	Salad dressings	

*Please note: Only certified cross contaminant free oats may be considered gluten- free.

Unsafe: These contain gluten

Barley	Emmer	Malt	Semolina
Bulgur	Filler	Malt flavouring	Spelt (Dinkel)
Cereal binder	Flour (unspecified)	Oats (unless certified cross-contaminant free)	Triticale
Couscous	Farro	Oat gum	Wheat
Durum	Graham flour	Roux	Wheat germ
Einkorn	Kamut	Rye	

Being Gluten-Free in a Wheaty Home

What if one person in the home needs a gluten-free diet, but the rest do not? Perhaps that person is you. What do you do? While each home will approach this situation differently, there are various issues to be addressed and options to be considered. I caution against the prescriptive approach. Telling someone, "You are sick and this is your medicine so choke it down," or saying, "If I must eat gluten-free food you all will," is a recipe for isolation, deprivation, cheating and the recurrence of symptoms.

We all need to remember how deeply ingrained wheat and bread are in the social fabric of our society. "Breaking bread," is synonymous with eating together; the Lord's Prayer says, "Give us this day our daily bread;" and most homes have an appliance whose sole purpose is to crisp up slices of the stuff. Given these realities, we need to come up with solutions that address the social and emotional needs of the entire home.

Considering the needs of everyone in the home becomes a balancing act between deprivation and resentment. While the wheat-eater(s) may feel resentful over unwanted dietary restrictions, the gluten-free member(s) will certainly feel deprived watching others enjoy their old wheaty favorites. If the person requiring the diet is a child, how will he feel watching the rest of the family enjoy their wheat laden 'normal' food while he is regulated to eating his 'special' food? Even a three year old understands that 'special' food is different from what everyone else is having. A true story told to me by an individual diagnosed with celiac disease as a toddler recounted his family enjoying fully loaded take-out pizza while he had tomato sauce and cheese on a rice cake. The fact that this person, now in his forties, felt the need to share this incident years later makes the cruelty of the situation very clear.

Gluten-free eating is a reality to be discussed in a respectful, empathic manner. The family dinner table is not the place to foster isolation. Here are some suggestions to consider during an open, honest conversation on the topic of maintaining a mixed gluten-free/wheaty household:

- ✓ **The person who cooks the meals will be faced with additional work** when preparing two different versions of each meal; one with gluten, one without. Is he prepared to assume this extra burden and is he knowledgeable enough about gluten-free cooking to do this safely? If it is the 'family cook' who needs to be gluten-free, is it reasonable or fair to expect this person to cook food that will make him sick?

- ✓ Is the **temptation** of having restricted foods in the house going to be a problem? Could a moment of weakness lead to cheating because the restricted foods are readily available? If only certain foods will be tempting perhaps only those foods need to be considered or removed.

- ✓ **What can other family members do** to make preparing and eating gluten-free foods easier? Perhaps a more empathetic way to deal with the "pizza" scenario above is simply to enjoy the restricted foods when away from home or when the person who needs to follow a gluten-free diet is not present. Just as it is perfectly acceptable for everyone to eat different menu items in a restaurant, this would be a great opportunity for the wheat-eaters in the family to indulge without upsetting the gluten-free family member.

- ✓ **Cross contamination is a major issue** to consider in a mixed gluten-free/wheaty kitchen. Extremely small amounts of gluten can illicit responses from susceptible people. Any contact with utensils, toasters, grills and cutting boards can leave a small amount of residual gluten behind. Crumbs left in butter, jam or other condiments are also a problem. Does the idea of two sets of utensils and appliances work for you?

- ✓ **Is a poorer standard of fare acceptable** for the gluten-free family member? Sadly, when the decision is made to modify only the gluten-free family member's diet, this is commonly the result. For example, if the family pancakes are wheaty what is the likelihood that a second batch of gluten-free pancakes will be prepared? Most likely, the gluten-free family member will end up with a frozen toaster waffle or the like. Realistically, examples such as this are likely to be repeated for most meals and snacks throughout the day.

- ✓ **A gluten-free diet is not harmful to those who can eat wheat,** but gluten does harm those who need to be gluten-free. This fact should weigh heavily on all decisions regarding meal planning. I suggest you try cooking gluten-free for the whole family at mealtimes. With the help of the recipes in this book you may find that the accommodations that need to be made are small enough that the switch isn't a hardship for anyone.

The Gluten-Free Label

More and more food manufacturers are producing gluten-free products. However, it is important to note that some gluten-free products are a secondary line manufactured by a parent company that produces wheaty products in the same facility, thus raising the possibility of cross contamination within the factory. Regardless of who manufacturers the gluten-free products, they vary greatly in quality, but frequently have similarly elevated prices.

The tax deduction available in Canada and the United States for individuals with medical costs due to gluten-free dietary restrictions has made these inflated prices more manageable for those diagnosed with celiac disease. However, those with ineligible diagnoses must bear the full cost themselves. This economic reality has inspired me to seek out products that are gluten-free, although not marketed as such. Throughout my research I have found many items of excellent quality including: crackers, soy sauce, salad dressings, baking ingredients, condiments and seasonings; all at about half the cost of similar gluten-free labeled products. In short, if an item is not an obvious gluten containing product, read the label. You might be pleasantly surprised to find some new, tasty, affordable options available to you.

Sadly, the gluten-free label is no more an absolute guarantee of purity than is the absence of any of the terms gluten hides behind in the listed ingredients. This uncertainty can create a tendency towards paranoia regarding hidden gluten in processed products; an understandable reaction to labels with sketchy information and chemical names that confound all but the chemists among us. Modified food starch? Natural flavour? Seasoning? The list goes on. Lists of gluten-free products are available through celiac associations, but unfortunately, such lists are not usually comprehensive, are difficult to keep up to date, nor do they reflect regional differences found in national or multi-national brands. This leaves us to contact these companies ourselves.

Most products have 1-800 numbers or email addresses printed somewhere on their label. I encourage you to contact the company directly and ask if any grain or malt products are used in the production, storage or packaging of the product. If they answer, "Yes," then ask, "what grains are used?" *Do not ask if the product contains gluten.* While researching this book I spoke with two different customer service representatives for the same multi-national corporation. Each representative gave conflicting answers regarding a natural flavour in ice cream, based upon how I asked the question. In another survey I conducted, when asked if their products contained gluten, a group of ten manufacturers answered, "No," but seven changed their answer to, "yes," when asked if they contained malt or grain products. In all seven cases the grains involved had gluten. *Clearly many of the spokespersons for the food manufacturing companies do not always know what gluten is and what it is derived from.*

How you ask your questions of the manufacturer is at least as important as *what* you ask. Be polite and direct stating that you have enjoyed their products in the past, but need to know if you can continue to eat them due to recent dietary restrictions. At this point in the discussion it is best to avoid mentioning all the foods you can not eat, or the dire reactions possible when ingesting gluten, as it tends to put manufacturers on the 'legal liability' defensive. If your conversation with the manufacturer takes on a legal tone the company representative will likely say, "It may contain," any or all of the items you have listed in order to limit their legal liability. This does not necessarily mean the product contains gluten, just that they are protecting their company from potential legal action.

Overall, I have found that working collaboratively with manufacturers has resulted in my obtaining the most beneficial information about the products I was investigating. Keeping this in mind, always remember that it is your responsibility to ensure that other people fully understand your dietary needs. Do not assume that company representatives fully understand your gluten-free needs, or take their knowledge for granted unless it is demonstrated to your satisfaction.

Within this book, I have deliberately chosen not to endorse any products. Often products are re-made to be 'new and improved', possibly with the addition of cheap and plentiful gluten containing ingredients. I do not wish to mislead anyone regarding the gluten-free status of any product. It is up to you to frequently re-check the ingredients list on products as they do periodically change without notice. I also feel strongly that endorsement of any brands or products would have a detrimental effect on the integrity of this book. You can be assured that all ingredients have been chosen solely on their merits of taste, texture, appearance, nutrition and economy; not for any potential economic or political benefits to the author. My goal is to write a book that is informative and helpful, giving you a comprehensive view of how to prepare delicious gluten-free foods. I believe I have accomplished this goal; I hope you agree.

Eating Out Gluten-Free: A Chef's Perspective

'Good guys' do wear white hats. The vast majority of chefs will work very hard to ensure you receive a great meal that will not make you ill. Chefs generally have a creative temperament and a desire to please their patrons. Asking for help and including the chef in your decision making always works better than telling people what to do. If you can make your gluten-free request a creative challenge for the chef, even better. You may end up with the most spectacular meal you have ever had.

In order to ensure a safe, gluten-free meal two basic challenges need to be overcome; cross contamination control measures and clarity of communication. First, the chef must have knowledge of cross contamination control measures. Chefs in quality restaurants are thoroughly trained in cross contamination control measures because of possible anaphylactic allergic reactions that may occur to some patrons and the associated legal liability.

Unfortunately, some of the cross contamination control measures suggested by several celiac association websites are entirely unworkable in a restaurant setting. Shutting off ventilation fans and keeping an entirely separate work area for gluten-free dishes are not feasible solutions. Separate deep fryers and toasters are also unrealistic expectations. For this reason it is safest to stick to items which can be prepared on the stovetop in a pot or pan, or in the oven. By choosing a reputable establishment with good sanitation procedures and a highly trained chef your worries can be alleviated.

Second, you must communicate your needs to the chef in a manner which does not leave room for ambiguity and does not take for granted an intimate knowledge of gluten-free protocols. The gluten- free diet is only one of dozens of possible dietary restrictions a chef must cater to everyday, so the idea that restaurant staff in any establishment will know everything about all types of dietary restrictions, allergies, and even religious strictures is an unreasonable expectation. It is wisest to communicate your needs fully with no expectation of prior knowledge, because the knowledge they have may include errors, omissions, or out of date information.

I recommend using a written form of communication such as the restaurant card *(found on p. 23)* to ensure that your message gets to the chef without errors or omissions. When information is unclear dangerous assumptions may be made, which in this case may have disastrous consequences. Ensuring clear communication and reducing your risk of cross-contamination should resolve most of the challenges you may encounter when dining out.

Tips for Restaurant Dining

To avoid some other possible challenges when dining out a basic understanding of how restaurants operate will go a long way toward ensuring you receive a great meal that is safe for you to eat. If you picture a restaurant kitchen as an assembly line it will give you a more informed perspective.

Here are a few tips to increase your chances of getting what you need from a restaurant kitchen with the least possible worry.

✓ **Clearly communicate your needs.** Kitchen staff can't help you if they don't know what you need. The most important part of this is to *communicate with the right person.* Regardless of how charming or knowledgeable your server is, they do not prepare the food. We don't tell the mailman the message we want them to deliver; we write it in a letter. The servers in a restaurant are the messengers between the kitchen and the patrons. Detailed instructions need to be written out to prevent errors. When ordering gluten-free meals the restaurant card is this letter.

✓ **Always use the restaurant card.** If the server includes your restaurant card with your order it will ensure that the chef knows the order is for you and not another table. This is important because your restaurant card is a gluten-free protocol 'cheat sheet' explaining what you can't have as well as making suggestions regarding items the chef can use to prepare your meal. *Leave the card with the chef* in the hope that it will be used to educate all restaurant staff that may not be aware of what can and cannot be included within gluten-free meals. This will also help the next gluten-free diner who comes in to the establishment less prepared than you. When dining out I have been frequently asked if the restaurant could keep the card for precisely this purpose. Truthfully, my first *useful* information on the gluten-free diet came to me in this way twenty five years ago when I was an apprentice chef.

✓ **Notify the kitchen of your dietary needs before you order your meal.** Do not take for granted that because your favorite home-cooked recipe for a dish is gluten-free that it will also be gluten-free in a restaurant. A chef's personal touch to make a dish 'better' may be problematic.

✓ **Try to eat in better quality restaurants.** Usually in better quality restaurants more of the products served are actually prepared in-house. This means there are fewer pre-prepared items brought in from outside suppliers that the kitchen staff have virtually no way of verifying as having 100% gluten-free status. Many moderate family restaurants purchase the majority of their food partially pre-prepared and it is only finished / heated at service time. Pre-made soups, sauces, seasoning mixes, coatings, entrees and desserts are all likely to have hidden gluten in them. Even the cooks (Did you notice I didn't call them chefs?) don't know what is in the food they are serving. *Avoid this at all costs!*

✓ **Avoid buffets.** Buffets are a cross contamination nightmare. Diners with no knowledge of cross contamination dangers switch serving utensils and spill items from their plate onto other buffet items with startling regularity. If you must eat in an establishment which offers a buffet, request something directly from the kitchen. Most restaurateurs would rather prepare a separate meal for you than risk a food reaction in front of a dining room full of other patrons.

✓ **If possible, schedule your dining for off-peak times.** Restaurants have busy times and slower times. A hurried and harried chef is more likely to make an error (revert to the standard gluten containing dish) than one who has a moment to ensure your meal is safe. Professional kitchens can be extremely busy and the one thing that surprises most people is how few people actually cook all that food they see coming out to the dining room.

✓ **Call ahead during off peak times and speak directly to the chef.** As a chef I much prefer knowing in advance that a diner with special dietary requirements is coming into my restaurant. This enables me to create a pre-arranged plan to cater to those needs rather than having to 'wing it' when the diner arrives. If calling ahead is not possible, the restaurant card mentioned earlier is the next best thing.

✓ **Become a "regular."** When you find a restaurant that you like and will take care of your needs, frequent it often and bring your friends. This reinforces the concept that it is worthwhile to put in the extra effort to accommodate your gluten-free requirements. Frequently it is the person in the group with special dietary needs that chooses where the group goes to eat. Your repeat business rewards the establishment for their efforts. Being a regular also has some very personal rewards for you. I have spent many years working in private clubs where I knew many of the members by name and their dietary requirements. As a result I could cater to their needs easily and efficiently, eliminating any stress for my diners and myself. Any establishment that can allow you to get out of your own kitchen and not worry about your health deserves your support.

✓ **Read the menu as a list of ingredients.** This takes some practice so be patient with yourself as you develop this skill. If the dish you are considering has elements that won't work, ask for elements from other dishes as possible replacements. For example, if you are considering a chicken dish that comes with pasta smothered in a gluten-containing sauce, request that the gluten-free rice that accompanies the fish dish be used in lieu of the pasta. Most restaurants are very willing to make these minor changes as they use items that are readily available to them and are safe for you to eat.

- ✓ **Be flexible.** The chef may need to substitute several components of a dish in order to make it work. So long as the finished dish is safe to eat and retains the original character you were hoping for, let go of some of the details and enjoy it.

Remember, a restaurant that refuses to adapt to your needs doesn't deserve your business; walk out!

The Restaurant Card

Once you venture away from your own cooking, communicating your dietary needs will likely be your greatest challenge. In most cases, telling servers a detailed list of your dietary requirements with the hope that they will act as an accurate 'go-between' for you and the kitchen staff is a recipe for errors and gluten ingestion. Through my experience I have found the most efficient way to ensure my dietary needs are accurately relayed to the kitchen is to outline them in written form, and request that my server give this information to the cook or chef who will be preparing my meal.

As time constraints and bad handwriting can make this approach somewhat cumbersome, I suggest preparing a restaurant card in advance. A business card format works extremely well for this purpose as it is both useful and convenient. I strongly encourage you to adopt this restaurant card approach. When travelling, consider having the restaurant card translated into the language(s) of the locations you will be visiting. This will facilitate clear communication and minimize the likelihood of misunderstandings. Celiac associations usually produce some form of written communication and have it available already translated into several languages.

I prefer to customize my restaurant card. Below you will read the text for the restaurant card I use and I offer it to you for your own use. It provides a concise description of the gluten-free diet, tailored to answer the questions of anyone providing you with food. While the restaurant card does not include a complete list of all items of concern, it does provide enough information to enable someone with no prior knowledge of gluten-free cooking to prepare a meal that is safe to eat. Creating your own business card has an added benefit; you can customize it to include any other dietary restrictions you may have.

Gluten-Free Dining Card

> **I am gluten-intolerant.** If I eat any food product, additive, stabilizer, starch or seasoning or condiment containing even a trace of **most grains**, including wheat, oats, barley, rye, triticale, spelt, kamut, malt, or any derivatives of these grains, I will become ill. Please ensure that my food does not contain any of the ingredients listed above. **I am able to eat foods containing potatoes, rice, corn, fruit, vegetables, meats, dairy, fish and seafood.** Please assist me in ordering a meal I can safely enjoy.
> Thank you very much.

This text will fit onto a standard sized business card when printed in most basic 10 point fonts. Many home computing programs have a feature which enables easy printing of multiple copies of business cards. Pre-punched card stock can be used with any home printer allowing you to print more cards whenever you need them. Alternately, print shops frequently have very reasonable rates to print basic business cards when printed 500-1000 at a time.

The "I am able to eat" portion of the text is the most important because it suggests safe menu options. Once the kitchen staff is aware of what you can safely enjoy they can create a meal for you that showcases their abilities and fulfills your dietary request. However, be sure to double-check all pre-prepared condiments and sauces for hidden ingredients. You will also need to watch out for tricky items such as soy sauce and Worcestershire sauce, generally containing wheat or malt, but are often overlooked because most people have no understanding of what is in these everyday staples.

On the card, I have purposely not gone into detail about possible dire reactions from ingesting gluten. Adopting the approach of 'less said the better' for reasons of brevity and good taste seems to be more than adequate. Graphic descriptions of gluten-induced physiological reactions do not increase the likelihood of receiving a gluten-free meal. No reputable restaurateur will risk the possibility of a patron becoming ill in their establishment.

When I think back to my first professional experience cooking for a gluten-free client, it was a card similar to this that provided the information I needed to meet her needs. While using this card myself, I have frequently been asked by the cook or chef if the card can be kept in the kitchen. I have always answered, "Yes." This little gluten-free 'cheat-sheet' can go a long way toward educating its readers about gluten-free protocols. In this way, I am also helping out any other gluten-free diners who may come into the establishment in the future less prepared than I.

Travelling Gluten-Free

With a bit of practice and planning, maintaining a gluten-free diet at home can become relatively easy. By eliminating cross contamination issues and choosing products carefully, home can become a worry free haven from wheaty intruders. However, when you travel you lose much of the control you need over your diet and find yourself potentially at risk for gluten ingestion. The good news is that there are steps you can take to travel safely and enjoyably. Whether you choose to fly or drive; stay in hotels, condos, bed and breakfasts, or campgrounds; the following strategies are sure to keep you feeling healthy while away from home.

Before You Go

✓ **Have your restaurant card translated**
If you are travelling to an area where English is not commonly spoken, have your restaurant card translated. Cultural associations and clubs; universities, and translation services are all good places to look for help with this. Be sure a native speaker with knowledge of food terminology does the translation for you. A chef in a local ethnic restaurant representing the country you are planning to visit may be a great person to translate the card for you. From a chef's perspective, a good bottle of wine is a reasonable fee for this service and is well worth the peace of mind it can provide.

✓ **Airlines**
Although the airline industry is changing, on long flights most airlines can provide you with a gluten-free meal if you contact them well in advance. Be sure to check into this *before* you book your flight. To assist with this, fax or email a copy of your restaurant card text to the appropriate person or department preparing in-flight meals to ensure they have a full understanding of your needs. Even with these prior arrangements I suggest you pack a few rations in your carry-on

luggage. It never hurts to be over-prepared in case of errors, oversights or flight delays.

✓ **Contact local celiac associations**
Often the local celiac association in the area you are travelling to can be a great source of information. They should be able to recommend safe local restaurants, accommodations, and suppliers of gluten-free products.

✓ **Pack rations/mixes**
When you begin your travels pack the extra suitcase you will fill with souvenirs for your trip home with non-perishable, gluten-free supplies. Remember; do not include fresh fruits or vegetables if crossing international borders as customs officials will generally confiscate them. Gluten-free crackers, cookies, pretzels, granola bars and cereals are all acceptable and will go a long way when you are unable to readily find gluten-free products away from home. With some locally available fruit, cheese, and vegetables; you will be able to avoid any risky situations without starving. If you are travelling to accommodations where you can cook for yourself, pack pre-measured and mixed dry ingredients for foods like Stovetop Bread *(p. 120)* and Pancakes *(p. 52)*. Include the instructions to complete the recipes on the packages and you will be able to easily enjoy the comforts of home. If staying in bed and breakfast accommodations, you could even offer some pancake mix or cereal to your host to ensure you don't just eat eggs, potatoes, and fruit every morning.

✓ **Ship supplies ahead**
For extended trips, ship supplies ahead to pre-arranged drops. You can make arrangements with hotels to receive and hold the supplies for your arrival. Have a friend at home ship future packages to you so that they will arrive a few days ahead of when you need them.

✓ **Consult guidebooks and web sites**
Travellers' guidebooks and the Internet are increasingly including contact information for accommodations and restaurants providing gluten-free options. Email, phone or fax these businesses in advance to arrange for a safe meal upon your arrival. Be sure to use your restaurant card text to make this easy for everyone.

The Internet may also have listings of gluten-free resources and shops selling gluten-free products in the areas you will be visiting. Knowing this in advance can save you a great deal of time in finding and hauling around your own supplies.

✓ **Contact resorts, cruise lines and restaurants in advance**
If you are travelling to a resort or on a cruise ship, be sure to contact their food services department in advance and inform them of your dietary information. Ensure they can meet your needs *before* booking your trip. If working with a travel agent who offers to do this for you, although well intended, unless your travel agent also follows a gluten-free diet I suggest you contact the establishment directly to ensure your information has been clearly and accurately presented. Once again, the information on your restaurant card will be invaluable when doing this. Ask what menu items could be prepared gluten-free to see whether you would enjoy the offerings or if they would be overly restricted. Most major resorts and cruise ships will be able to accommodate you very well with some advance notice.

While Travelling

Once the above preparations have been made, it should be relatively easy to enjoy your trip without worrying where your next meal is coming from. It has been my experience that advanced planning is the key to safely enjoying gluten-free meals while travelling. Unfortunately, despite all the pre-trip planning that can be done, things don't always work out as planned. Here are a few 'on the spot fixes' to help get you through unforeseen situations:

✓ **Shop the market and picnic**
Local markets can be a great way to eat while travelling. Fruit, cheese, cooked meats, seafood, potatoes and the occasional gluten-free grain product are all readily available in markets the world over. By eating simple, natural foods, you can prevent accidental ingestion of gluten even when language difficulties may exist. A plain piece of fruit will always be a safe bet. With your translated restaurant card in hand you can enjoy the sights and eat as the locals do, without the extra costs and time required for restaurant meals. A park bench picnic with a few gluten-free crackers from your own supplies, some cheese, fruit and a bottle of water or wine is a great quick meal while travelling.

✓ **Convenience store survival**.
This is what you can do if you haven't followed any of the advice above and are stuck without any other options. Interestingly, I find that this last resort is usually used when I am fairly close to home. It is also important to note that the suggestions made here are not nutritionally sound; they are only to prevent the growling in your stomach from becoming so loud that you are unable to hear yourself think. In most countries, convenience stores are never far away. With a bit of careful reading to exclude gluten-containing ingredients, items such as chocolate bars, potato and corn chips, nuts, and ice-cream can all temporarily fill the void until better options can be found.

While indulging my own love for travel I have encountered many of the more novel approaches for eating gluten- free that I have presented here. Cuisines that are not wheat based have some of the best gluten- free options I have ever encountered. Travelling the world can be scary when regular food makes you sick. However, with a bit of forethought and some creativity, travel can still be delicious, nutritious, and a lot of fun.

You Are Invited…

It's party time and you have been invited to a dinner party, a wedding or a banquet. While dining at such functions may present some challenges, most can be overcome. First and foremost, always be honest; you do not have to suffer in silence. If you are truthful about your dietary needs your host will undoubtedly make a sincere effort to accommodate you. Any host would prefer knowing your needs in advance rather than wondering why you ate only ten percent of what was offered to you.

When attending a catered function you have a couple of options. In consultations with clients I regularly suggested they include a special dietary requirements request form within the reply envelope. By using this request form the host can pass your needs on to the caterer with ease. However, a follow-up call to the caterer a day before the event is still advisable.

Another option is to request the contact information for the caterer from the host, explaining that due to your specialized dietary needs you will happily take care of your own meal arrangements (leaving them time to plan the other party details). Contact the caterer a few days in advance to discuss your needs. You may wish to fax a copy of your restaurant card to the chef to ensure that the kitchen staff clearly knows your dietary requirements. As a chef with many years of banquet experience I came to expect 2-3% of my diners to require some sort of special dietary accommodations. You are not alone in making special requests and any caterer would prefer to know of your needs in advance rather than having to 'wing it' without notice.

For less formal occasions, here are some strategies to help get you through:

- ✓ **Never arrive famished.** I know this sounds pessimistic, but all too often a lack of understanding of what gluten is and where it is found can turn, "It's all taken care of," into "oh sorry, I guess you can't eat this."

- ✓ **Load your pockets or purse with rations.** A few gluten-free crackers can make a cocktail party bearable and will enable you to enjoy the gluten-free offerings that generally are served on bread or crackers.

- ✓ **Ask if you can contribute something to the meal.** If you 'pot-luck it' you can always eat what you brought, plus the few obviously gluten-free items available.

- ✓ **Bring your restaurant card.** Never take for granted that anyone has knowledge of the gluten-free diet protocol. Regardless of where you are your restaurant card is a valuable teaching tool.

Baking Gluten-Free

When removing gluten from your diet, baked goods are often the first to go. Still, there is no reason to miss out. You just need to get into the kitchen and bake gluten-free versions of the things you miss. Using some of the tips in this section it can be a lot less work than you may think to enjoy delicious fresh-baked treats whenever you want them.

A high-risen, light-textured loaf of bread is the ultimate goal of gluten-free bakers. Unfortunately, this is difficult to attain without gluten, the stretchy protein found in wheat that traps the bubbles of carbon dioxide produced by yeast or chemical leaveners, enabling the bread to rise. In fact, the super-light white bread that is a staple of the North American diet is often accomplished by adding extra gluten to wheat flour. This is not to say that good gluten-free bread isn't possible, it just means you will need to emulate the styles of bread that are more attainable. Hearty multi-grain loaves, European rye, and dense nut breads all lend themselves very well to gluten-free makeovers.

If you are still wanting light and spongy white bread this book includes white bread recipes that are very good, but I make no claim that they are indistinguishable from the gluten containing original. The types of flours used to bake gluten-free white bread do provide a slightly different flavour, and the lack of gluten results in a heavier texture. However, these recipes will be fresher, better tasting and more economical than any store bought gluten-free breads you might find.

Muffins, loaves, biscuits, cookies, pancakes and pastries are the easiest to remake in gluten-free forms. In many of these items the gluten has long been an obstacle to achieving a terrific end product. Any gluten based recipe calling for cake or pastry flour is a perfect candidate for a gluten-free conversion because the identified flours are used specifically for their low gluten content.

Some of the ingredients listed in gluten-free recipes within this book may seem strange and you may find yourself asking the question, "Do I really need to put that stuff in?" Xanthan gum, gelatine and all manner of flours you may have never heard of are the staples of a gluten-free kitchen. There is no magic all-purpose gluten-free flour that can copy wheat flour without help from various binders, protein sources, and other flours and starches. In order to recreate the characteristics of wheat flour, you need to blend together as many as six or seven ingredients. Attempts to abbreviate the number of ingredients will invariably compromise the quality in the finished product. This accounts for the apparent complexity of many gluten-free recipes whose wheaty counterparts have very few ingredients.

Tips for Easier Baking

To help make your gluten-free baking a little easier, here are a few shortcuts to make these extra ingredients less of a hassle:

- ✓ **Measure out the dry ingredients for multiple batches** of your favourite baked goods and keep them handy for quick use when needed. I use zip-type bags and write the recipe name, date, and information required to complete the recipe on the bag. This is a great time saving strategy because most of the time required to measure out ingredients is actually spent retrieving and returning all the items to the pantry.

- ✓ **Measure individual batches separately.** Do not measure out the dry ingredients for multiple batches together and then separate them after mixing. Some of the active ingredients such as xanthan gum and leaveners are a very small portion of the overall volume and missed spots in mixing can cause significant variability in the outcome.

- ✓ **"Just add water" (JAW) versions** of recipes for baked goods have been included within this book. I find them extremely convenient to have on hand either at home or when traveling.

Another challenge of gluten-free baking is its tendency to dry out more quickly than its wheaty counterparts. This is because gluten is very effective for sealing moisture into the cellular structure of baked goods. The conventional method of dealing with this problem is to freeze baked goods you will not consume within 1-2 days, keeping only as much as you plan to eat right away. However, this method has limited success with gluten-free foods because the moisture that evaporates out of freshly baked gluten-free items forms ice crystals during freezing. These ice crystals can turn the frozen product soggy when thawed.

A better tasting approach (which is commonly used in the food service industry) is to portion and freeze gluten-free dough and batter before baking. For recipes such as muffins or buns, bake only the amount you need for a day or two at a time. Freeze the remaining batter or dough in muffin cup liners or on parchment paper. Properly wrapped, most dough and batter will keep a few months in the freezer without loss of quality. Imagine a breakfast of fresh muffins baked while you get ready for your day. Just thaw the batter overnight in the refrigerator and pop it into the oven when you get up. With this method you can enjoy a greater variety of baked goods rather than eating the same thing day after day. By maintaining a small stock of dough and batter in your freezer you will never again be 'caught without' by unexpected guests, and most items can be thawed and baked in less than an hour. Many of the recipes in this book are compatible with the frozen dough method.

Working with Bread Machines

The bread machine has turned bread making from a practiced skill into an easy task that can be accomplished by even the most novice baker. Most home cooks today do not bake any bread because it is much easier to buy it. Spending the time to nurture the live yeast so it can turn a heavy gluey mess into light spongy bread is not a high priority for most people in our busy modern world. However, when you discover that you need your bread to be gluten-free you may find that your priorities change enough to make a bit of time to bake. The expensive, dry, frozen gluten-free bread available in supermarkets is even more likely to inspire you to bake your own bread.

Have no fear, the amount of time and effort required to coddle the yeast into making your bread rise has been dramatically reduced by the automatic bread machine. The sometimes odd shaped loaves with holes in parts of them from the removal of the various implements used to mix the dough may look a bit different than what we are accustomed to getting from the store, but be assured the bread will be fresh, will taste better and be more economical than anything you can buy.

Many models of bread machines are available from very simple units with relatively few features to pricey units with very complex capabilities. To gauge what you really need in a bread machine an understanding of what a bread machine must do to bake gluten-free breads is required.

The bread machine mixes/kneads the dough in a temperature controlled chamber for a set period of time. After this time has elapsed a heating element turns on and bakes the bread for the specified time. At the end of this time an alarm notifies you that the baking is complete. These requirements can be fulfilled by most of the simplest units available. *All you really need is a unit which has a rapid or single rise setting, and a choice of desired crust (light, medium or dark).*

Many units tout themselves as having a more powerful mixing motor. In gluten-free baking this powerful motor is unnecessary because gluten-free bread dough is much thinner and requires much less power to mix than the wheaty stuff these machines were designed to work with.

Gluten free flours are more prone to form dry clumps which do not mix into the dough than wheat flour. In order for the different gluten-free ingredients to act as a single compound just as wheat flour does, the dry ingredients must be thoroughly mixed before any wet ingredients are added. The need to mix the dry ingredients together before placing them in the machine provides us with an opportunity to prevent lumps of dry flour from remaining in your bread. Since you already have the mixed dry ingredients in a bowl, add the remaining wet ingredients and mix by hand until you can see all the lumps are gone. All sorts of proprietary solutions have been designed to try to overcome this mixing problem, but I haven't seen any that work as well for gluten-free breads as a

quick mix in a bowl before placing the ingredients in the machine. Although this is an extra step required for gluten-free breads, it ensures dry flour spots do not form as a result of the less than perfect mixing action of most machines.
Some units offer a huge range of programming possibilities which are also mostly unnecessary. The most useful function of these programming possibilities is to control the rising time of the dough. The baking times for the gluten-free breads in this book do not differ from wheaty ones and therefore, do not require tinkering.

Rather than controlling the rising time for the dough, as is suggested by the manufacturers of the more complex units, change the temperature of the liquids added into the machine. Use an instant read type meat thermometer (every kitchen needs one of these) to test the temperature of the liquids being added. The difference in the temperature of these liquids from refrigerator temperature up to 40°C/104°F provides a greater range of control over the rising time of the dough than even the most sophisticated machines allow. Start with the recommended ingredient temperatures suggested by the manufacturer of your particular unit. For breads not raised enough, increase the temperature of the liquid a bit each time you try the recipe up to, but not exceeding 40°C/104°F. This will speed up the action of the yeast causing the bread to rise more quickly. For over-raised breads, (ones that have a fallen or have a concave top) gradually lower the temperature of the liquids used each time you try the recipe to slow the growth of the yeast. Once you have found the optimal temperature of a particular recipe in your machine make note of that temperature on the recipe for consistently great results in the future.

Some bakers use changes in the amount of yeast, salt or sugar to speed up or slow down the rising of the dough. These approaches change the flavour of the bread in order to control the rising and therefore, are not advisable.

With a bread machine automating most of the processes of bread making, a fresh loaf of great gluten-free bread is easy to bake.

Following the Directions

For gluten-free cooking and baking the rules have changed. No matter how weird the instructions may seem in some of the recipes in this book, following them exactly will lead to the best results. When I took my chef's training, I learned that in order to produce the desired results there was only one way to cook and bake. I am sure many of my instructors would consider my abandonment of traditional techniques as a sacrilege, but when cooking and baking gluten-free the reality is that those methods no longer work.

Many of the recipes within this book include the rationale for the seemingly strange instructions which have been developed through intensive testing and numerous less than perfect initial results. At all costs resist the urge to fall back on the cooking and baking techniques used in gluten-based recipes. Many of the cornerstone techniques of regular wheaty cooking and baking are designed entirely to make best use of gluten or to minimize its effects. In developing this book I have had to completely rewrite that list of rules.

The New Gluten-Free Rules:

- ✓ **Some gluten-free recipes require extra steps for best results.** Pre-mixing dry ingredients for all gluten-free baking is an absolute must. Because several types of flour and xanthan gum must be thoroughly combined in order to simulate the gluten-like properties of wheat flour, all components must be completely mixed to ensure they behave as a single new compound.

- ✓ **Bread machines can save you a great deal of fuss** and make better bread than most commercial gluten-free bakeries. However, once again you need to thoroughly pre-mix all dry ingredients in order to achieve the desired results. If the dry ingredients are not thoroughly mixed you will end up with lumps that the bread machine will be unable to get out.

- ✓ **When making soups and sauces there are gluten-free techniques that will save time and reduce fat.** Unlike traditional wheaty roux which is high in fat and needs to be simmered for at least 20 minutes to eliminate the starchy taste; once the low-fat, gluten-free thickener has come to a low boil the starchy taste is gone. This means gluten-free thickeners can be mixed into the sauce or soup ingredients while they are still cold. Alternatively, the gluten-free thickener can be mixed with some cold liquids to prevent lumps forming before adding it to the hot stock. As for the fat, if you want the extra richness of butter or alternate, feel free to add it in, but it is no longer a necessity.

- ✓ **Gluten-free flours absorb liquid differently than wheat flour.** Some gluten-free flours take considerable time to hydrate fully. For some recipes you may need to wait a few minutes for the gluten-free flours to absorb the liquid and make the batter or dough workable. Variations in the milling of gluten-free flours can also cause variations in the amount of liquid required in a recipe.

✓ **Gluten-free flours absorb fat differently than wheat flour.** Some gluten-free flours, especially rice flour, will not soften fully in mixtures such as muffin batters or cookie doughs where the amount of liquid is restricted in favour of butter or alternates. This is the cause of the gritty texture in a lot of products based on rice flour.

✓ **The texture of gluten-free dough and batter will be very different** from their wheaty counterparts. If gluten-free bread dough is made as stiff as wheat dough the resulting bread will be heavy and dry. This is the problem with most store-bought gluten-free bread as it is mass produced using equipment designed for wheaty breads. Gluten-free bread dough made like a thick, but not stiff, batter will yield a loaf most resembling the gluten filled original.

✓ **Handling gluten-free dough requires different methods.** Using a small amount of water rather than extra flour or fat to prevent the dough from sticking to your hands will result in a nicer, less starchy-tasting finished product. This method makes a huge difference to the outcomes of the Stovetop Bread *(p. 120)* and Pizza Dough *(p. 112)* recipes.

✓ **Gluten-free baked products do not harden up in the oven** the same way their wheaty counterparts do. Therefore, they often require cooling time before they can be handled. Items such as cookies and brownies will crumble if they are handled while still hot, but will have the same texture as wheaty ones once they have cooled.

Where is the Gluten-Free Flour Mix?

Where is the gluten-free flour mix? The answer is there is no such 'mix' in this book! During my research I have encountered all sorts of pre-mixes, but none of them resulted in final products that met my standards. Early in my recipe research and development I created several gluten-free flour blends, but found that I could never get as good a result with them as when I was able to individually manipulate all the variables to optimize the outcomes. As a result, each recipe within this book lists individual ingredients and amounts to create the best quality product.

In gluten-free baking, the all-purpose flour replacement concept is flawed. The same mixture of flours can have very different outcomes depending on the amount of fat, liquid and protein added; as well as the technique used to prepare the recipe. In addition, the interplay of variables when several flours are combined in an attempt to mimic wheat flour makes a general purpose gluten-free flour mix a poor choice. Using a gluten-free flour mix also makes it necessary to keep more of the various gluten-free flours on hand in order to have all the required blends for different types of recipes. Furthermore, unless painstaking care is taken to completely mix these flour blends the outcomes are unreliable. When mixing several different gluten-free flours, the majority of which are white powders, it is very difficult to tell if the resulting blend is fully mixed. Any pockets of the various flours left unmixed will lead to inconsistent outcomes.

It is important to me that you are able to consistently create high quality products that you are proud to serve. To help ensure this outcome, when mixing the various flours required for each recipe you know you will always have the exact proportion of ingredients in each batch as called for in the recipe. While the recipes may seem to be less complex when only one gluten-free flour mix is called for, the preparation of that gluten-free flour mix is really just an additional step done at another time; not a time saver. Rather than working from a less than ideal gluten-free mix try some of the time saving tips offered in, "Baking Gluten-Free" (p. 29).

The Gluten-Free Pantry

When you first try gluten-free baking you may not recognize many of the ingredients; but fear not, these new items bring with them great taste and nutrition. Whether masquerading as wheaty items or showing off their own charms, they will provide you with a wide variety of delicious alternatives. All the gluten-free grains and binders listed below have been approved by the Canadian Celiac Association, and can be found in health food stores, some supermarkets, or through online mail-order houses.

Gluten-Free Grains and Binders

Amaranth
This ancient grain from Central America was a staple of the Aztecs. These tiny grains are high in protein and have a nutty flavour. They can be cooked into breakfast porridge or used to add texture to breads. Amaranth flour is commonly

available in health food stores and is often combined with other flours to improve their nutrition and taste. Amaranth can also be puffed like rice or popcorn (only if it is very fresh), and is available as puffed amaranth cakes in Central American markets. They make a great emergency snack item.

Arrowroot

This white starchy flour is ground from the root of a plant native to the Caribbean. It has a neutral taste and is frequently used as a thickener for sauces. Arrowroot can be exchanged with equal volumes of cornstarch for those who are intolerant of corn.

Bean Flours

Bean flours have both benefits and pitfalls. They are very high in protein and can arguably be used to make baked goods most like wheaty ones in appearance and texture. However, they are one of the more expensive gluten-free flours available; they have relatively strong flavours, and they have the side effects beans are famous for. For persons with gastrointestinal difficulties bean flours can be a further irritant.

The following are the most common bean flours used in gluten-free baking:

- ✓ **Garbanzo (chick pea) flour,** also known as **chana flour,** is often used in Indian cooking.

- ✓ **Garfava flour** is a commercially prepared mixture of garbanzo flour and fava bean flour. I mention this flour with a caution. Fava bean flour is nearly indigestible to many people, particularly those of Mediterranean descent who carry a genetic sensitivity to the toxicity of the undercooked bean and the plant's pollen. If this concern does not affect you, this mixture is one of the most palatable bean flours available.

- ✓ **Romano/Cranberry bean flour** is strong tasting flour that should only be considered for use in heavily spiced and highly flavoured dishes. I do not use this product in any of the recipes in this book.

- ✓ **Soy flour** is high in protein and has a relatively mild taste compared to its other 'beany' cousins. Whole soy flour is high in fat, but defatted soy flour is now becoming readily available. When combined with other flours it gives excellent results. Soy flour can become rancid quite easily so it must be stored in the refrigerator or freezer.

Buckwheat

Despite its unfortunate name, buckwheat isn't in the wheat family at all and is gluten-free. In China, Russia and Japan, buckwheat has long been a staple. It can be made into a side dish in place of rice or milled into flour where it traditionally finds its way into pancakes and soba noodles. Because of its strong flavour, buckwheat is frequently mixed with other flours. Hulled (light) buckwheat flour has a much milder flavour.

Cornstarch

Cornstarch is cheap, easy to find and tastes bland. This versatile ingredient plays a major role in the recipes in this book that emulate wheaty products. If corn is a problem for you, it can be replaced with equal parts potato starch or arrowroot starch.

Cornmeal

Dried kernels of corn (yellow, white or blue) are milled to different degrees for different uses.

- ✓ **Yellow corn** milled to a texture of coarse sand is the standard in most North American cooking. In this form it is commonly used in cornbreads, Mexican cooking and as a coating for fried foods. A coarser grind is used to make polenta in Italian cooking.

- ✓ **White cornmeal** is well known to the people of the southern United States as grits, and is also a staple of South African cooking.

- ✓ **Blue corn,** which can sometimes be reddish in colour, is most commonly used in the making of tortillas where its taste and texture are generally indistinguishable from yellow.

Corn Flour

Cornmeal can be milled into finely textured flour. It can be mixed with other flours for baking and for dredging products before frying. When used as a part of baking mixes it gives the finished product a more natural, wheaty appearance.

Guar Gum

Commonly used in some early gluten-free recipes as a sticky gluten replacement, guar gum has two major drawbacks. It is a highly effective laxative which makes it a poor choice for anyone with a sensitive digestive system. It also has a telltale flavour that shows up whenever it is used. None of the recipes in this book call for guar gum. It is only included here as an option if someone cannot tolerate xanthan gum. To replace xanthan gum with guar gum, about 30 percent more guar gum is necessary.

Millet

One of the first grains to be domesticated by humans, millet has a myriad of uses around the world. It can be eaten as a cooked grain, milled into flour for baking, or fermented into a beer-like beverage. Millet is naturally alkaline so it is easy to digest. This mildly sweet nutty tasting flour is very nutritious and high in protein. It can be used effectively as a garnish grain in breads and as a portion of the flour in baked goods.

Nut Flour/Meal

Almond, chestnut and other nut flours are welcome additions to many gluten-free recipes. In any given recipe up to twenty percent of the flours used can be replaced with nut flours to enhance flavour and nutrition. However, care must be taken to reduce the amount of fat in baked goods due to the high oil content in nut flours. Nut flours must always be stored in the refrigerator or freezer. The Almond Bread recipe *(p. 128)* showcases the charms of almond flour.

Oats/Oat Flour

Recent research has proven that pure oats can be included in a gluten-free diet. However, I include oats in this book with this caution. In North America, the farming, storage and processing of wheat and oats are usually done using the same equipment, thus increasing the probability of cross contamination of oats with wheat. Be sure that the oats you choose are certified cross contaminant free. Oats and oat flour have great nutritional qualities as well as the familiar flavour that makes some of those old favourite recipes possible again.

Potato Starch

Potato starch is bland, white filler used in gluten-free baking. Although nutritionally not a fabulous choice, it does help give baked products a smoother texture. Much of the early gluten-free baking relied heavily on it, having its roots in Jewish cooking where grains are prohibited during some religious holidays. This grain-free experience was readily adopted by gluten-free cooks, and potato starch found its way into many early gluten-free cookbooks. It can be used interchangeably with cornstarch if you cannot tolerate corn.

Potato Flour

Potato flour is very different from potato starch and the two *cannot* be used interchangeably. This flour imparts a very noticeable potato flavour and will produce heavier baking, not a desired trait in most recipes. It does have value in helping to retain moisture in baked goods.

Quinoa

This ancient food from the Andes is a great gluten-free option, containing all the necessary amino acids to be considered a complete food. The small disk-shaped seeds have a bitter, soapy coating which *must* be thoroughly rinsed before cooking. While cooking, the bran layer peels away from the grain providing an interesting variation in texture. Quinoa flour is relatively bland with only a slightly bitter taste, and can enhance gluten-free baking when mixed with other flours. Make sure the flour you buy has been de-bittered to avoid disappointment.

Rice Flour

Rice flour is the traditional base grain used in most gluten-free baking. However, different techniques used in milling rice into flour cause inconsistencies between brands. North American brands tend to be quite coarse. When used in baking they require the addition of more liquid and an increased wait time before baking in order to achieve proper results. Asian milled rice flours are generally milled much finer, require less liquid, and are less likely to yield a gritty end product.

Rice flour is available in three varieties, each with their own characteristics:

✓ **White rice flour** is the most common bland, white filler used in gluten-free baking. It tends to result in a gritty texture, often recognized as the telltale sign of gluten-free baking. This grit does not soften well in the presence of fats. (Risotto uses this quirk to prevent the rice grains from becoming mushy.) White rice flour must be used in recipes with sufficient liquid and cooking time to allow the rice to soften. Baked goods that do not include much liquid and have a high fat content, such as cookies and muffins, are poor choices for white rice flour. Baking made with white rice flour can also have a rather surreal translucent white colour which is not very appealing to the eye.

✓ **Brown rice flour** contains the bran of the rice and is more nutritious than white rice flour. The slight bran taste is nearly undetectable in most baked goods. The tan colour and opaque appearance of brown rice flour allow it to have a more natural, wheaty appearance when used in baking. Brown rice flour should be stored in the refrigerator or freezer as there is a tendency for the flavour to become stronger over time, and the rice flour will eventually become rancid.

✓ **Sweet rice flour** is a confusing name because it does not accurately describe the properties of the flour. It is not sweet; it is simply made from a type of rice used for making sweets in Asian cooking. To further confuse consumers, sweet rice flour is also known as **glutinous rice flour**. This is a poor choice of name because glutinous rice flour contains no gluten, although it is very sticky. It is traditionally used in making Asian rice noodles because of its natural elasticity. Despite its unfortunate name sweet rice flour has some very useful traits, behaving quite differently from white or brown rice flour. Because it is milled from softer and starchier rice, the resulting flour is smoother, combines more readily with fats and has a less gritty texture. As a thickener for soups and sauces it most closely mimics the traits of wheat flour, with the added benefit of being freeze and thaw stable. Sweet rice flour is used extensively in this book whenever its elasticity or thickening properties are called for.

Sorghum Flour

White sorghum, a relatively new strain of sorghum grown for human consumption, is nutritionally comparable to wheat flour and has a light tan colour. It has a mild molasses-like taste which makes it a welcome addition to many types of bread. It works well in baking, but is best used when mixed with other flours.

Teff

This ancient grain from Ethiopia is tiny, but packs a powerful punch in both nutrition and sweet nutty taste. Traditionally used to make injera, the sourdough flatbread essential to Ethiopian meals, teff is also a great addition to cooked cereals and breads. The flour tends to be somewhat gritty in texture due to its high exterior bran content in relation to its soft grain interior. It should be used where this texture will not detract from the finished product.

Xanthan Gum

Xanthan gum is the, "Magic pixie dust," of gluten-free baking. It is the replacement to the 'glue' in gluten. Xanthan gum is a very sticky substance sold in powder form, and is a highly effective binder used to hold gluten-free products together. Only tiny amounts are required to drastically alter the texture of baked goods. It is *extremely* important to fully pre-mix all dry ingredients in gluten-free baking to ensure the xanthan gum is evenly distributed, thus making the best use of its stickiness. Without it, most recipes will just crumble. If you are concerned about this product please consider that you have probably been eating it for years in commercially prepared products such as salad dressings, ice-cream and yogurt.

Helpful Hints

Have you ever wondered how a restaurant can serve its customers much more quickly than you can prepare the same dish at home? Preparation is the answer. To save running around at mealtimes restaurants pre-blanch vegetables, prepare desserts in advance, and use elements of a dish that have been previously made in larger batches and stored in the freezer. When cooking at home, you too can use all these proven, time-saving strategies.

Pro-tips

Whether you are cooking gluten-free or wheaty, here are a few handy pro-tips for making food preparation easier:

✓ **Portion out** things like muffin batter and cookie dough using an ice-cream scoop with a thumb-activated release. These scoops are available in a wide variety of sizes, and can be purchased from kitchen shops and restaurant supply companies. By ensuring even sizing you also ensure even cooking or baking. As an added bonus, for those needing to carefully calculate carbohydrate values (such as those with diabetes) this tip gives a consistent carbohydrate value to each item.

✓ **Freeze portions of dough** for foods such as muffins and cookies in their raw dough state and thaw later, when needed. This gives you the option of having warm, fresh baked goods without the usual preparation time. This also gets around the fact that gluten-free baking tends to dry out faster than wheaty baking.

✓ **Prepare several batches at once.** Measure the dry ingredients needed for baked goods and keep them in storage containers or zip-type bags until needed. Remember to mark each container thoroughly and include the instructions needed to complete the recipe. *Resist the urge to mix multiple batches of a recipe in the same bowl and then divide it.* With the tiny amounts of certain ingredients such as salt, xanthan gum, and leaveners; the slightest missed spot in mixing can create inconsistent results.

Measuring the dry ingredients for many individual recipes is a terrific time-saver since most of the time required to measure ingredients for baking is spent in taking everything out of the pantry and returning it.

✓ **Purchase products according to value and taste,** rather than brand name or price. Although a premium product may be worth the elevated cost, often the only difference between it and its less expensive competitor is the money spent on advertising. You can easily judge taste by your own standards, but value is a more complex matter. By balancing taste and quality with price, you can decide on the value of a product.

When determining value you also need to consider the intended use of a product. For example, using an excellent bottle of wine for cooking becomes a poor value because the subtleties you pay extra for are destroyed by heat. However, it should be noted that certain better quality products such as tomato paste, grated cheese and ice cream do not contain some of the cheap, gluten-containing fillers found in less expensive products. By reading the ingredients, you can usually tell when these extras have been added. These fillers often rob the product of the fullest flavour, making it necessary to use more of the product in a recipe in order to achieve the best results. Needing to use more of a less expensive product often makes the more expensive better quality product a better value.

✓ **Flatten out cutlets** of meat or chicken by placing small pieces between two layers of plastic wrap and pounding them with a mallet or heavy flat-bottomed pot or pan. The result will be a more tender and quicker cooking cutlet. This technique is useful for scaloppini, piccata, paillard or carpaccio.

✓ **Freeze small quantities** of sauces and stews for use in daily dinners or when unexpected guests arrive. Sandwich size zip-type bags work well for this, and the wide flat shape that results from freezing flat makes them quick to defrost.

✓ **Keep the bones, trimmings and drippings from meat, fish or seafood.** These can be kept in a container in the freezer. Add onions, celery and carrots remaining from other recipes or going soft in the fridge, and soon you will have the makings of a wonderful stock from things you might otherwise have thrown away. Stronger flavored vegetables such as broccoli and asparagus also make tasty soup stocks, but should not be included in basic stocks because they overpower the other flavours.

✓ **Flexible silicone baking mats are great for rolling delicate pastry.** Gluten-free pastry is a bit more finicky to handle than wheaty pastry so roll it out on a silicone baking mat; then roll up the mat and the pastry together to transfer it to the pie plate. Simply turn the roll over and unroll for trouble free pastry. The silicone mats don't slide around on counters while rolling making the whole process easier than the frequently suggested wax paper method.

Tools and Equipment

No matter what kind of cooking you are doing it is important to have the proper tools and equipment. Here are a few hints on choosing and maintaining your kitchen utensils to give optimum results:

✓ **Meat thermometers** (not the type that stays in the oven) will guarantee that both overdone and undercooked meats become a thing of the past. To know exactly how far along the cooking is, insert the probe for about 30 seconds into the thickest part of the meat, not touching any bone. The first roast you don't ruin will pay for this little gadget. I don't know a chef who doesn't use one.

✓ **Cookware:** Beware the word, "Professional" describing any cookware. Ironically, the professional equipment used in restaurants is usually not flashy or expensive. It is functional and gets the job done properly and efficiently. Cookware used by television chefs is there because more often than not a sponsor paid for it.

- o Non-stick Teflon cookware should be viewed as semi-disposable. For things such omelets they are great, but most don't hold up to the rigors of frequent use.
- o The jury is still out on the health risks of cooking in bare aluminum pots. Also, because this soft metal tends to scratch and dent, cleaning is difficult and burning of food more likely.

- Look for cookware with a heavy bottom and a stoutly attached handle that can go into an oven repeatedly without damage. A stainless steel pot or pan with a thick disk of metal on the bottom is a great solution at a reasonable cost. Thick copper pots with stainless steel interiors are the crème de la crème of cookware, but the cost can be prohibitive.

✓ **Baking sheets** come in many variations. Non-stick, air-core and silicone mats are all touted as professional solutions to burnt bottoms and sticking. In every professional kitchen I have ever worked in the solution to burning and sticking has always been the same: Basic aluminum pans lined with bakers' parchment. I have yet to find anything that will stick to it. When preparing something that is a nightmare to clean (like glazed ribs) just toss the paper and save the scrubbing. If burning on the bottom is a problem, double up the pans to create your own air-core pans at a fraction of the cost and with greater versatility. For baked goods such as cookies, bakers' parchment can be re-used until it browns and becomes brittle.

✓ **Cutting boards** are indispensable for all sorts of food preparation, but they can also be one of the most dangerous items in the kitchen. Improperly cleaned cutting boards are one of the most common causes of food poisoning. In a mixed gluten-free/wheaty kitchen they can also become a source of cross-contamination. I firmly believe that plastic cutting boards are best. Pebbled glass cutting boards dull knives at an unparalleled rate and can be unsafe as the knife blade tends to skate across the surface. Plastic cutting boards can be sanitized in a dishwasher while wooden boards cannot. Notice I didn't write "washed" because the high heat required for killing illness-causing bacteria usually cannot be achieved by hand washing. The only other way to ensure cutting boards are sanitized is by the use of chemicals such as bleach. However, chemicals can leave behind a residue that can be passed on to food. For those who think a dishwasher is a frill, consider this. If a dishwasher breaks down in a restaurant, a health inspector will shut down the establishment until the machine has been repaired.

Choose a cutting board that is only an inch or two bigger than the length of the blade of your chef's chopping knife. For example, an 8 inch (20cm) chef's knife needs a cutting board that is only 10 inches (25cm) in width. When you find a cutting board that meets your needs buy at least two. Preparing raw meats and salads on the same board, even with a quick wash between, is asking for trouble. Ensure your cutting board is stable by spreading a damp kitchen cloth or paper towel underneath to prevent sliding. A cutting board that can move around while in use is an accident waiting to happen. The new flexible plastic cutting boards are great for transferring chopped vegetables, etc to the cooking pot because they can bend to form a spout enabling easy pouring. Unfortunately, with regular use they don't tend to last as long as the firmer plastic boards.

✓ **Knives** are the trademark tool of a chef. The choice of a knife is a very personal one. Manufacturers of cooking knives make an overwhelming variety of shapes and sizes for all purposes. Find something that fits your hand well and feels comfortable to use. If a knife is too heavy in either the handle or the blade it will not balance well in your hand. This will cause your hands and wrists to become easily fatigued. A knife is only as good as its edge, so it must be kept sharp. A dull knife seems to cut the person holding it better than anything else.

✓ **Measuring** is the key to consistency, especially in baking. Care and attention paid to measuring accurately will reward you with the same results every time. Choose measuring utensils that are durable with easy to read markings. For liquid measures the Pyrex type measuring cups are very handy because they enable use in the microwave to warm liquids, and to melt foods such as butter and chocolate. The sliding type teaspoon/ tablespoon measures alleviate all the fumbling needed to find just the right size measuring spoon.

✓ **Power tools** make cooking much easier. Mixers, blenders and food processors can make cooking much less of a chore. Choose heavy duty models with a range of available options and attachments. My mixer has attachments for mixing as well as slicing, shredding, grinding, pasta rolling and milling grains. Immersion blenders are a great tool for making pureed soups, dressings and sauces; and can be used when these items are hot. Using a standard bar type blender with hot liquids is a recipe for a dangerous, scalding mess.

Recipe Conversions

Most people have a repertoire of favourite recipes which "work" for the whole family, or at least the majority. When adopting a gluten-free diet many believe that their family favourites need to be removed from the menu, but this isn't necessarily true. The old family recipes and cookbooks which have served you well have not become useless; they just need a few modifications to convert their great recipes into gluten-free favourites.

New trends in food come and go with remarkable speed. As a result it is impossible to create a cookbook which caters to all the new trends. Truthfully, there are very few new ideas in cooking; most new trends are simply variations on what has been done before. By providing you with methods to convert recipes which contain only small amounts of gluten, your favourite recipes can be easily adapted and enjoyed as these new ideas come along.

In the, "Substitutions," below you will find strategies for replacing gluten when it used as a thickener, binder, coating or pasta. In many recipes for soups, sauces, stews and casseroles the gluten is simply the binder or thickener to hold together an otherwise watery mess into a hearty meal. With a few substitutions you might be surprised how easily you can bring back your repertoire of favourites or enjoy the interesting 'new' trends that come along.

Substitutions

- ✓ **Replacing wheat flour as a thickener**
  In many soups, stews and sauces a mixture of fat (butter, oil, lard...) and wheat flour is cooked to varying degrees to both thicken and colour a sauce. This mixture, known by its French name, "Roux," is simply a method devised to overcome the drawbacks of using wheat flour as a thickener. The extra fat required to prevent wheat flour from forming lumps is unnecessary when using sweet rice flour. The extra cooking time required to remove the starchy taste from a wheaty roux is not required when using sweet rice flour because its starchy taste cooks out immediately upon boiling.

  The natural inclination for most cooks when replacing wheat flour as a thickener is to use cornstarch which has some benefits, but also some drawbacks. Cornstarch looses its ability to thicken properly in the presence of an acid or during prolonged cooking. Cornstarch is also not freeze/thaw stable and any products made with it will separate upon thawing.

Tapioca starch is very well suited to thickening puddings and custard fillings, but tends to give a strange texture to hot dishes. Other gluten-free flours tend to impart colours, flavours or gritty textures which are not desired in finished products when trying to recreate recipes originally thickened with wheat.

✓ **Replacing wheat flour used as a thickener in sauces and soups**
Replace wheat flour with an equal amount of sweet rice flour. Mixing the sweet rice flour with a little bit of cold liquid to form a slurry before adding it into the dish will prevent the formation of lumps and keep the fat content much lower. If the extra fat/butter is desired in the dish it can easily be added, but it is no longer required.

✓ **Replacing wheat flour as a binder**
Ground meats for items such as; meatballs, meatloaf, and hamburgers all benefit from some sort of binder to help them hold together and retain moisture. The traditional bread or cracker crumbs can be replaced with gluten-free versions of the same, but an easier option is available from your pantry of gluten-free flours. *A small amount of brown rice flour works well to bind ground meats without adding any noticeable flavour.* Generally about 1 tbsp (15ml) will serve to bind 1 lb (450g) of ground lean meat. Use slightly more if the meat is fatty.

✓ **Replacing wheat flour as a coating**
Delicate products which are to be fried or baked frequently require something to hold them together during cooking or prevent them from becoming dry. Please see "Batters and Coatings" *(p. 230)* for many suggestions to replace wheat flour and to add some extra interest to your favourite meals.

✓ **Replacing wheat pasta, couscous and bulgur**
For most of us pasta products are a regular part of our diet and would surely be missed. Please refer to "Grains, Pastas and Side Dishes" *(p. 136)* for many options to replace wheat pasta, and some international alternatives to wheat noodles.

The conversion of gluten based, grain heavy recipes to gluten-free versions is generally quite complex, requiring a complete re-do of the recipes. Therefore, I have tried to create gluten-free versions of as many of the wheaty, grain heavy recipes as possible. Try the recipes as written in this book first to get an idea of the taste and texture of the basic recipe. Then feel free to use these recipes as a basis for customization. In a book such as this I couldn't possibly cater to all the individual tastes of my readers so I shall leave the fine tuning of flavours to you.

Nutritional Information

The nutritional information provided within this book is intended to inform you of the nutritional value of the recipes as written. Due care has been taken for these values to be as accurate as possible. However, errors and oversights can occur, and variations in the ingredients purchased may cause different nutritional values than those listed. For example, your choices in the fat, sugar and/or sodium content of ingredients can cause significant changes to the nutritional value of your batch of the recipes listed. Also, any of the variations listed will undoubtedly alter the nutritional profile of the recipes. Choosing alternates such as margarine instead of butter; or soy, rice or nut milk to replace dairy will have little effect on the recipe's taste and texture, but may have a noticeable effect on the recipe's nutritional content. Please note, none of the recipes in this book have been altered in any way to make them appear any more or less nutritious than the wheaty recipes they have been adapted from. Such alterations would compromise their quality.

All of the nutritional analyses have been calculated based upon the values of the raw ingredients and do not take into account the possible changes to these values caused by cooking. Unless otherwise stated, lower fat, sugar and sodium ingredients were used within the recipes. In recipes where the cooking technique, temperature and choice of ingredients can have a significant impact upon the nutritional values, the nutritional calculations have not been included. Please take these values as intended; as a guideline to help balance your diet to your nutritional needs.

Remember, the nutritional value of all the food you can't bear to eat will always be zero. Don't deprive yourself of delicious, gluten-free foods; experiment and enjoy the foods you crave, gluten-free.

Breakfast and Brunch

I am not a morning person. Anyone who knows me will see the irony in having a chapter in my book relating to a meal I prefer to sleep through. In fact, for many chefs, working the breakfast shift is considered cruel and unusual punishment. However, whether you are like me and prefer to sleep late or you are an early riser, the recipes in this chapter are sure to please. In case your breakfast is served a little late, be assured that the pancakes and all the other recipes in this chapter taste terrific any time of the day.

The first meal of the day, regardless of what the clock reads, has been proven to be the most important meal in order to have an alert, productive day. However, breakfast and brunch can be tough to handle gluten-free. Muffins, bagels, granola, most cereals, pancakes and waffles, just to mention just a few, are all wheaty items. The traditional breakfast items of bacon, eggs and hash brown potatoes are generally gluten-free, but nutritionally they should only be enjoyed in moderation.

Fortunately, some great breakfast choices are mercifully gluten-free. Try fruit, yogurt and gluten-free cereals as they are, or try layering them into a parfait glass and dress up these great breakfast staples. Smoothies are another way of combining these items into an easy, delicious breakfast. These quick and simple breakfast solutions are a great choice when time is an issue.

There are many great gluten-free versions of traditional breakfast and brunch specialties within this chapter. Some recipes are better suited to leisurely brunches, while others can be prepared quickly and enjoyed every day. Many of these recipes have even fooled wheat-eaters into thinking they were 'regular' brunch items. Cook some up, and make breakfast and brunch pleasurable again.

Buttermilk Pancakes

Served for breakfast or brunch, these pancakes are sure to please. Most of my testers can't tell these aren't wheaty.

¾ cup	corn starch *or* potato starch	185 ml
½ cup	brown rice flour	125 ml
¼ cup	tapioca starch	60 ml
1 ½ tsp	baking powder	8 ml
¾ tsp	baking soda	4 ml
¾ tsp	salt	4 ml
⅓ tsp	xanthan gum	2 ml
3	eggs	3
2 tbsp	vegetable oil	30 ml
1 cup	buttermilk *or* non-dairy substitute with ¼ tsp (2 ml) vinegar	250 ml

Instructions:

1. **Fully mix all dry ingredients**. Try measuring out multiple batches so you will have some on hand for future convenience. Be sure to mark the container with the instructions.
2. **Add wet ingredients and stir to fully incorporate.** The batter will take on its proper thickness only after a few minutes standing. If the batter is too thick or thin (variations in milling of the various flours or in the liquid used can cause this,) use water to thin slightly or corn starch/potato starch to thicken slightly.
3. **Cook as you would any pancake.** This recipe also works for waffles.

Yield: 15, 4 inch (10cm) pancakes

Nutritional Information

Calculations based upon the basic recipe excluding
optional ingredients and variations.

Per 4 inch (10 cm) pancake

energy	86 calories/360 kJ
protein	2 g
fat	3 g
carbohydrate	13 g
sodium	247 mg
potassium	51 mg
calcium	52 mg
iron	trace mg

Variations:

These pancakes are a special "sleep-in" favourite at my house. In their basic form or dressed up with variations, they are always a hit. Here are a few ideas to get you started:

✓ **Berry Pancakes**

Sprinkle a few fresh or frozen berries of your choice on the top of each pancake right after you place the batter into the pan.

✓ **Banana Pancakes**

Chop a banana into small pieces and mix it into the batter for a great tropical treat.

✓ **Apple Cinnamon Pancakes**

Add a chopped apple and a teaspoon of cinnamon to the batter. With a little maple syrup this is a perfect cool morning breakfast.

✓ **Waffles**

Prepare the batter as you would for pancakes, but cook it in a waffle iron for crisp light waffles. Top them as you wish and enjoy immediately.

Pro-tip: If you undercook them just slightly they can be frozen for later use as toaster waffles.

✓ **Pancake Breakfast Sandwiches**

Build yourself a breakfast sandwich on pancakes. While not a new idea, it is a good one.

Egg-Free Pancakes

With this recipe it is possible to have pancakes that are free of gluten, corn, soy, egg and dairy; all in a format that only needs oil and water to finish it. Whether you use it at home or take it with you for camping or travel, this is sure to become a favourite because of its convenience.

¾ cup	corn starch or potato starch	185 ml
½ cup	brown rice flour	125 ml
¼ cup	tapioca starch	60 ml
1 tsp	unflavoured gelatine *or* soy protein isolate	5 ml
1 ½ tbsp	egg replacer	22 ml
1 ½ tsp	baking powder	8 ml
¾ tsp	baking soda	4 ml
¾ tsp	salt	4 ml
⅓ tsp	xanthan gum	2 ml
3 tbsp	vegetable oil	45 ml
1 ¼ cups	water	310 ml

Instructions:

1. **Fully mix all dry ingredients.**
   Pro-tip: Try measuring out multiple batches so you will have some on hand for future convenience. Be sure to mark the container with the instructions.

2. **Add wet ingredients and stir to fully incorporate.** The batter will take on its proper thickness only after a few minutes standing. If the batter is too thick or thin (variations in milling of the various flours or in the liquid used can cause this), use water to thin slightly or corn starch/potato starch to thicken slightly.

3. **Cook on slightly lower heat** and for a longer time than standard pancakes. This recipe also works well for waffles.

Yield: 15, 4 inch (10 cm) pancakes

Nutritional Information

Calculations based upon the basic recipe excluding
optional ingredients and variations.

Per 4 inch (10 cm) pancake

energy	79 calories/331 kJ
protein	trace g
fat	3 g
carbohydrate	13 g
sodium	223 mg
potassium	16 mg
calcium	29 mg
iron	trace mg

Variations:

See pancake variations on *page 53*.

Helpful Hint:

Make up this recipe as a dry ready mix to take along when traveling almost anywhere. Whether you choose to stay in bed and breakfast accommodations or hotels, just print the directions to finish them and provide them to the kitchen staff wherever you're staying. This makes the monotony of bacon and eggs for breakfast a thing of the past. When camping or fishing, these pancakes are a great staple to have on hand, especially when the fish aren't biting.

Crepes

Wrap these around a variety of fillings to create breakfasts, entrees or desserts. Or try some of the variations below to expand the uses for this recipe.

½ cup	corn starch *or* potato starch	125 ml
⅓ cup	brown rice flour	85 ml
¼ cup	tapioca starch	60 ml
½ tsp	xanthan gum	3 ml
¼ tsp	salt	2 ml
½ tsp	sugar	3 ml
4	eggs	4
2 cups	milk *or* non-dairy alternate	500 ml
2 tbsp	vegetable oil	30 ml
¼ - ½ cup	water	60-125 ml

Instructions:

1. **Mix dry ingredients fully;** then add eggs and mix into a paste.
2. **Beat in all the liquids a bit at a time** until a smooth very thin batter forms.
3. **Preheat a 10 inch (25 cm) fry pan** or crepe pan over medium heat. Apply a sparse coating of cooking spray or wipe with a little vegetable oil.
4. **Quickly pour a scant ¼ cup (60 ml) of batter** into the pan while tilting and swirling it to spread the batter over the whole surface (this takes some practice, but is worth learning). Return the pan to the heat and cook until the edges brown slightly and the surface no longer appears wet. Depending on how hot your pan is, this may take less than a minute.
5. **Loosen the edges** all the way around with a thin spatula or palette knife and flip the crepe over. Cook 30-45 seconds on the other side until a few delicate golden brown spots form. Remove the crepe from the pan and immediately refill it as described above. Repeat until all the batter has been cooked.
6. **As the crepes come out of the pan** they can be stacked on a plate without risk of sticking together. They can be kept warm for use right away, kept covered in the refrigerator for up to a week, or frozen for later use.

Yield: about 20 crepes

Nutritional Information

Calculations based upon the basic recipe excluding
optional ingredients and variations.

Per crepe

energy	67 calories/280 kJ
protein	2 g
fat	3 g
carbohydrate	8 g
sodium	50 mg
potassium	55 mg
calcium	34 mg
iron	trace mg

Variations:

Crepes are a classic staple of continental dining with many traditional uses and variations. The following are some great uses for this gluten-free version:

✓ **Herb or Spice Crepes**

Add any herb or spice that suits your purposes. Try chilli powder, curry, chives or basil to give your crepes a personal touch.

✓ **Chocolate Crepes**

Add ¼ cup (60 ml) cocoa and 1 tbsp (15 ml) sugar to the batter for bittersweet chocolate crepes which are a great foil to sweet filings. Another option is to add ¼ cup (60 ml) cocoa powder and ¼ cup (60 ml) sugar for sweet chocolate crepes.

✓ **Stuffed Crepes**

For a great dressed up entrée, stuff the crepes with scrambled eggs, vegetable ragouts, creamed or curried seafood, or poultry.

✓ **Sandwich Wraps**

Prepare the crepes with a generous ¼ cup (70 ml) of batter (to make them a bit stronger) and use as you would a flour tortilla to prepare sandwich wraps.

✓ **Layered Desserts**

Build up a low cake-like dessert by layering the crepes with fruit fillings, icing or caramel sauce. Cut in wedges to serve.

✓ **Crisps**

Cut crepes into any desired shape and bake on a baking sheet lined with parchment paper until crisped. Great theme garnishes for desserts can be made in this way. Imagine a pair of clock hands for a New Year's dessert or a simple fan shape to decorate ice cream.

Buckwheat Crepes

Great for more than just breakfast, this staple of continental cooking has many uses. The buckwheat flavour adds a depth of character not found in regular crepes.

½ cup	light buckwheat flour	125 ml
¼ cup	brown rice flour	60 ml
¼ cup	tapioca starch	60 ml
½ tsp	xanthan gum	3 ml
¼ tsp	salt	2 ml
½ tsp	sugar	3 ml
4	eggs	4
2 cups	milk *or* non-dairy alternate	500 ml
2 tbsp	vegetable oil	30 ml
¼ cup	water	60 ml

Instructions:

1. **Mix dry ingredients fully,** then add eggs and mix to a paste.
2. **Beat in all the liquids a bit at a time** until a smooth very thin batter forms.
3. **Preheat a 10 inch (25 cm) fry pan** or crepe pan over medium heat. Apply a sparse coating of cooking spray or wipe with a very small amount of vegetable oil.
4. **Quickly pour a scant ¼ cup (60 ml) of batter** into the pan while tilting and swirling it to spread the batter over the whole surface (this takes some practice but is worth learning). Return the pan to the heat and cook until the edges brown slightly and the surface no longer appears wet. Depending on how hot your pan is, this may take less than a minute.
5. **Loosen the edges** all the way around with a thin spatula or palette knife and flip the crepe over. Cook 30-45 seconds on the other side until a few delicate golden brown spots form. Remove the crepe from the pan and immediately refill it as described above. Repeat until all the batter has been cooked.
6. **As the crepes come out of the pan** they can be stacked on a plate without risk of sticking together. They can be eaten warm right away, kept covered in the refrigerator for up to a week or frozen for later use.

Yield: about 20 crepes

Variations:

See crepes variations on *page 57*.

Nutritional Information
Calculations based upon the basic recipe excluding
optional ingredients and variations.
Per crepe

energy	20 calories/84 kJ
protein	2 g
fat	3 g
carbohydrate	6 g
sodium	50 mg
potassium	71 mg
calcium	35 mg
iron	trace mg

Buttermilk Biscuits

Soft and flaky, these biscuits are great with jam and butter for breakfast or baked on top of stews for an easy alternative to pot pies.

1 cup	tapioca starch	250 ml
2/3 cup	brown rice flour	165 ml
2/3 cup	corn starch	165 ml
2 ¼ tsp	baking powder	12 ml
½ tsp	salt	3 ml
2 tbsp	cold butter *or* non-dairy alternate	30 ml
1 cup	buttermilk *or* non-dairy alternate	250 ml

Instructions:
1. **Mix the first group of ingredients** in a bowl to fully combine.
2. **Rub in butter or alternate** with your hands until a coarse meal is formed.
3. **Add in the buttermilk or alternate** and mix until fully combined.
4. **Separate the dough** into evenly sized portions. Use a thumb release type ice cream scoop to do this easily. Place on a baking sheet lined with baker's parchment, allowing a bit of room for expansion. Flatten each portion to a disk about ½ - ¾ inch (1 - 2 cm) thick and 2 ½ inches (6 cm) round. Bake in a preheated 450°F (230°C) oven for 12-14 minutes. Place on a rack to cool.

Yield: about 12, 2 ½ inch (6 cm) round shaped biscuits

Nutritional Information

Calculations based upon the basic recipe excluding optional ingredients and variations. Per biscuit

energy	118 calories/494 kJ
protein	1 g
fat	2 g
carbohydrate	23 g
sodium	223 mg
potassium	57 mg
calcium	77 mg
iron	trace mg

Variations:

Biscuits have long been a quick and easy alternative to bread, and are a great accompaniment to sweet or savoury dishes. From breakfast to dinner, biscuits have a role to play. Here are just a few ideas to make biscuits a versatile staple in your kitchen.

- ✓ **Biscuit Topped Stews**

  Drop the dough from a spoon or scoop to cover the surface of a casserole of hot stew. Bake until gently browned and enjoy this easy alternative to pot pies.

- ✓ **Biscuit Breakfast Sandwiches**

  Split the biscuits top and bottom and use them for breakfast sandwiches. Some fast food restaurants even make wheaty versions of this.

- ✓ **Biscuits with Berries and Cream**

  Split the biscuits top and bottom and cover them with fresh berries and whipped cream for a variation on strawberry shortcake.

- ✓ **Biscuits with Butter and Jam**

  This is probably the best known use of biscuits for breakfast and is always a favourite.

- ✓ **Biscuit Cases**

  Prepare the biscuits in a size large enough to be used as an entrée and stuff them with stew to provide a great plate presentation and an alternative to potatoes or rice.

- ✓ **Biscuit French Toast**

  Split the biscuits top and bottom and use them instead of bread for French toast. This is also a great use for biscuits that have been around awhile.

Scones

For an English breakfast or high tea, these are sure to please.

¾ cup	corn starch	185 ml
¾ cup	brown rice flour	185 ml
¾ cup	tapioca starch	185 ml
2 ½ tsp	baking powder	13 ml
2 tbsp	brown sugar	30 ml
½ tsp	xanthan gum	3 ml
½ tsp	salt	3 ml
¼ cup	cold butter *or* non-dairy alternate	60 ml
2	eggs	2
⅓ - ½ cup	buttermilk *or* non-dairy alternate	85 - 125 ml

Instructions:

1. **Mix the first group of ingredients** in a bowl to fully combine.
2. **Rub in butter or alternate** with your hands until a coarse meal is formed.
3. **Add in the buttermilk or alternate** and mix until fully combined.
4. **Separate the dough** into evenly-sized portions.

Pro-tip: Use a thumb release type ice cream scoop to do this easily. Place on a baking sheet lined with bakers' parchment, allowing a bit of room for expansion. Flatten each to a disk about ½ - ¾ inch (1 - 2 cm) thick and 2 ½ inch (6 cm) round. Bake the scones in a preheated 375ºF (190ºC) oven for 14 - 16 minutes. Place on a rack to cool.

Yield: about 12, 2 ½ inch (6 cm) round size

Nutritional Information

Calculations based upon the basic recipe excluding
optional ingredients and variations.

Per scone

energy	145 calories/607 kJ
protein	2 g
fat	5 g
carbohydrate	24 g
sodium	248 mg
potassium	55 mg
calcium	72 mg
iron	trace mg

Variations:

No traditional English breakfast or tea would be complete without scones and
Devon cream. Now avoiding gluten doesn't mean going without. Here are a few
ideas to add a little extra to this recipe.

✓ **Dried Fruit Scones**

Try adding ¾ cup (185 ml) raisins, currants, cranberries or other dried
fruits to the dough before forming.

✓ **Fresh Berry Scones**

Try adding ¾ cup (185 ml) blueberries, raspberries or chopped
strawberries to the dough before forming.

✓ **Mixed Peel Scones**

Try adding ½ cup (125 ml) mixed candied citrus peel to the dough before
forming.

✓ **See Variations for Buttermilk Biscuits (***page 61)*

63

English Muffins

Just toasted or made into Eggs Benedict,
these are sure to please.

1 cup	corn starch	250 ml
2/3 cup	brown rice flour	165 ml
1/3 cup	potato starch	85 ml
1 ½ tsp	baking powder	8 ml
1 tsp	baking soda	5 ml
1 tsp	unflavoured gelatine	5 ml
2 tbsp	sugar	30 ml
1 tbsp	instant dry yeast	15 ml
½ tsp	xanthan gum	3 ml
1 cup	milk or non-dairy alternate	250 ml
1	egg	1
¼ cup	melted butter *or* non-dairy alternate	60 ml
½ tsp	cider vinegar	3 ml

Instructions

1. **Mix together all dry ingredients** fully in a mixer, then add all wet ingredients and beat to a smooth batter (about 1 minute.)
2. **Scoop into 8, greased 4 inch (10 cm) English muffin rings** set on a baking sheet lined with baker's parchment. Allow to rise in a warm, draft free area until the dough has risen to nearly fill the rings.
3. **Bake at 350°F (180°C)** for about 15 minutes or until just starting to turn golden on the top.
4. **Turn them over and bake a further 5 minutes**.
5. **Remove from the oven** and wait about 2 minutes before removing from the rings.

Yield: 8, 4 inch (10 cm) round English muffins

Nutritional Information

Calculations based upon the basic recipe excluding optional ingredients and variations.

Per muffin

energy	226 calories/946 kJ
protein	3 g
fat	8 g
carbohydrate	36 g
sodium	334 mg
potassium	124 mg
calcium	94 mg
iron	1 mg

Variations:

This classic breakfast item is very versatile. Here are just a few ideas to make English muffins a useful staple in your kitchen:

✓ **English Muffin Breakfast Sandwich**

This isn't a new idea, but it is a popular one. Split the muffin top and bottom, toast it and load it up any way you like. Fried egg, ham, cheese and a tomato slice is a good start.

✓ **English Muffin Mini Pizza**

Split the muffin top and bottom and top as you would a pizza crust. This is a great snack for the kids and they can even help make their own.

✓ **Eggs Benedict and variations**

The perennial brunch favourite of a toasted English muffin topped with back bacon, a poached egg and hollandaise sauce is a great use for this recipe.

   ○ Replace the back bacon with smoked salmon.
   ○ Replace the back bacon with sautéed spinach and the hollandaise with a cheese sauce.

Whatever you put on top, these muffins are sure to be up to the task of making a great brunch dish.

GF- Ola

"Granola without the grain?" you bet; and it still makes a great breakfast. You control the amount of sugar and it doesn't have all the added fat of the commercial brands. By altering the recipe with the variations suggested the possibilities are endless.

2 cups	rolled soy, millet *or* buckwheat *or* oats*	500 ml
2 cups	slivered almonds *or* other nuts	500 ml
1 cup	unsweetened shredded coconut	250 ml
1 cup	sunflower seeds	250 ml
¼ - ¾ cup	brown sugar	60 -180 ml
½ cup	water	125 ml
1 cup	raisins	250 ml
1 cup	dried fruit (cranberries, cherries, blueberries, apricots...)	250 ml
2 cups	gluten-free flake cereal *or* nutty rice	500 ml

*Be sure the oats are certified gluten-free.

Instructions:
1. **Mix together** all the ingredients in the first grouping in a large bowl and set aside.
2. **Bring the water and sugar to a boil** and add to the first set of ingredients.
3. **Mix thoroughly,** but gently, until fully combined.
4. **Spread the mixture out evenly**, no more than ¼ inch (7mm) thick on bakers' parchment lined baking trays.
5. **Bake** at 300ºF (150ºC) for 20-25 minutes until golden. If the edges are browning up more quickly than the rest, stir the edges into the centre periodically for even toasting.
6. **Allow to cool** completely before mixing in the remaining ingredients. When mixed, store in an air-tight container. This cereal should last about a month on the pantry shelf, depending on your choice of nuts.

Yield: 10 cups (2.5 litres)

Nutritional Information

Calculations based upon the basic recipe using the first ingredients listed,
excluding optional ingredients and variations.

Per ½ cup (125 ml) serving

energy	230 calories/962 kJ
protein	5 g
fat	14 g
carbohydrate	22 g
sodium	31 mg
potassium	396 mg
calcium	63 mg
iron	2 mg

Variations:

This gluten free granola recipe is a basic guide which is easy to customize to suit your tastes. Try different dried fruits, nuts and seeds; and vary the other cereals added to it to customize this recipe.

- ✓ Try keeping small bags of it on hand to use as emergency rations when away from home.
- ✓ Enjoy as is or with milk.
- ✓ To dress this up a bit in the Swiss style, mix in yogurt and some grated apple.
- ✓ Toss some into a green salad to add some crunch.
- ✓ Layer it with some yogurt in tall glasses to create an attractive breakfast parfait.

Cheese Soufflé

This brunch dish is full of hot air and loved for it.
It is also very unforgiving of waiting to be served, so be sure to
pay it due respect by waiting fork in hand until it is ready.

2 cups	milk *or* non-dairy alternate	500 ml
¼ cup	onion finely chopped	60 ml
½ cup	tapioca starch	125 ml
⅓ cup	brown rice flour	85 ml
¼ cup	corn starch	60 ml
½ tsp	xanthan gum	3 ml
1 cup	grated sharp cheese such as Cheddar, Gruyere, Swiss, *or* Blue	250 ml
4	eggs (*separated*)	4
½ tsp	salt (*if desired*)	3 ml

Instructions:

1. **Combine all the ingredients in the first group cold** in a saucepan; then bring to a simmer for 5 minutes to allow the flavours to develop. Stir frequently to prevent burning.

Alternately, this can be made over a double boiler to prevent burning.

2. **Remove from the heat and allow to cool slightly** while separating the eggs.
3. **Whip the whites and the salt** to firm, but not dry looking peaks.
4. **Stir the yolks and the cheese into the cooked mixture.**
5. **Fold the beaten egg whites into the cooked mixture** until fully combined.
6. **Transfer the soufflé batter** into greased soufflé cups or a straight-sided 2 litre/quart oven-proof casserole dish.
7. **Place the soufflé into a preheated 375ºF (190ºC) oven** until puffed to about double the size, is nicely browned on top and golden brown on the exposed sides. This will be about 45-50 minutes for the 1 quart (2 litre) size, less for smaller sizes.

Pro-tip: **Serve immediately** for best results because the soufflé will begin to fall within a few minutes. It will still taste great, but the presentation will suffer.

Yield: 6 portions

Nutritional Information

Calculations based upon the basic recipe excluding
optional ingredients and variations.

Per 1 cup (250 ml) serving

energy	258 calories/1079 kJ
protein	12 g
fat	12 g
carbohydrate	25 g
sodium	195 mg
potassium	213 mg
calcium	250 mg
iron	1 mg

Variations:

I originally attempted this dish as a challenge from a friend who thought it
would be impossible to make gluten-free. Fortunately, to the surprise of both of
us, it worked well. Soufflés aren't nearly as finicky as they are made out to be,
and they make a great brunch dish. Try changing the cheeses and adding herbs
and spices to give a bit of variety to this dish. Also check *page 326* for dessert
versions.

Lunch Options

Lunch tends to be the meal which causes the most stress and receives the least effort. Its placement in the middle of the day usually requires quick preparation and eating, simply because of the time constraints associated with it. However, when "grabbing a quick sandwich" includes baking bread, the "quick" part of the statement is in serious jeopardy. Yes, a sandwich can make a great lunch, but we owe it to ourselves to explore faster, simpler, wonderful international solutions to the 'brown bag blahs'. With a thermos, soups and stews are perfect take along foods. Most offices now have microwave ovens that can turn dinner leftovers into great lunches. This chapter offers some other quick and easy solutions to making lunch either at home or when brown bagging it.

The sandwich concept exists in other cultures around the world that do not use bread. The Japanese sushi roll is simply a cold rice-based "sandwich," as is the Vietnamese rice roll. Both involve no more work than putting together a good sandwich. Gluten-free crepes make a great basis for wraps, and with the addition of herbs and spices to the batter, the flavour variations are nearly limitless. Corn tortillas form the basis for many Central American sandwich replacements. Calzones and empanadas are other sandwich substitutes that can add interest to your lunch.

Salads can also make great lunches. The traditional chef or Cobb salad with all the toppings to round it out into a full meal is a great lunch. Try taco salads with tortilla chips, salsa, ground beef and refried beans for a hearty choice. Consider deli favourite salads such as potato, bean, rice and gluten-free pasta. Cold noodle salads can be made with a startling array of gluten-free noodles. Noodles made from yams, tofu, rice, potato, arrowroot, corn, sweet potato, mung beans, tapioca and buckwheat are all available in Asian markets. Gluten-free granola bars, crackers, corn chips, rice cakes and pretzels can make a quick and easy cocktail nibbles-style lunch. All the basic food groups can easily be supplied in separate parts. Add cheese or meat, fruit and veggies for a portable lunch without a lot of work.

Gluten-free lunches don't have to be a problem. With a few solutions borrowed from other cultures and a bit of creativity, we can enjoy brown bag lunches without the blahs.

Sushi Rolls

Sushi doesn't have to be raw fish and seaweed.
Sushi rolls really are just another bread-free sandwich idea and
aren't all that difficult to make. You can put together sushi rolls
as fast as a sandwich and have a great lunch
without the effort of baking bread.

3 cups	fresh cooked sushi rice, *page 154*	750 ml
2 tbsp	seasoned rice vinegar *or* flavoured vinegar of your choice with ¼ tsp (2 ml) salt and 1 tsp (5 ml) sugar dissolved in it	30 ml
3 sheets	dried nori *(if desired)*	3 sheets
	fillings of your choice *(see below for ideas)*	

Instructions:

1. **Prepare the rice** following the recipe on *page 154*.
2. **Stir in the vinegar mixture and any other desired seasoning** while the rice is still warm. Consider using chilli powder, curry or herbs.
3. **Allow the rice to cool** to about room temperature before continuing.
4. **Place about 1 cup (250 ml) of sushi rice on a sheet of nori or plastic wrap,** spreading it out to cover about two-thirds of the sheet approximately ¼ inch (7 mm) thick.
5. **Place the garnish of your choice** in a line that will form the centre of the roll on the side of the rice opposite the rice-free part of the nori or plastic wrap.
6. **Roll toward the plain, rice-free part of the sheet.** This rice-free flap helps hold the sushi together while it cools and sets.

Pro-tip: **Roll it up using a sushi rolling mat**. These bamboo mats held together with string are found in Asian markets and are very inexpensive. Roll from the long side of the sheet for thinner sushi rolls and from the shorter side for thicker rolls. Using both hands to apply gentle pressure, roll the sushi mat a first time to allow the roll to form. Then loosen the sushi mat and re-roll it a second time a bit tighter to make the roll firmer and easier to handle.

7. **Wrap and refrigerate the rolls** to chill them fully before cutting. It is possible to cut them immediately, but when warm they are much more difficult to cut without crumbling.

Pro-tip: **To cut the rolls** moisten the blade of a very sharp knife with water between each slice to prevent sticking. Sushi chefs use a clean wet kitchen towel to wipe the blade after each slice.

Nutritional Information
Due to the variations inherent in this recipe,
nutritional calculations are not possible.

Variations:
This classic Japanese sandwich replacement can really be a quick and easy way to make lunch. Almost anything you can make into a cold sandwich can be used. However, unless you know a fabulous fish monger don't even try making the raw fish varieties as only the freshest and highest quality raw fish will do. Fortunately, there are many other options available.

- ✓ You can make Japanese-style sushi or make the flavour your own.
- ✓ Use plastic wrap to roll the rice and fillings if you don't like the nori, or if it doesn't suit the flavour of your creation.
- ✓ Change the vinegar to change the flavours. Choose a vinegar flavour that complements your fillings, such as tarragon vinegar with chicken and raspberry vinegar with shrimp.
- ✓ Try cooked shrimp, crab, canned or smoked salmon, omelette, chicken, tuna or steak.
- ✓ For some extra flavour, add pickled ginger, wasabi, mustard, chutney, barbeque sauce or hot sauce.
- ✓ To round out your rolls, add some avocadoes, peppers, onions, shredded lettuce, mango, fresh fruit or sprouts.
- ✓ Southwest seasoned beef and peppers make for a Tex-Mex style sushi.
- ✓ Curried rice and chicken with mango slices create a taste of India.
- ✓ Choose ham and cheese with a bit of Dijon mustard and you are in for a treat.

Rice Paper Rolls

This Vietnamese sandwich replacement may not be authentic, but it is a great way to make lunch. Not used for writing, this paper is actually a very thin noodle, perfect to stuff with a variety of fillings.

1 oz	rice vermicelli	25 g
½ lb	cooked shrimp, crab *or* whatever you like	225 g
1 ½ cups	shredded vegetables *(try carrots, cucumber, scallions, bell peppers, or lettuce)*	375 ml
to taste	salt, pepper, sugar and rice vinegar	to taste
10 - 12 sprigs	fresh herbs *(try cilantro or basil)*	10 - 12 sprigs
4 - 5 sheets	8 - 10 inch (20 - 25 cm) round rice paper *(found in Asian markets)*	4 - 5 sheets

Instructions:

1. **Place rice vermicelli in a large flat dish** and cover with very hot, but not boiling water. Allow to soak for about 10 minutes or until softened. Drain well and reserve the noodles in the colander used to drain them. Reserve the large flat dish for further use in step 3.

2. **While noodles are soaking prepare shredded vegetables.** Season them with a little sugar and vinegar to give a sweet and sour balance. Adjust seasoning with salt and pepper to taste.

3. **To assemble rice paper rolls** fill the large flat dish with hot water and lay out a clean kitchen towel on your work surface nearby. Put a single sheet of rice paper into the water at a time for about 10 - 15 seconds before placing it on the towel.

Pro-tip: Do not let the rice paper soak much longer as it will become unmanageable. Do not be concerned if it is still a bit firm. It will continue to soften as you work with it.

4. **Place about ¼ - ¹/₅ of your prepared fillings** in the centre of the rice paper and roll over one edge about a third of the way.
5. **Fold the sides in** burrito-style before rolling the rest of the way, using firm pressure to roll it fairly tight. Repeat until all the filling is used. Resist the urge to overstuff the rolls; the extra filling will just end up in your lap.
6. **Wrap tightly** in plastic wrap and refrigerate.

Pro-tip: **To cut the rolls** moisten the blade of a very sharp knife with water between each slice to prevent sticking. Cut the rolls in half on a long diagonal to show off the colourful ingredients, or slice the rolls into smaller pieces for use as appetizers.

Nutritional Information
Due to the variations inherent in this recipe,
nutritional calculations are not possible.

Variations:

Rice paper rolls are simply another international sandwich replacement concept. Follow the Vietnamese style described above, or fill it as you would any sandwich for an easy take-along lunch. The rice vermicelli can be replaced by cooked rice or any other cooked gluten-free grain. See Sushi Roll variations *(page 73)* for some ideas.

Rice paper rolls are generally served with a dip. For a traditional dip, try the recipe below or branch out and try anything you like.

Vietnamese Dipping sauce

2 tbsp	water	30 ml
2 tbsp	sugar	30 ml
2 tbsp	lime juice	30 ml
2 tbsp	fish sauce (nam pla)	30 ml
	(available in Asian markets)	
½ tsp	fresh grated ginger	3 ml
½ tsp	fresh red chilli or dried hot pepper flakes	3 ml

Instructions:

Stir together all ingredients until sugar is dissolved. Allow to sit at least 20 minutes for the full flavour to develop. **Yield:** about 4 ounces (110 ml)

Easy Hot Lunches

Most quick lunches are bread based making a quick lunch a difficult thing to accomplish without baking bread regularly. Some international solutions and novel uses of regular household staples can make a hot lunch quick and easy. Here are a few ideas to get you started.

- ✓ **Left-overs and planned-overs**
  Use your dinner left-overs to save cooking lunch. Or better yet, when preparing dishes which reheat well, plan to make extra so you have what I call "planned-overs." If you rotate these items so that you don't eat them for dinner and then for lunch the next day they won't even seem like left-overs.

- ✓ **Quesadillas**
  Grilled cheese sandwiches with a Spanish accent, quesadillas are a great solution when I need a quick lunch for my kids. Place combinations of cheese, cooked meats, seafood … or perhaps scrambled eggs, peppers and onions between two corn tortillas and grill over medium/low heat on both sides until the cheese has melted. Cut into wedges and enjoy with sour cream and salsa. This concept can be used with any hot sandwich fillings such as basic ham and cheese, or roast beef and Cheddar, but 'pizzadillas' are my kids' all-time favourite.

- ✓ **Tortilla Pie**
  Alternate tortillas with a variety of fillings to make a lasagne-type layered casserole with a Spanish accent. Cooked and seasoned ground beef, chicken or pork, cheese, refried beans, sautéed peppers and onions all make for an easy one dish meal. Bake or microwave until the cheese has melted and it is hot all the way through.

- ✓ **Baked potato melts**
  The classic hot open faced sandwich remade without the bread. Cut open a baked potato and top it with tuna, salmon or shrimp salads. Sprinkle over a bit of grated cheese of your choice and broil or microwave to melt the cheese. Sandwich meats and chilli also work well for this.

- ✓ **Omelettes**
  A few eggs or egg whites combined with leftover potatoes, vegetables, pasta, meats, cheese or seafood can make a hearty omelette a quick and easy lunch.

Muffins

For many people muffins are a 'grab and go' convenience food. They fill the need for something quick and easy to eat while on the way out the door or while on a quick coffee break. Unfortunately, when the muffins need to be gluten-free they are not readily available in the corner bakery or convenience store. The good news is that by using a few chefs' tricks you can make your kitchen into that convenient corner bakery.

Upon looking at the recipes within this section you will notice that it contains recipes for muffins only, no loaves are included. Loaves do not turn out as well as muffins because without the extra structure that gluten provides, they can be difficult to slice without some crumbling. The differences between recipes for a muffin and a loaf of the same type are minimal, but when baking gluten-free products there are other factors to be considered. The crust surrounding a muffin provides a more manageable structure for handling. It also makes for a lighter-textured product. Furthermore, muffins can be frozen for later use and thawed very quickly.

You can also portion the batter and freeze it in its raw state. Simply thaw the batter overnight in the refrigerator and pop it into the oven when you get up. Imagine having the exact number of fresh baked muffins you need with no running around. Chefs have been using this trick for years. If you keep a small stock of different muffin batters frozen in reserve, you can even offer impromptu guests a choice of different flavours without any extra effort.

This section includes muffin recipes based upon several different flours. The stronger flavoured muffins utilize a soy flour combination to make use of its great texture and moistness, while minimizing its bean taste. The more subtly flavoured recipes are based upon rice flour, cornstarch and tapioca starch which do not have strong flavours that would overpower the milder flavoured muffins. Bake up a batch, or two, and enjoy.

Apple Crisp Muffins

These muffins are the result of a marriage
between coffee cake and apple crisp.

	topping	
½ cup	brown sugar	125 ml
¼ cup	soft butter *or* non-dairy alternate	60 ml
2 tbsp	sweet rice flour	30 ml
2 tbsp	tapioca starch	30 ml
1 tsp	cinnamon	5 ml
½ cup	rolled soybeans, millet *or* buckwheat	125 ml
	muffin batter	
1 cup	soy flour	250 ml
½ cup	potato starch	125 ml
½ cup	sweet rice flour	125 ml
¾ cup	sugar	185 ml
1 tbsp	baking powder	15 ml
½ tsp	xanthan gum	3 ml
½ tsp	salt	3 ml
½ tsp	cinnamon	3 ml
1	egg	1
⅓ cup	milk *or* non-dairy alternate	85 ml
⅓ cup	oil, melted butter *or* non-dairy alternate	85 ml
1 cup	shredded apple	250 ml

Instructions:

1. **Rub together the first group of ingredients** for the topping in a small bowl until crumby. Add in the rolled grain of your choice and mix gently to incorporate without breaking the flakes. Set aside.
2. **Mix together all ingredients** in the first group of the muffin batter ingredients and set aside.
3. **Beat the next group of muffin batter ingredients** in a mixer until frothy.

80

4. **Mix dry with wet** to moisten fully; then mix on high for 1 minute before stirring in the apple.
5. **Divide batter** into 12 greased/sprayed muffin cups.

Pro-tip: Thumb release ice cream scoops are available in a wide variety of sizes and are   ideal for easy and consistent portioning of soft doughs and batters. This recipe can be made up and promptly frozen in paper muffin cup liners to allow fresh baked muffins a few at a time whenever you wish. Thaw overnight in the refrigerator or 1 hour at room temperature.

6. **Top each muffin** with some of the topping mixture.
7. **Bake** at 375°F (190°C) for 20 - 25 minutes.

Yield: 12 standard sized muffins

Nutritional Information

Calculations based upon the basic recipe excluding optional ingredients and variations.

Per 1 muffin

energy	285 calories/1192 kJ
protein	6 g
fat	14 g
carbohydrate	32 g
sodium	262 mg
potassium	372 mg
calcium	125 mg
iron	1 mg

Variations:

Try replacing the apples with pears. Consider changing the spices. Cardamom, nutmeg, cloves or star anise all make for interesting variations.

Banana Muffins

These muffins stay moist and freeze well, so double the recipe to have some on hand.

1 cup	soy flour	250 ml
½ cup	potato starch *or* corn starch	125 ml
½ cup	sweet rice flour	125 ml
¹/₂ tsp	xanthan gum	3 ml
1 ½ tsp	baking soda	8 ml
1 ½ tsp	baking powder	8 ml
½ tsp	salt	3 ml
¾ tsp	ground ginger	4 ml
2	eggs	2
¼ cup	water or orange juice	60 ml
½ cup	oil, melted butter *or* non-dairy alternate	125 ml
¾ cup	sugar	185 ml
¾ cup	mashed banana	185 ml
1 cup	blueberries, cranberries… fresh *or* frozen (*optional*)	250 ml

Instructions:

1. **Mix together ingredients** in the first group and set aside.
2. **Beat eggs** in the bowl of a mixer until frothy.
3. **Beat in** the next group of ingredients.
4. **Mix dry ingredients with wet** to moisten fully; then mix on high for 1 minute before stirring in the berries.
5. **Divide batter** into 12 greased/sprayed muffin cups.

Pro-tip: Thumb release ice cream scoops are available in a wide variety of sizes and are ideal for easy and consistent portioning of soft doughs and batters.

6. **Bake** at 375ºF (190ºC) for 20 - 25 minutes.

Yield: 12 standard-sized muffins

Nutritional Information
Calculations based upon the basic recipe excluding
optional ingredients and variations.
Per 1 muffin

energy	223 calories/933 kJ
protein	4 g
fat	11 g
carbohydrate	24 g
sodium	318 mg
potassium	250 mg
calcium	54 mg
iron	1 mg

Variations:

Try adding berries of your choice such as blueberries, cranberries or raspberries.
Consider a change in the spice used. Cardamom, nutmeg, cloves and star anise
are all worth a try.

Basic Muffin Batter

This basic muffin recipe can be the basis for hundreds of variations. Dress it up any way you like.

1 cup	corn starch *or* potato starch	250 ml
1 cup	tapioca starch	250 ml
½ tsp	xanthan gum	3 ml
1 ½ tsp	baking soda	8 ml
1 ½ tsp	baking powder	8 ml
½ tsp	salt	3 ml
2	eggs	2
²/₃ cup	milk *or* non-dairy alternate	185 ml
¹/₃ cup	oil, melted butter *or* non-dairy alternate	85 ml
½ - ²/₃ cup	sugar *(depending on how sweet your additions are)*	125 – 165 ml
1 tsp	vanilla extract	5 ml
	see variations below	

Instructions:

1. **Mix together** the first group of ingredients and set aside.
2. **Beat the next group of ingredients** in the bowl of a mixer until frothy.
3. **Mix dry with wet** to moisten fully; then mix on high for 1 minute before stirring in any optional variations.
4. **Divide batter** into 12 greased/sprayed muffin cups.

Pro-tip: Thumb release ice cream scoops are available in a wide variety of sizes and are ideal for easy and consistent portioning of soft doughs and batters. This recipe can be made up and promptly frozen in paper muffin cup liners to allow fresh baked muffins a few at a time whenever you wish. Simply thaw overnight in the refrigerator or 1 hour at room temperature before baking.

5. **Bake** at 375ºF (190ºC) for 20 - 25 minutes.

Yield: 10 standard-sized muffins without any additional fruit
        12 standard-sized muffins with 1 cup added fruit

Nutritional Information

Calculations based upon the basic recipe excluding
optional ingredients and variations.

Per muffin

energy	180 calories/753 kJ
protein	1 g
fat	7 g
carbohydrate	28 g
sodium	324 mg
potassium	30 mg
calcium	54 mg
iron	trace mg

Variations:

With this recipe and a bit of imagination, many types of muffins are possible.
Here are just a few ideas to get you started.

- ✓ **Berry Muffins**
  Try adding up to 1 cup (250 ml) berries of your choice such as
  blueberries, cranberries or raspberries. Either fresh or frozen work well.
- ✓ **Veggie Muffins**
  Try adding up to 1 cup (250 ml) grated moist vegetables such as
  zucchini, carrots, sweet potato, squash or pumpkin for a moist and
  flavourful change.
- ✓ **Spice Muffins**
  Add ¼ cup (60 ml) liquid of your choice and consider changing the
  spices used. Cardamom, nutmeg, cloves and star anise are all worth a
  try.
- ✓ **Lemon Poppy Seed Muffins**
  Try adding the juice and zest of half a lemon and ½ cup (125 ml) of
  poppy seeds for lemon poppy seed muffins.
- ✓ **Marmalade Muffins**
  Stir in ½ cup (125 ml) of Seville orange marmalade for a great bitter-
  sweet variation.
- ✓ **Chocolate Chip Muffins**
  Change the sugar to brown sugar and add up to 1 cup (250 ml) chocolate
  chips. You can even try white chocolate, butterscotch or peanut butter
  chips as long as they are gluten-free.

Carrot Raisin Muffins

These muffins are a great way to add a few vegetables to breakfast or snacks. They stay moist and freeze well either baked or as batter.

1 cup	soy flour	250 ml
½ cup	potato starch *or* corn starch	125 ml
½ cup	sweet rice flour	125 ml
½ tsp	xanthan gum	3 ml
1 ½ tsp	baking powder	8 ml
¾ tsp	baking soda	4 ml
½ tsp	salt	3 ml
¼ tsp	nutmeg	3 ml
¾ tsp	cinnamon	4 ml
2	eggs	2
⅔ cup	oil, melted butter *or* non-dairy alternate	165 ml
¾ cup	brown sugar	185 ml
⅓ cup	orange juice	
1 cup	grated carrots *(lightly packed)*	250 ml
¾ cup	raisins *or* currants	185 ml
½ cup	chopped nuts *(optional)*	125 ml

Instructions:

1. **Mix together ingredients** in the first group and set aside.
2. **Beat the eggs, oil or alternate and sugar** in the bowl of a mixer until creamy.
3. **Beat in** the third group of ingredients.
4. **Mix dry with wet** to moisten fully; then mix on high for 1 minute before stirring in the nuts, if using them.
5. **Divide batter** into 12 greased/sprayed muffin cups.

Pro-tip: Thumb release ice cream scoops are available in a wide variety of sizes and are ideal for easy and consistent portioning of soft doughs and batters.

6. **Bake** at 375ºF (190ºC) for 20 - 25 minutes.

Yield: 12 standard-sized muffins

Nutritional Information
Calculations based upon the basic recipe excluding
optional ingredients and variations.
Per 1 muffin

energy	259 calories/1084 kJ
protein	4 g
fat	14 g
carbohydrate	29 g
sodium	247 mg
potassium	340 mg
calcium	71 mg
iron	1 mg

Variations:

Consider a change in the spice used. Cardamom, allspice, ginger, cloves and star anise are all worth a try. Try replacing the carrots with winter squash or sweet potato for an interesting variation.

Corn Muffins

Not a sweet tasting muffin, these are a tasty alternative to dinner rolls, especially with Tex-Mex or Cajun food.

1 cup	corn meal	250 ml
¾ cup	corn flour	185 ml
½ cup	tapioca starch	125 ml
⅓ cup	sugar	85 ml
1 ½ tbsp	baking powder	22 ml
½ tsp	xanthan gum	3 ml
½ tsp	salt	3 ml
1	egg	1
⅓ cup	vegetable oil	85 ml
1 cup	milk *or* non-dairy alternate	250 ml

Instructions:

1. **Mix together** the first group of ingredients and set aside.
2. **Beat the next group of ingredients** in the bowl of a mixer until frothy.
3. **Mix dry with wet** to moisten fully; then mix on high for 1 minute before stirring in any optional variations.
4. **Divide batter** into 12 greased/sprayed muffin cups.

Pro-tip: Thumb release ice cream scoops are available in a wide variety of sizes and are ideal for easy and consistent portioning of soft doughs and batters. This recipe can be made up and promptly frozen in paper muffin cup liners, to allow fresh baked muffins a few at a time whenever you wish. Simply thaw overnight in the refrigerator or 1 hour at room temperature before baking.

5. **Bake** at 400ºF (200ºC) for 20 - 25 minutes. Allow to cool 5 minutes before removing from the pan to ease removal. Serve warm with butter.

Yield: 12 standard-sized muffins

Nutritional Information
Calculations based upon the basic recipe excluding
optional ingredients and variations.
Per muffin

energy	179 calories/749 kJ
protein	3 g
fat	8 g
carbohydrate	26 g
sodium	287 mg
potassium	77 mg
calcium	129 mg
iron	1 mg

Variations:

This classic cornbread is suitable for any of the usual variations. Here are just a few ideas to get you started.

✓ **Double Corn Muffins**

Add ¾ cup (185 ml) sweet corn kernels to add a bit of texture to the muffins.

✓ **Bacon Corn Muffins**

Add ½ cup (125 ml) crumbled crisp bacon to add a little flavour.

✓ **Sweet Pepper Corn Muffins**

Add ½ cup (125 ml) colourful finely chopped sweet peppers for a great splash of colour and flavour.

✓ **Hot Pepper Corn Muffins**

Add what you dare of finely diced hot peppers such as Jalapeño, Serrano or Chipotle.

✓ **Herbed Corn Muffins**

Add any herb that suits the dish you will be serving the muffins with. Rosemary, thyme and oregano are especially good.

Java Date Muffins

A full flavoured muffin that pairs well with morning coffee

1 ½ cups	chopped dates	375 ml
1 cup	hot coffee	250 ml
1 cup	corn starch	250 ml
½ cup	tapioca starch	125 ml
1 tsp	baking soda	5 ml
2 tsp	baking powder	10 ml
1 tsp	xanthan gum	5 ml
½ tsp	salt	3 ml
2	eggs	2
½ cup	sugar	125 ml
1/3 cup	butter, oil *or* non-dairy alternate	85 ml
¾ cup	yogurt *or* soft tofu	185 ml
½ cup	chopped nuts (*optional*)	125 ml

Instructions:

1. **Combine** the chopped dates and coffee. Mix fully and leave to cool.
2. **Measure and mix** together all ingredients in the next group and set aside.
3. **Beat the third group of ingredients** in the bowl of a mixer until fluffy.
4. **Mix dry with wet** to moisten fully; then mix on high for 1 minute before stirring in the dates. If using chopped nuts, add them last to prevent breaking them up too much.
5. **Divide batter** into 12 greased/sprayed muffin cups.

Pro-tip: Thumb release ice cream scoops are available in a wide variety of sizes and are ideal for easy and consistent portioning of soft doughs and batters. This recipe can be made up and promptly frozen in paper muffin cup liners to allow fresh baked muffins a few at a time whenever you wish. Thaw overnight in the refrigerator or 1 hour at room temperature.

6. **Bake** at 400ºF (200ºC) for 20 - 25 minutes. Allow to cool 5 minutes before removing from the pan to ease removal.

Yield: 12 standard-sized muffins

Nutritional Information

Calculations based upon the basic recipe excluding
optional ingredients and variations.

Per 1 muffin

energy	217 calories/908 kJ
protein	2 g
fat	6 g
carbohydrate	40 g
sodium	345 mg
potassium	190 mg
calcium	77 mg
iron	1 mg

Pumpkin Spice Muffins

This is a moist muffin with a pumpkin pie flavour.
These muffins stay moist and freeze well so
double the recipe to have some on hand.

1 cup	soy flour	250 ml
½ cup	potato starch *or* corn starch	125 ml
½ cup	sweet rice flour	125 ml
½ tsp	xanthan gum	3 ml
2 ½ tsp	baking powder	13 ml
½ tsp	salt	3 ml
1 ½ tsp	pumpkin pie spice	8 ml
2	eggs	2
½ cup	oil, melted butter *or* non-dairy alternate	125 ml
¾ cup	brown sugar	185 ml
1 cup	canned pumpkin *or* steamed fresh with excess liquid wrung out	250 ml
1 cup	raisins *or* currants (*optional*)	250 ml

Instructions:

1. **Mix together ingredients** in the first group and set aside.
2. **Beat the eggs, oil or alternate and sugar** in the bowl of a mixer until creamy.
3. **Beat in** the third group of ingredients.
4. **Mix dry ingredients with wet** to moisten fully; then mix on high for 1 minute before stirring in the raisins or currants, if using.
5. **Divide batter** into 12 greased/sprayed muffin cups.

Pro-tip: Thumb release ice cream scoops are available in a wide variety of sizes and are ideal for easy and consistent portioning of soft doughs and batters.

6. **Bake** at 375ºF (190ºC) for 20 - 25 minutes.

Yield: 12 standard-sized muffins

Nutritional Information

Calculations based upon the basic recipe excluding
optional ingredients and variations.

Per 1 muffin

energy	205 calories/908 kJ
protein	2 g
fat	11g
carbohydrate	22 g
sodium	206 mg
potassium	266 mg
calcium	90mg
iron	1 mg

Raisin and Bran Muffins

This perennial favourite tastes just as good made with rice bran and flax seed.

1 cup	brown rice flour	250 ml
2/3 cup	cornstarch	165 ml
1/3 cup	tapioca starch	85 ml
1/2 cup	milled flax seed	125 ml
1/2 cup	rice bran	125 ml
2 tsp	baking powder	10 ml
1 tsp	baking soda	5 ml
1 tsp	xanthan gum	5 ml
1/2 tsp	salt	3 ml
2	eggs	2
1/3 cup	melted butter, oil *or* non-dairy alternate	85 ml
3/4 cup	yogurt *or* soft tofu	185 ml
1/4 cup	molasses	60 ml
1/4 cup	brown sugar	60 ml
3/4 cup	cold coffee *or* water	185 ml
1 cup	raisins	250 ml

Instructions:

1. **Mix together ingredients** in the first group and set aside.
2. **Beat eggs until frothy** in the bowl of a mixer.
3. **Beat in** the next group of ingredients.
4. **Mix dry ingredients with wet** to moisten fully; then mix on high for 1 minute before stirring in the raisins.
5. **Divide batter** into 12 greased/sprayed muffin cups.

Pro-tip: Thumb release ice cream scoops are available in a wide variety of sizes and are ideal for easy and consistent portioning of soft doughs and batters. This recipe can be made up and promptly frozen in paper muffin cup liners to allow fresh baked muffins a few at a time whenever you wish. Thaw overnight in the refrigerator or 1 hour at room temperature.

6. **Bake** at 375ºF (190ºC) for 20 - 25 minutes.

Yield: 12 standard sized muffins

Nutritional Information
Calculations based upon the basic recipe excluding optional ingredients and variations.
Per 1 muffin

energy	265 calories/1109 kJ
protein	5 g
fat	10 g
carbohydrate	42 g
sodium	353 mg
potassium	399 mg
calcium	109 mg
iron	2 mg

Zucchini Coconut Muffins

These muffins are a great way to use up extra zucchini at harvest time. They stay moist and freeze well either baked or as batter

1 cup	soy flour	250 ml
½ cup	potato starch *or* corn starch	125 ml
½ cup	sweet rice flour	125 ml
½ tsp	xanthan gum	3 ml
1 ½ tsp	baking soda	8 ml
¾ tsp	baking powder	4 ml
½ tsp	salt	3 ml
½ tsp	nutmeg	3 ml
¾ tsp	cinnamon	4 ml
2	eggs	2
²/₃ cup	oil, melted butter *or* non-dairy alternate	165 ml
¾ cup	sugar	185 ml
1 cup	grated zucchini	250 ml
¾ cup	grated coconut	185 ml
½ cup	chopped nuts (*optional*)	125 ml

Instructions:

1. **Mix together ingredients** in the first group and set aside.
2. **Beat the eggs, oil or alternate and sugar** in the bowl of a mixer until creamy.
3. **Beat in** the third group of ingredients.
4. **Mix dry with wet** to moisten fully; then mix on high for 1 minute before stirring in the nuts, if using.
5. **Divide batter** into 12 greased/sprayed muffin cups.

Pro-tip: Thumb release ice cream scoops are available in a wide variety of sizes and are ideal for easy and consistent portioning of soft doughs and batters.

6. **Bake** at 375ºF (190ºC) for 20 - 25 minutes.

Yield: 12 standard-sized muffins

Nutritional Information

Calculations based upon the basic recipe excluding
optional ingredients and variations.

Per 1 muffin

energy	258 calories/1079 kJ
protein	4 g
fat	16 g
carbohydrate	25 g
sodium	289 mg
potassium	236 mg
calcium	40 mg
iron	1 mg

Variations:

Try adding raisins or currants. Simply soak them in water for a few minutes and drain fully before adding them in step 4. Consider a change in the spice used. Cardamom, nutmeg, cloves and star anise are all worth a try.

Zucchini Raisin Muffins

This is a great moist muffin that helps use up the inevitable excess of zucchini in the fall. These muffins also freeze well either baked or as batter.

1 cup	soy flour	250 ml
½ cup	potato starch *or* corn starch	125 ml
½ cup	sweet rice flour	125 ml
½ tsp	xanthan gum	3 ml
1 ½ tsp	baking powder	8 ml
1 ½ tsp	baking soda	8 ml
½ tsp	salt	3 ml
1 tsp	cinnamon	5 ml
1 cup	raisins	250 ml
2	eggs	2
1/3 cup	oil, melted butter *or* non-dairy alternate	85 ml
1 cup	sugar	250 ml
1 tsp	vanilla extract	5 ml
1 cup	grated zucchini	250 ml

Instructions:

1. **Mix together ingredients** in the first group and set aside.
2. **Beat eggs** in the bowl of a mixer until frothy.
3. **Beat in** the next group of ingredients.
4. **Mix dry with wet** to moisten fully; then mix on high for 1 minute before stirring in the zucchini.
5. **Divide batter** into 12 greased/sprayed muffin cups.

Pro-tip: Thumb release ice cream scoops are available in a wide variety of sizes and are ideal for easy and consistent portioning of soft doughs and batters. This recipe can be made up and promptly frozen in paper muffin cup liners to allow fresh baked muffins a few at a time whenever you wish. Thaw overnight in the refrigerator or 1 hour at room temperature.

6. **Bake** at 375ºF (190ºC) for 20 - 25 minutes.

Yield: 12 standard-sized muffins

Nutritional Information

Calculations based upon the basic recipe excluding
optional ingredients and variations.

Per 1 muffin

energy	238 calories/996 kJ
protein	4 g
fat	8 g
carbohydrate	35 g
sodium	320 mg
potassium	309 mg
calcium	63 mg
iron	1 mg

Variations:

Try adding berries of your choice such as blueberries, cranberries or raspberries. Consider a change in the spice used. Cardamom, nutmeg, cloves and star anise are all worth a try.

Breads and Flat-Breads

For those who must avoid gluten it is a cruel irony that the most common staple food in many parts of the world is bread. The ease with which wheat can be formed into hundreds of varieties of bread has ensured that bread is at the core of most meals. While researching this book, I came across the following unattributed quote in the notes I made while studying to be a chef, "Wheat is the most essential grain used in bread making, because it is the only cereal that contains the proper combination of glutenin and gliadin. When combined with water these properties form gluten, essential for retaining the gas produced by yeast. No other grain can replace wheat in bread making."

Well here I am over twenty years later proving that where there's a will, there's a way. While according to a gluten-filled perspective the quote is true, it does have a few loopholes for gluten-free individuals to exploit. By using a combination of different gluten-free grains, protein sources and food gum, we can replace the wheat in bread making.

The consistency of gluten-free bread dough is quite different from regular wheaty dough. The thin sticky dough required to yield gluten-free breads most like their wheaty cousins require different methods to mix, knead and form. The instructions given differ significantly from those used for making wheat-based breads, but be assured these new methods yield the closest facsimiles to wheat breads. Many of the recipes in this chapter have been designed to be made either with a bread machine or a heavy duty mixer. Therefore, you can have the convenience of a bread machine or the versatility of forming and raising the dough any way you wish.

This chapter contains recipes for basic breads with numerous variations. Try the recipes as written first before trying the variations listed, or any other variations you may be considering. Try preparing and forming the dough into any size or shape you need, then freeze it before it has a chance to rise. The next time you need bread you can thaw and proof (raise) the dough without any further work. This method allows you to enjoy fresh baked breads daily, instead of dry or frozen ones. Bread is a staple of many cuisines of the world and the need to be gluten-free doesn't change that fact. I hope these basic recipes and international specialty breads make 'going without' a thing of the past for you. Bake well and often to make the gluten-free lifestyle one without deprivation.

Bagels

Yes it is true; it is possible to make gluten-free bagels!
They tend to crack a bit when they bake, but have
an enjoyable chewy texture and a crisp crust.

1 cup	brown rice flour	250 ml
1 cup	tapioca flour	250 ml
½ cup	potato starch	125 ml
½ cup	sweet rice flour	125 ml
1 tbsp	xanthan gum	15 ml
1 tsp	salt	5 ml
1 ½ tbsp	sugar	22 ml
1 tbsp	unflavored gelatin	15 ml
1 ½ tbsp	instant rise yeast	22 ml
½ tsp	cider vinegar	3 ml
1 tbsp	vegetable oil	15 ml
1 cup	milk *or* non-dairy alternate	250 ml
3	eggs	3
1	egg white *(for brushing on top)*	1

Instructions:

1. **Mix dry ingredients** in a heavy-duty mixer with a flat paddle installed. In a separate container, beat eggs until frothy.

Pro-tip: An immersion blender works well for this purpose.

2. **Warm the milk** or alternate to about 120ºF (40ºC) (this will feel very much like a warm bath) and combine it with the other wet ingredients.

3. **Add the wet to the dry** and mix on low/medium for about 3 minutes. Soft, slightly sticky dough will form.

4. **Divide the dough** into 8 balls. Poke a finger through the centre of each ball and gently form the dough over your finger into the classic bagel shape.

5. **Place the bagels** on a baking sheet covered with bakers' parchment, allowing a bit of room for them to rise.

6. **Allow them to rise** in a warm, draft free area until they are 1 ½ times their original size.

7. **Drop the bagels into lightly salted boiling water** for about 10 seconds each and remove immediately. Place the bagels back on the parchment lined baking sheet.

8. **Brush the top of each bagel** with a bit of beaten egg white. Bake at 375ºF (190ºC) for about 25 minutes until golden brown.

Yield: about 8 sandwich-sized bagels.

Nutritional Information
Calculations based upon the basic recipe excluding optional ingredients and variations.
Per bagel, about 3 ¼ oz (90 g) serving

energy	262calories/1096 kJ
protein	8 g
fat	5 g
carbohydrate	42 g
sodium	316 mg
potassium	181 mg
calcium	52 mg
iron	1 mg

Variations:
The list of variations possible is easily as long as the lineups at some great bagel shops. This recipe is a blank canvas ready to accept your favorite variations.
- ✓ Add herbs, dried fruits or berries, spices or any number of gluten-free seeds and grains.
- ✓ If you are in the mood for a little indulgence try adding chocolate chips, toffee or your favorite nuts.
- ✓ Numerous fast food restaurants have adopted the bagel as the basis for a quick, on the go, breakfast sandwich. Try your own version, for breakfast or brunch. For me, a poppy seed bagel with lox and cream cheese is a perfect brunch, but the choice is yours.

Calzones

Calzones, pizza pockets and empanadas are all names for roughly the same thing – a bread pocket filled with whatever suits you. Although they are a bit of work to make initially, a little planning can provide all the convenience of the store-bought stuff without the gluten.

1 ½ cups	brown rice flour	375 ml
1 ¼ cups	cornstarch	310 ml
1 cup	tapioca starch	250 ml
1 tbsp	sugar	15 ml
1 tbsp	instant rise yeast	15 ml
1 tbsp	xanthan gum	15 ml
¾ tsp	salt	
1 ½ tsp	baking powder *(make sure yours is gluten-free)*	8 ml
1	egg	1
1 ⅓ cups	milk *or* non-dairy alternate	335 ml
3 tbsp	vegetable oil	30 ml
1	beaten egg	1

Instructions:

1. **Mix dry ingredients** in a heavy-duty mixer with the dough hook installed. In a separate container, beat the egg until frothy.

Pro-tip: I use an immersion blender for this) and combine with the other wet ingredients.

2. **Add the wet ingredients to the dry** and mix on low/medium for about 5 minutes. A fairly firm dough will form.

3. **Form dough** into a round flat disk. Cut the dough into 8 wedges as you would a pie. This shape makes the forming of 8 equal-sized calzones easiest. Shape each wedge into a ball before rolling it out into a circle about 8 inches (20 cm) round. Cover the dough you are not immediately working with to prevent drying.

4. **Fill the dough** with just enough filling to cover about $1/3$ of the surface of the dough rounds about 1 inch (2.5 cm) thick. Take care to leave a margin of about 1 inch (2.5 cm) around the edge with no filling to seal the dough. *See variations below for filling ideas.*

5. Brush the beaten egg onto the outer margin of the dough. Fold the dough over on itself to form a half moon shape and press the edges together to seal the package. Brush with vegetable oil or beaten egg.

6. Cover with plastic wrap on a baking sheet lined with bakers' parchment and leave to rise in a warm draft-free area until the dough puffs up to 1 ½ times its thickness along the edges.

7. **Bake** the calzones in a 375ºF (190ºC) oven, 15 - 20 minutes or until golden brown.

Pro-tip: If you are intending to save the calzones for later, you may wish to leave them a bit pale so they will not become over-baked when you reheat them in the oven.

8. **Remove from oven**. Enjoy warm right away or save them for later in the refrigerator or freezer. Reheat in your oven or microwave.

Yield: 8 meal sized calzones

Nutritional Information

Calculations based upon the basic recipe excluding
optional ingredients and variations.
Per 1 calzone

energy	324 calories/1356 kJ
protein	5 g
fat	8 g
carbohydrate	59 g
sodium	331 mg
potassium	193 mg
calcium	112 mg
iron	1 mg

Variations:

✓ **Empanadas**
Wrap up spicy beef and peppers for a Central and South American flavour.

✓ **Pizza Pockets**
Load it up with all your favorite pizza toppings.

✓ **Appetizers**
The full size is a meal for one, but when made in smaller sizes they make great hot appetizers.

Cinnamon Raisin Rolls

The flavour and aroma of these rolls will make your morning!

1 cup	brown sugar	250 ml
½ cup	softened butter *or* non-dairy alternate	125 ml
½ cup	raisins	125 ml
1 tbsp	cinnamon	15 ml
1 ½ cups	tapioca starch	375 ml
1 ½ cups	brown rice flour	375 ml
1 cup	cornstarch	250 ml
1 tbsp	xanthan gum	15 ml
1 tsp	salt	5 ml
1 ½ tbsp	sugar	22 ml
1 tsp	gelatine	5 ml
1 tbsp	instant rise yeast	15 ml
3	eggs	3
¾ tsp	cider vinegar	4 ml
1 ¼ cups	milk *or* non-dairy alternate	375 ml

Instructions:

1. **Mix the first group of ingredients** together and set aside.
2. **Mix the second group of ingredients** in a heavy-duty mixer with a flat paddle installed. In a separate container, beat the eggs and vinegar until frothy.

Pro-tip: An immersion blender works well for this.

3. **Combine** the eggs with the other wet ingredients.
4. **Add the wet to the dry** and mix on low/medium for about 3 minutes. Soft dough will form.
5. **On a work surface dusted with tapioca starch. Spread the dough** to form a large rectangle with outer dimensions about 16 x 10 inches (40 x 25 cm), and a thickness of ¼ inch (7 mm).
6. **Spread the reserved sugar raisin mixture** over the rectangle, leaving a 2 inch (5 cm) strip along the longer side.
7. **Roll up the dough** so the strip with no sugar raisin mixture can seal against the roll to help hold it together.

8. **Slice the roll** into 1 ½ inch (4 cm) thick slices and set them into a 9 x 13 inch (33 x 21 cm) pan. Allow the dough to rise in a warm, draft free area until it is nearly double its original size.

9. **Bake at 375ºF (190ºC)** for about 30 minutes until golden brown.

Yield: 12 rolls

Nutritional Information
Calculations based upon the basic recipe excluding
optional ingredients and variations.
Per 1 roll

energy	334 calories/1397 kJ
protein	4 g
fat	10 g
carbohydrate	59 g
sodium	475 mg
potassium	224 mg
calcium	165 mg
iron	2 mg

Variations:

✓ **Cranberry Ginger Rolls**
   Replace the raisins with dried cranberries and the cinnamon with ground ginger for a tasty change from the regular recipe.

✓ **Cheese Rolls**
   Replace the raisin and sugar filling with any grated cheese you enjoy. Sharp Cheddar, Swiss, Raclette or even Blue cheese can make a savory variation from the sweet original.

✓ **Nutty Rolls**
   Replace the raisins with your favourite nuts to create a nutty version.

Corn Tortillas

Fresh soft corn tortillas are the flatbread basis of Mexican cooking and a great gluten-free staple. Many of the commercially available brands are loaded with preservatives and tend to be hard and dry. If you don't have a good Latin American market in your neighbourhood, this recipe will have you enjoying tortillas the way they were meant to taste.

2 cups	ground corn masa *This is whole grain corn that has been specially ground and dehydrated, with a small amount of lime added. The lime makes nutrients such as calcium in the corn easier to digest. It is available in Latin American markets or well stocked supermarkets.*	500 ml
½ tsp	salt	3 ml
1 ⅛ cups +	water	280 ml +

Instructions:

1. **Measure and mix** all ingredients in a heavy duty mixer with the flat paddle installed. Continue mixing until a firm dough forms. If it seems a bit dry or crumbly, add about 1 tablespoon (15 ml) of water at a time, allowing the dough to mix together completely before adding any more water. When the right amount of water has been added, the dough will naturally clump together.

2. **Divide the dough** into 12 balls. Cover dough balls with a damp cloth to prevent drying while you cook the tortillas one at a time. With a bit of practice you can roll or press the next tortilla in the time it takes to cook one.

3. **Flatten out each ball** with your hands before placing it between two sheets of bakers' parchment or plastic wrap.

4. **Roll out dough** or press it with a tortilla press until the tortillas are about 6 inches (15 cm) in diameter.

If your tortillas aren't the perfectly round circles you may be accustomed to, don't despair. The machine-made commercially prepared ones are cut into that shape. While you can go to the trouble of cutting them to shape, I prefer to just leave them as is. A tortilla press is worth the investment if you find you like making your own tortillas.

5. **Peel the tortilla carefully off** the bakers' parchment or plastic wrap onto your hand.

6. **Drop the tortilla flat onto a very hot ungreased pan** or griddle and cook about 20 seconds per side or until small spots of brown appear on the surface and the tortilla loses its wet dough look.

7. **Remove from the pan and cover** to keep the tortillas soft and pliable.

Yield: 12, 6 inch (15 cm) tortillas

Nutritional Information

Calculations based upon the basic recipe excluding optional ingredients and variations.

Per tortilla

energy	70 calories/293 kJ
protein	1 g
fat	1 g
carbohydrate	15 g
sodium	90 mg
potassium	61 mg
calcium	2 mg
iron	trace

Variations:

With entire cookbooks based on corn tortillas, the possibilities are nearly endless. Here are a few easy ideas to get you started, and any Mexican cookbook will be sure to add many more.

✓ **Quesadillas**

Grilled cheese sandwiches with a Spanish accent, quesadillas are a great solution when I need a quick lunch for my kids. Place cheese with any combination of cooked meats, seafood, scrambled eggs, peppers, onions, or other vegetables between two tortillas and grill over medium/low heat on both sides until the cheese has melted. Cut into wedges and enjoy with sour cream and salsa. This concept can be used with any hot sandwich fillings such as basic ham and cheese, or corned beef and Swiss.

✓ **Tortilla Pie**

Alternate tortillas with a variety of fillings to make a lasagne-type layered casserole with a Spanish flair. Cooked and seasoned ground beef, chicken or pork, cheese, refried beans, sautéed peppers and onions all make for an easy one dish dinner. Bake until the cheese has melted and it is hot all the way through.

Naan Bread

This Indian flatbread is traditionally cooked in a tandoori oven, but an inexpensive pizza stone in your oven does a great job of reviving this Indian classic. The method is a bit of work, but if you miss this staple of Indian take-out, you are in for a treat.

1 ½ cups	brown rice flour	375 ml
1 ¼ cups	cornstarch	310 ml
1 cup	tapioca starch	250 ml
1 tbsp	sugar	15 ml
1 tbsp	instant rise yeast	15 ml
1 tbsp	xanthan gum	15 ml
¾ tsp	salt	
1 ½ tsp	baking powder *(make sure yours is gluten-free)*	8 ml
1	egg	1
1 ⅓ cups	plain yogurt *or* soft tofu	335 ml
3 tbsp	vegetable oil	30 ml

Instructions:

1. **Mix dry ingredients** in a heavy-duty mixer with the dough hook installed. In a separate container, beat the egg until frothy.
Pro-tip: An immersion blender works well for this.

2. **Combine** eggs with the other wet ingredients.

3. **Add the wet to the dry** and mix on low/medium for about five minutes. A fairly firm dough will form.

4. **Form dough** into a round flat disk. Cut the dough into six wedges as you would a pie. This shape makes forming the traditional shape of the naan easiest. Cover the dough you are not immediately working with to prevent drying. Roll each wedge out into the traditional teardrop shape about 10 x 5 inches (25 x 12 cm).

5. **Cover the formed dough** with plastic wrap and leave to rise in a warm, draft free area until it puffs up to 1 ½ times its thickness.

6. **Bake** by placing the naan, one at a time, onto a pizza stone preheated in a 500°F (260°C) oven. Bake 3 - 4 minutes or until puffy with brown spots.

7. **Remove from oven**, brush with clarified butter (ghee) or alternate, if desired. Keep the naan soft and warm by wrapping it in a clean kitchen towel while you bake the remaining dough. Best enjoyed warm.

Yield: 6 naan

Nutritional Information

Calculations based upon the basic recipe excluding optional ingredients and variations.

Per naan

energy	431 calories/1803 kJ
protein	6 g
fat	11 g
carbohydrate	78 g
sodium	429 mg
potassium	248 mg
calcium	145 mg
iron	1 mg

Variations:

✓ **Dried Fruit**

Add a ½ cup (125 ml) chopped raisins and dried apricots along with 1 tsp (5 ml) ground cardamom to the dough. This variation is so good you may want it for dessert.

✓ **Savoury**

Just before the basic naan is baked, try sprinkling on chopped coriander (cilantro) leaves or crushed garlic.

Pizza Dough

Make up some of these crusts ahead of time and freeze them. While not quite as convenient as take-out, a bit of forward planning makes them just as fast!

2 cups	brown rice flour	500 ml
²/₃ cup	potato starch *or* corn starch	165 ml
¹/₃ cup	tapioca starch	80 ml
2 tbsp	sugar	30 ml
1 tbsp	xanthan gum	15 ml
1 tsp	unflavored gelatin	5 ml
¾ tsp	salt	3 ml
1 tbsp	rapid rise (instant) yeast	15 ml
1 ½ cups	milk *or* non-dairy alternate, 110°F (40°C)	375 ml
2	eggs	2
¼ cup	olive oil	60 ml

Instructions:

1. **Mix together all dry ingredients** in an electric mixer using the flat paddles, *not* the dough hook.
2. **Add the wet ingredients** and beat 1 minute on high. **Note:** The dough will look quite different from regular pizza dough. This is due to the different flours used and is necessary in order to achieve the desired outcome.
3. **Split dough** into three equal portions for thin crust pizzas; two for thick crust style pizzas.
4. **Press into non-stick pans** (do not use a pizza stone or perforated pizza pan) that have been coated with cooking spray. Use a wet hand to form the dough into the desired pizza shell shape.
Pro-tip: Re-wetting your hand frequently will prevent the dough from sticking to you.
5. **Allow dough to rise** in a warm, but not hot, area for 20 - 30 minutes, or until it is 1 ½ times as thick.
6. **The pizza dough can be topped** as you wish to bake right away, or baked without toppings to be kept for use later. With toppings; bake at 400°F (200°C) for about 20 minutes, or until nicely browned.

7. **To prepare the plain shells** for use later, bake at 325°F (165°C) for about 15 minutes until baked, but not browned. The pre-baked pizza crust can be kept a few days in the refrigerator or frozen.

Yield: 3, 12 inch (30 cm) thin crust pizzas or 2, 12 inch (30 cm) thick crust pizzas

Nutritional Information
Calculations based upon the basic recipe excluding
optional ingredients and variations.
Per ⅛ slice of 1 thick crust pizza

energy	158 calories/661 kJ
protein	3 g
fat	5 g
carbohydrate	26 g
sodium	122 mg
potassium	115 mg
calcium	34 mg
iron	1 mg

Variations:

The variations in toppings are only limited by your imagination. You can stick to the traditional favourites or try some new combinations, possibly creating a new masterpiece. Any kind of gluten-free meats, cheeses or vegetables can be combined with whatever type of sauce you like.

✓ **Cheese Crust**
   Add ¾ cup (185 ml) grated cheese of your choice into the dough to add a bit of extra flavour.

✓ **Herb Crust**
   Add some herbs to the dough to add a bit of extra flavour. Try basil, oregano, and fennel seed for a classic Italian flavour.

✓ **Dessert pizza**
   Top the dough with thin slices of apples or pears and sprinkle with sugar and cinnamon, or other sweet spices. The resulting "pie" is different from the ones at your local pizzeria, but it sure is tasty.

Soda Crackers

When the commercially prepared rice crackers just won't do, this recipe will put the saltines back in your soup. With the variations below all manner of 'dressed up' crackers are possible.

1 cup	corn starch	250 ml
²/₃ cup	brown rice flour	165 ml
¹/₃ cup	tapioca starch	85 ml
1 tsp	baking powder	5 ml
1 tsp	xanthan gum	5 ml
¹/₃ cup	cold butter *or* non-dairy alternate	85 ml
1 cup	milk *or* non-dairy alternate	250 g
to taste	coarse salt *(if desired)*	to taste

Instructions:

1. **Measure and mix** the first group of ingredients and set aside.
2. **Rub in butter or alternate** with your hands until a coarse meal is formed. Add the remaining ingredients and mix until just barely combined to form a dough.
3. **Roll dough to about ¹/₁₆ inch (1.5 mm) thickness** between two sheets of bakers' parchment. Peel off the top sheet by pulling it at a low angle across the surface so it folds back upon itself as it comes away from the rolled dough.
4. **Cut dough** into the familiar square shape and poke holes in its surface with a fork to prevent large air pockets from forming during baking. If you like, sprinkle on some coarse salt at this point.
5. **Bake at 375ºF (190ºC)** on a baking sheet lined with bakers' parchment until lightly golden. This will take 10 - 12 minutes for average-sized crackers. The crackers will be a bit soft when you remove them from the oven. Allow to cool slightly before handling. The crackers will not take on their final texture until they have cooled about an hour at room temperature.

Yield: about 4 dozen standard-sized crackers

Nutritional Information
Calculations based upon the basic recipe excluding
optional ingredients and variations.
Per standard sized cracker

energy	34 calories/142 kJ
protein	trace
fat	1 g
carbohydrate	5 g
sodium	26 mg
potassium	15 mg
calcium	13 mg
iron	trace

Variations:

Just like their wheaty cousins, this soda cracker replacement can be crumbled into soups and chowders, or topped with peanut butter and raisins for a great kids' snack. With a few additions and a little extra care in shaping the dough, it can also become a great base for more 'dressed up' crackers.

✓ **Cheese Crackers**

Add ½ cup (125 ml) of very sharp cheese, such as Cheddar to the dough to liven up the colour and flavour.

✓ **Garlic and Herb Crackers**

Add a clove or two of finely chopped garlic to the dough, along with some herbs of your choice.

✓ **Sesame Crackers**

Add ½ cup (125 ml) of raw sesame seeds to the dough to give the crackers a pleasing crunch. If you are a big fan of sesame seeds, you could even top them with more sesame seeds.

✓ **Multigrain Crackers**

Add ½ cup (125 ml) of small gluten-free seeds such as flax, teff, poppy seed or millet to the dough. Your crackers will have a great appearance and some extra whole grain goodness as well.

✓ **Hazelnut crackers**

Add ½ cup (125 ml) of ground hazelnuts to the dough. The rich nutty flavour is great with wine and cheese.

Yeast-Free Stovetop Bread

(Home version)

A backpackers best friend, but with a prep time of only 20 minutes you will find this useful at home as well. Its low round shape makes it great to split the top and bottom for sandwiches. This is the recipe I fall back on when I need some bread in a hurry.

¾ cup	cornstarch	185 ml
½ cup	brown rice flour	125 ml
¼ cup	tapioca starch	60 ml
2 tsp	baking powder	10 ml
1 tsp	xanthan gum	5 ml
½ tsp	salt	3 ml
1	egg	1
1 cup	milk *or* non-dairy alternate	250 ml
1 tsp	butter *or* non-dairy alternate	5 ml

Instructions:

1. **Mix dry ingredients fully;** then add egg and milk and mix into very soft, sticky dough.
2. **Melt butter or alternate** in a 10 inch (25cm) fry pan with a lid; swirl pan to grease evenly.
3. **Spread dough out evenly** in the pan.

Pro-tip: A wet hand works well for this as you can feel when the dough begins to stick and you need to re-wet your hand.

4. **Cover with the lid** and place on the stovetop on medium-low (about 25 - 30% power on most stoves) for 12 - 15 minutes until the top loses its wet sheen.
5. **Turn over and cook a further 5 minutes** on the other side or until lightly browned. Cool fully before cutting.

Yield: 1, 10 inch (25 cm) round x 1 inch (2.5 cm) thick bread

Nutritional Information
Calculations based upon the basic recipe excluding optional ingredients and variations.
Per ⅙ of recipe

energy	160 calories/669 kJ
protein	3 g
fat	2 g
carbohydrate	32 g
sodium	379 mg
potassium	111 mg
calcium	147 mg
iron	1 mg

Variations:

As with any basic bread recipe the possible variations are nearly endless. You can safely add up to ¾ cup (185 ml) of dry ingredients like herbs, spices, nuts, dried fruits, seeds or gluten-free grains. The beauty of this recipe is that you can still make bread without an oven. For camping or travel this bread can be a lifesaver.

The low rounded shape of this bread presents some interesting possibilities.
- ✓ It makes great grilled Italian **Panini sandwiches**. Enjoy it cut into individual sandwiches filled as you like, or make it as one large sandwich to share.
- ✓ Try loading it up with your favourites as an **oversized burger** and cut it in wedges to share among friends. Cut in small wedges to use as a great appetizer or snack for a group.
- ✓ Cut in small wedges and toast in the oven. Serve with your favourite dip. Spinach dip, bruscetta, hummus or whatever you like will taste great on these. They also make perfect **bases for canapés.**

Just Add Water Stovetop Bread
(Low allergen version)

A backpackers best friend, with quick stovetop cooking time and a "just add water" format. This recipe is also an allergy sufferers dream. It can be made without eggs, dairy, soy, corn, and yeast. Its low round shape makes it great to split the top and bottom for sandwiches.

¾ cup	cornstarch *or* potato starch	185 ml
½ cup	brown rice flour	125 ml
¼ cup	tapioca starch	60 ml
2 tsp	baking powder	10 ml
1 ½ tsp	egg replacer	8 ml
1 tsp	xanthan gum	5 ml
½ tsp	salt	3 ml
1 tsp	vegetable oil	5 ml
1 cup + 2 tbsp	water	280 ml
1 tsp	butter *or* vegetable oil	5 ml

Instructions:

1. **Mix dry ingredients fully;** then add water and the first 1 tsp (5 ml) vegetable oil. Mix into a very soft sticky dough.
2. **Place the second 1 tsp (5 ml) vegetable oil** in a 10 inch (25 cm) fry pan with a lid; swirl pan to grease evenly.
3. **Spread dough out evenly** in the pan.

Pro-tip: A wet hand works well for this as you can feel when the dough begins to stick and you need to re-wet your hand.

4. **Cover with the lid** and place on the stovetop on medium-low (about 25 - 30% power on most stoves) for 12 - 15 minutes until the top loses its wet sheen.
5. **Turn over and cook a further 5 minutes** on the other side or until lightly browned. Cool fully before cutting.

Yield: 1, 10 inch (25 cm) round x 1 inch (2.5 cm) thick bread

Nutritional Information
Calculations based upon the basic recipe excluding
optional ingredients and variations.
Per ¹/₆ of recipe

energy	142 calories/594 kJ
protein	1 g
fat	2 g
carbohydrate	30 g
sodium	346 mg
potassium	39 mg
calcium	94 mg
iron	1 mg

Variations:

Please see variations for Yeast-Free Stovetop Bread (*p. 120*)

Brown Yeast-Free Stovetop Bread
(Home version)

A backpackers best friend, but with a prep time of only 20 minutes, you will find this useful at home as well. Its low round shape makes it great to split top and bottom for sandwiches, and the sorghum and brown rice formula has whole grain taste and nutrition.

½ cup	sorghum flour	125 ml
½ cup	brown rice flour	125 ml
½ cup	tapioca starch	125 ml
2 tsp	baking powder	10 ml
1 tsp	xanthan gum	5 ml
½ tsp	salt	3 ml
1	egg	1
1 cup	milk *or* non-dairy alternate	250 ml
1 tsp	butter *or* non-dairy alternate	5 ml

Instructions:

1. **Mix dry ingredients fully,** then add egg and milk and mix into a very soft sticky dough.
2. **Melt butter or alternate** in a 25 cm (10 inch) fry pan with a lid; swirl pan to grease evenly.
3. **Spread dough out evenly** in the pan.
Pro-tip: A wet hand works well for this as you can feel when the dough begins to stick and you need to re-wet your hand.
4. **Cover with the lid** and place on the stovetop on medium-low (about 25 - 30% power on most stoves) for 12 - 15 minutes until the top loses its wet sheen.
5. **Turn over and cook a further 5 minutes** on the other side or until lightly browned. Cool fully before cutting.

Yield: 1, 10 inch (25 cm) round x 1 inch (2.5 cm) thickness

Nutritional Information
Calculations based upon the basic recipe excluding
optional ingredients and variations.
Per $^1/_6$ of recipe

energy	149 calories/623 kJ
protein	4 g
fat	3 g
carbohydrate	29 g
sodium	378 mg
potassium	145 mg
calcium	149 mg
iron	1 mg

Variations:

Please see variations for Yeast-Free Stovetop Bread (*p. 120*)

Egg-Free Dairy-Free French Bread

If you need to avoid eggs and dairy this bread is for you. It doesn't rise quite as high as the other French bread in this book, but it is a good alternative for anyone unable to tolerate eggs and dairy, as well as gluten.

Medium 1 ½ lb loaf	Large 2 lb loaf		Medium 680 g loaf	Large 900g loaf
1 cup +2 tbsp	1 ½ cups	tapioca flour	280 ml	375 ml
¾ cup	1 cup	brown rice flour	185 ml	250 ml
¾ cup	1 cup	potato starch *or* cornstarch	185 ml	250 ml
2 tsp	1 tbsp	xanthan gum	10 ml	15 ml
¾ tsp	1 tsp	salt	3 ml	5 ml
1 ½ tbsp	2 tbsp	sugar	22 ml	30ml
2 tsp	1 tbsp	instant rise yeast	10 ml	15 ml
1 ½ tsp	2 tsp	gelatine	7 ml	10 ml
1 ½ tsp	2 tbsp	egg replacer	7 ml	30 ml
¾ tsp	1 tsp	cider vinegar	3 ml	5 ml
2 tbsp	3 tbsp	vegetable oil	30 ml	45 ml
1 ½ cups	2 cups	water	350 ml	500 ml

Bread Machine Instructions:

1. **Measure and mix dry ingredients** and set aside. Follow the directions given for your particular bread machine regarding appropriate temperatures for ingredients. See "Working with Bread Machines" *(p. 31)* for best results.
2. **Beat eggs.** Add them, along with milk or alternate, honey, oil and vinegar to the dry ingredients.
3. **Mix to fully incorporate the flours** before transferring dough to the bread machine.

Pro-tip: Resist the urge to skip this step. Gluten-free flours tend to be harder to incorporate and the machine will likely not get out all the lumps.

4. **Set the machine** on single rise (rapid) setting and choose dark crust. When the machine has completed its cycle, remove bread immediately and place

on a cooling rack. It is best to wait until the bread has cooled fully before slicing.

Hand Made Instructions:

1. **Mix dry ingredients** in a heavy-duty mixer with a flat paddle installed. Warm the water to about 120°F (40°C) (this will feel very much like a nice warm bath) and combine it with the other wet ingredients.
2. **Add the wet to the dry** and mix on low/medium for about three minutes. Soft, sticky dough will form.
Pro-tip: Handle dough with wet hands to prevent sticking.
3. **Form dough** into any shape you desire such as sandwich loaves, baguettes or buns.
4. **Place the formed dough** to rise in a warm, draft free area until nearly double the original size.
5. **To produce one large loaf, bake at 375°F (190°C)** for about 40 minutes until golden brown. For other shapes and sizes of buns or breads, bake until golden brown.

Nutritional Information
Calculations based upon the basic recipe excluding optional ingredients and variations.
Per slice, approximately 2 2/3 oz (75 g)

energy	180 calories/753 kJ
protein	2 g
fat	4 g
carbohydrate	35 g
sodium	185 mg
potassium	89 mg
calcium	5 mg
iron	1 mg

Variations:

This bread is a great solution for those with egg and dairy allergies, and has many other uses as well. This recipe can also make great pizza, sandwich bread and with the addition of other seeds, nuts and dried fruits, it can bring a great deal of variety to your meals. This recipe made up as raisin bread is a wonderful breakfast indulgence without the allergy worries.

French Bread

If you miss soft white breads with crispy crusts, this is for you.
This recipe makes the lightest, softest gluten-free bread
my testers have ever tasted.

Medium 1 ½ lb loaf	Large 2 lb loaf		Medium 680 g loaf	Large 900g loaf
1 cup +2 tbsp	1 ½ cups	tapioca flour	280 ml	375 ml
¾ cup	1 cup	brown rice flour	185 ml	250 ml
¾ cup	1 cup	potato starch *or* cornstarch	185 ml	250 ml
2 tsp	1 tbsp	xanthan gum	10 ml	15 ml
¾ tsp	1 tsp	salt	3 ml	5 ml
1 tbsp	1 ½ tbsp	sugar	15 ml	22 ml
2 tsp	1 tbsp	instant rise yeast	10 ml	15 ml
1 egg +1 egg white	2	eggs	1 egg +1 egg white	2
¾ tsp	1 tsp	cider vinegar	3 ml	5 ml
1 ½ tsp	2 tbsp	vegetable oil	22 ml	30 ml
1 ⅓ cups WATER + SUGAR	1 ¾ cups	milk *or* non-dairy alternate warmed to 110ºF (40ºC)	325 ml	435 ml
¾	1	egg white, for brushing on top (*optional*)	¾	1

Bread Machine Instructions:

1. **Measure and mix dry ingredients** and set aside. Follow the directions given for your particular bread machine regarding appropriate temperatures for ingredients. See "Working with Bread Machines" *(p. 31)* for best results.
2. **Beat eggs.** Add them, along with milk or alternate, oil and vinegar to the dry ingredients bowl.
3. **Mix to fully incorporate the flours** before transferring dough to the bread machine.

Pro-tip: Resist the urge to skip this step. Gluten-free flours tend to be harder to incorporate and the machine will likely not get out all the lumps.

4. **Set the machine** on single rise (rapid) setting and choose dark crust. When the machine has completed its cycle, remove bread immediately and place on a cooling rack. It is best to wait until the bread has cooled fully before slicing.

Hand Made Instructions:

1. **Mix dry ingredients** in a heavy-duty mixer with a flat paddle installed. In a separate container, beat eggs until frothy.

Pro-tip: An immersion blender works well for this.

2. **Warm the milk** or alternate to about 120°F (40°C). This will feel very much like a warm bath and combine it with the other wet ingredients.

3. **Add the wet to the dry** and mix on low/medium for about three minutes. Soft, sticky dough will form.

Pro-tip: Handle dough with wet hands to prevent sticking.

4. **Form dough** into any shape you desire, such as sandwich loaves, baguettes or buns.

5. **Place the formed dough** to rise in a warm, draft free area until nearly double the original size. For a crisper crust, brush with lightly beaten egg white.

6. **To produce one large loaf, bake at 375°F (190°C)** for about 40 minutes until golden brown. For other shapes and sizes of buns or breads, bake until golden brown.

Nutritional Information

Calculations based upon the basic recipe excluding
optional ingredients and variations.
Per slice, approximately 2 2/3 oz (75 g)

energy	193 calories/808 kJ
protein	3 g
fat	4 g
carbohydrate	38 g
sodium	206 mg
potassium	123 mg
calcium	51 mg
iron	1 mg

Mock Multigrain Rye

If you miss those heavy, dark, grainy breads of Europe, this recipe is for you. The heavier texture of the gluten-free flours is right at home with this style of bread.

Medium 1 ½ lb loaf	Large 2 lb loaf		Medium 680 g loaf	Large 900g loaf
1 cup +2 tbsp	1 ½ cups	brown rice flour	280 ml	375 ml
½ cup	¾ cup	tapioca starch	140 ml	185 ml
⅓ cup	½ cup	cornstarch	95 ml	125 ml
⅓ cup	½ cup	sorghum flour	95 ml	125 ml
3 tbsp	¼ cup	coarsely milled flax seed (*You can do this yourself in a coffee grinder.*)	45 ml	60 ml
½ cup	¾ cup	any of the following *or* a combination: sunflower seeds, whole millet, whole amaranth, sesame seeds, whole teff, green pumpkin seeds	140 ml	185 ml
¾ tsp	1 tsp	grated orange peel (*optional*)	3 ml	5 ml
1 ½ tbsp	2 tbsp	cocoa powder	22 ml	30 ml
3 tbsp	¼ cup	molasses	45 ml	60 ml
¾ tsp	1tsp	salt	3 ml	5 ml
2 tsp	1 tbsp	xanthan gum	10 ml	15 ml
2 tsp	1 tbsp	instant dry yeast	10 ml	15 ml
1 ½ cups	2 cups	water *or* coffee	375 ml	500 ml
1 egg +1 white	2	eggs	1 egg +1 white	2
1 ½ tbsp	2 tbsp	vegetable oil	22 ml	30 ml
¾ tsp	1 tsp	cider vinegar	3 ml	5 ml

Bread Machine Instructions:

1. **Measure and mix dry ingredients** and set aside. Follow the directions given for your particular bread machine regarding appropriate temperatures for ingredients. See "Working with Bread Machines" (*p. 31*) for best results.

126

2. **Beat eggs.** Add them, along with the water or coffee, oil and vinegar to the dry ingredients bowl.

3. **Mix to fully incorporate the flours** before transferring dough to the bread machine.

Pro-tip: Resist the urge to skip this step. Gluten-free flours tend to be harder to incorporate and the machine will likely not get out all the lumps.

4. **Set the machine** on single rise (rapid) setting and choose dark crust. When the machine has completed its cycle, remove the bread immediately and place on a cooling rack. It is best to wait until the bread has cooled fully before slicing.

Hand Made Instructions:

1. **Mix dry ingredients** in a heavy-duty mixer with a flat paddle installed. In a separate container, beat eggs until frothy.

Pro-tip: An immersion blender works well for this.

2. **Warm the water** or coffee to about 120°F (40°C). This will feel very much like a nice warm bath, and combine it with the other wet ingredients.

3. **Add the wet to the dry** and mix on low/medium for about three minutes. Soft, sticky dough will form.

Pro-tip: Handle dough with wet hands to prevent sticking.

4. **Form dough** into any shape you desire, such as sandwich loaves, baguettes or buns.

5. **Place the formed dough** to rise in a warm, draft free area until nearly double the original size. For a crisper crust, brush with lightly beaten egg white.

6. **To produce one large loaf, bake at 375°F (190°C)** for about 40 minutes until golden brown. For other shapes and sizes of buns or breads, bake until golden brown.

Nutritional Information

Calculations based upon the basic recipe excluding
optional ingredients and variations.
Per slice, about 2 ⅔ oz (75 g)

energy	255 calories/1067 kJ
protein	6 g
fat	9 g
carbohydrate	39 g
sodium	195 mg
potassium	301 mg
calcium	42 mg
iron	2 mg

Almond Bread

This bread is reminiscent of some of the European dessert breads without being sweet.

Medium 1 ½ lb loaf	Large 2 lb loaf		Medium 680 g loaf	Large 900g loaf
1 cup+ 2 tbsp	1 ½ cup	almond meal	280 ml	375 ml
¾ cup	1 cup	brown rice flour	185 ml	250 ml
¾ cup	1 cup	tapioca starch	185 ml	250 ml
⅓ cup	½ cup	potato starch	85 ml	125 ml
2 tsp	1 tbsp	xanthan gum	10 ml	15 ml
¾ tsp	1 tsp	salt	3 ml	5 ml
2 tsp	1 tbsp	rapid rise yeast	10 ml	15 ml
1 ½ tbsp	2 tbsp	sugar	22 ml	30 ml
1 egg +1 white	2	eggs	1 egg +1 white	2
1 ½ tbsp	2 tbsp	vegetable oil	22 ml	30 ml
1 cup +2 tbsp	1½ cups	milk *or* non-dairy alternate	280 ml	375 ml
¾ tsp	1 tsp	cider vinegar	3 ml	5 ml

Bread Machine Instructions:

1. **Measure and mix dry ingredients** and set aside. Follow the directions given for your particular bread machine regarding appropriate temperatures for ingredients. See "Working with Bread Machines" *(p. 31)* for best results.

2. **Beat eggs.** Add them, along with milk or alternate, oil and vinegar to the dry ingredients bowl.

3. **Mix to fully incorporate the flours** before transferring dough to the bread machine.

Pro-tip: Resist the urge to skip this step. Gluten-free flours tend to be harder to incorporate and the machine will likely not get out all the lumps.

4. **Set the machine** on single rise (rapid) setting and choose dark crust. When the machine has completed its cycle, remove the bread immediately and place on a cooling rack. It is best to wait until the bread has cooled fully before slicing.

Hand Made Instructions:

1. **Mix dry ingredients** in a heavy-duty mixer with a flat paddle installed. In a separate container, beat eggs until frothy.

Pro-tip: An immersion blender works well for this.

2. **Warm the milk** or alternate to about 120°F (40°C). This will feel very much like a warm bath and combine it with the other wet ingredients.

3. **Add the wet to the dry** and mix on low/medium for about three minutes. Soft, sticky dough will form.

Pro-tip: Handle dough with wet hands to prevent sticking.

4. **Form dough** into any shape you desire, such as sandwich loaves, baguettes or buns.

5. **Place the formed dough** to rise in a warm, draft free area until nearly double the original size. For a crisper crust, brush with lightly beaten egg white.

6. **To produce one large loaf, bake at 375°F (190°C)** for about 40 minutes until golden brown. For other shapes and sizes of buns or breads, bake until golden brown.

Nutritional Information

Calculations based upon the basic recipe excluding optional ingredients and variations.

Per slice, approximately 2 2/3 oz (75g)

energy	232 calories/971 kJ
protein	11 g
fat	7 g
carbohydrate	33 g
sodium	210 mg
potassium	361 mg
calcium	119 mg
iron	2 mg

Variations:

This recipe is the basis for the gluten-free Stollen *(p. 258)* in the "Holidays" chapter of this book. The addition of dried fruits and other nuts adds a great deal of interest and options for variety to this already interesting bread. Some of my favourite variations are adding 3/4 cup (185 ml) chopped dried apricots and ½ tsp (3 ml) of cardamom or ¾ cup (185 ml) diced dried apples and a ½ a tsp (3 ml) of cinnamon. Whether you try my variations or come up with your own, this recipe is a great basis for breaking out of the plain bread blahs.

Honey Brown Bread

A great choice for breakfast or in a sandwich,
this recipe is sure to become a favorite.

Medium 1 ½ lb loaf	Large 2 lb loaf		Medium 680 g loaf	Large 900g loaf
1 ½ cups	2 cups	brown rice flour	375 ml	500 ml
⅓ cup	½ cup	potato starch	85 ml	125 ml
⅓ cup	½ cup	tapioca starch	85 ml	125 ml
⅓ cup	½ cup	coarsely milled flax seed. (*You can do this yourself in a coffee grinder.*)	85 ml	125 ml
¾ tsp	1 tsp	salt	3 ml	5 ml
2 tsp	1 tbsp	xanthan gum	10 ml	15 ml
2 tsp	1 tbsp	rapid rise yeast	10 ml	15 ml
1 egg +1 white	2	eggs	1 egg +1 white	2
1 ⅓ cups	1 ¾ cups	milk *or* non-dairy alternate warmed to 110ºF (40ºC)	330 ml	440 ml
¼ cup	⅓ cup	honey	60 ml	85 ml
1 ½ tbsp	2 tbsp	cooking oil	22 ml	30 ml
¾ tsp	1 tsp	cider vinegar	3 ml	5 ml

Bread Machine Instructions:

1. **Measure and mix dry ingredients** and set aside. Follow the directions given for your particular bread machine regarding appropriate temperatures for ingredients. See Working with Bread Machines *(p. 31)* for best results.

2. **Beat eggs.** Add them, along with the rest of the wet ingredients to the dry ingredients bowl.

3. **Mix to fully incorporate the flours** before transferring dough to the bread machine.

Pro-tip: Resist the urge to skip this step. Gluten-free flours tend to be harder to incorporate and the machine will likely not get out all the lumps.

4. **Set the machine** on single rise (rapid) setting and choose dark crust. When the machine has completed its cycle, remove the bread immediately and place on a cooling rack. It is best to wait until the bread has cooled fully before slicing.

Hand Made Instructions:

1. **Mix dry ingredients** in a heavy-duty mixer with a flat paddle installed. In a separate container, beat eggs until frothy.
   Pro-tip: An immersion blender works well for this.
2. **Warm the milk** or alternate to about 120°F (40°C) (this will feel very much like a warm bath) and combine it with the other wet ingredients.
3. **Add the wet to the dry** and mix on low/medium for about three minutes. Soft, sticky dough will form. Handle dough with wet hands to prevent sticking.
4. **Form dough** into any shape you desire, such as sandwich loaves, baguettes or buns.
5. **Place the formed dough** to rise in a warm, draft free area until nearly double the original size. For a crisper crust, brush with lightly beaten egg white.
6. **To produce one large loaf, bake at 375°F (190°C)** for about 40 minutes until golden brown. For other shapes and sizes of buns or breads, bake until golden brown.

Nutritional Information

Calculations based upon the basic recipe excluding optional ingredients and variations.

Per slice, approximately 2 ⅔ (75g)

energy	242 calories/1013 kJ
protein	6 g
fat	6 g
carbohydrate	42 g
sodium	210 mg
potassium	210mg
calcium	66 mg
iron	1 mg

Variations:

This recipe is great as a basis for **cinnamon raisin** or **cranberry orange bread**. Just add ¾ cup (185 ml) raisins and 1 tsp (5 ml) cinnamon or ¾ cup (185 ml) dried cranberries and the zest of a small orange to make a great whole grain flavoured breads with a surprise inside to please the kid in all of us.

Brown Rice Sorghum Bread

A great whole wheat sandwich bread replacement, this bread stays nice and soft even when chilled.

Medium 1 ½ lb loaf	Large 2 lb loaf		Medium 680 g loaf	Large 900g loaf
1 ½ cups	2 cups	brown rice flour	350 ml	500 ml
¾ cup	1 cup	sorghum flour	185 ml	250 ml
¾ cup	1 cup	tapioca starch	185 ml	250 ml
1 ½ tbsp	2 tbsp	sugar	20 ml	30 ml
2 tsp	1 tbsp	xanthan gum	10 ml	15 ml
2 tsp	1 tbsp	instant dry yeast	10ml	15 ml
¾ tsp	1 tsp	unflavoured gelatine	3 ml	5 ml
¾ tsp	1 tsp	salt	3 ml	5 ml
1 ½ cups	2 cups	milk *or* non-dairy alternate	350 ml	500 ml
1 egg +1 white	2	eggs	1 egg +1 white	2
1 ½ tbsp	2 tbsp	oil	30 ml	45 ml
¾ tsp	1 tsp	cider vinegar	3 ml	1 tsp

Bread Machine Instructions:

1. **Measure and mix dry ingredients** and set aside. Follow the directions given for your particular bread machine regarding the appropriate temperatures for ingredients. See "Working with Bread Machines" *(p. 31)* for best results.

2. **Beat eggs.** Add them, along with milk or alternate, oil and vinegar to the dry ingredients.

3. **Mix to fully incorporate the flours** before transferring dough to the bread machine.

Pro-tip: Resist the urge to skip this step. Gluten-free flours tend to be harder to incorporate and the machine will likely not get out all the lumps.

4. **Set the machine** on single rise (rapid) setting and choose dark crust. When the machine has completed its cycle, remove bread immediately and place on a cooling rack. It is best to wait until the bread has cooled fully before slicing.

Hand Made Instructions:

1. **Mix dry ingredients** in a heavy-duty mixer with a flat paddle installed. In a separate container, beat eggs until frothy.

Pro-tip: An immersion blender works well for this.

2. Warm the milk or alternate to about 120ºF (40ºC). This will feel very much like a warm bath, and combine it with the other wet ingredients.

3. **Add the wet to the dry** and mix on low/medium for about three minutes. Soft, sticky dough will form.

Pro-tip: Handle dough with wet hands to prevent sticking.

4. **Form dough** into any shape you desire, such as sandwich loaves, baguettes or buns.

5. **Place the formed dough** to rise in a warm, draft free area until nearly double the original size. For a crisper crust, brush with lightly beaten egg white.

6. **To produce one large loaf, bake at 375ºF (190ºC)** for about 40 minutes until golden brown. For other shapes and sizes of buns or breads, bake until golden brown.

Nutritional Information

Calculations based upon the basic recipe excluding optional ingredients and variations.

Per slice (approximately 2 ⅔ oz (75 g)

energy	222 calories/882 kJ
protein	6g
fat	5 g
carbohydrate	41 g
sodium	211 mg
potassium	203 mg
calcium	61 mg
iron	1 mg

Variations:

This is the bread I frequently turn to when I need to make sandwiches the next day. I like to bake up this bread in mini loaf pans and slice them twice the long way to make triple-decker sandwiches like clubhouses.

Dairy-Free Sorghum and Corn Bread

This dairy-free bread has plenty of whole grain taste and a nice soft texture.

Medium 1 ½ lb loaf	Large 2 lb loaf		Medium 680 g loaf	Large 900g loaf
1 cup +2 tbsp	1 ½ cups	brown rice flour	280 ml	375 ml
½ cup	¾ cup	sorghum flour	140 ml	185 ml
⅓ cup	½ cup	corn flour	95 ml	125 ml
3 tbsp	¼ cup	ground flax seed	45 ml	60 ml
3 tbsp	¼ cup	brown sugar	45 ml	60 ml
2 tsp	1 tbsp	xanthan gum	10 ml	15 ml
¾ tsp	1 tsp	salt	3 ml	5 ml
2 tsp	1 tbsp	instant yeast	10 ml	15 ml
1 egg +1 white	2	eggs	1 egg +1 white	2
⅞ cup	1 ¼ cup	soy milk, *or* nut milk, *or* water plus 1 tsp gelatine	225 ml	310 ml
1 ½ tbsp	2 tbsp	vegetable oil	22 ml	30 ml
¾ tsp	1 tsp	cider vinegar	3 ml	5 ml

Bread Machine Instructions:

1. **Measure and mix dry ingredients** and set aside. Follow the directions given for your particular bread machine regarding the appropriate temperatures for ingredients. See "Working with Bread Machines" *(p. 31)* for best results.

2. **Beat eggs.** Add them, along with the rest of the wet ingredients to the dry ingredients.

3. **Mix to fully incorporate the flours** before transferring dough to the bread machine.

Pro-tip: Resist the urge to skip this step. Gluten-free flours tend to be harder to incorporate and the machine will likely not get out all the lumps.

4. **Set the machine** on single rise (rapid) setting and choose dark crust. When the machine has completed its cycle, remove the bread immediately and

place on a cooling rack. It is best to wait until the bread has cooled fully before slicing.

Hand Made Instructions:

1. **Mix dry ingredients** in a heavy-duty mixer with a flat paddle installed. In a separate container, beat eggs until frothy.

Pro-tip: An immersion blender works well for this.

2. **Combine eggs** with the other wet ingredients.

3. **Add the wet to the dry** and mix on low/medium for about three minutes. Soft, sticky dough will form.

Pro-tip: Handle dough with wet hands to prevent sticking.

4. **Form dough** into any shape you desire, such as sandwich loaves, baguettes, or buns.

5. **Place the formed dough** to rise in a warm, draft free area until nearly double the original size. For a crisper crust, brush with lightly beaten egg white.

6. **To produce one large loaf, bake at 375ºF (190ºC)** for about 40 minutes until golden brown. When baking other shapes and sizes of buns or breads, bake until golden brown or until they sound hollow when tapped.

Nutritional Information
Calculations based upon the basic recipe excluding optional ingredients and variations.
Per slice, approximately 2 ²/₃ oz (75 g serving

energy	184 calories/770 kJ
protein	5 g
fat	6 g
carbohydrate	30 g
sodium	195 mg
potassium	196 mg
calcium	20 mg
iron	1 mg

Variations:

This recipe is great as a basis for light coloured, multigrain bread variations. Just add ¾ cup (185 ml) gluten-free grains and seeds such as teff, millet, amaranth, oats, sunflower seeds or green pumpkin seeds to make great whole grain breads with that extra crunch that tells us that they are good for us.

Gluten-Free Grains, Pastas and Side Dishes

Grains and pastas are the ever-present humble side dishes. At best they can aspire to the role of, "Best supporting actor," in a meal. They never get top billing on the menu, but they are always there. We never seem to set out to eat the grains and pastas that make up the bulk of the diet for most cultures in the world. All too frequently we take them for granted. The need to remove the common gluten-based varieties from our diet forces us to look at new options to fill that other part of our plate.

Fortunately for those of us who need to avoid gluten, many cultures have found gluten-free alternates. Great gluten-free grains and starches that originally came from Asia, Africa, South America, North America and Europe are now readily available for us to enjoy. Amaranth, buckwheat, corn, millet, quinoa, rice, sorghum and teff are all options worth a try. Many of these lesser known grains (at least in North America) are very flavourful and nutritious, adding variety to our diet and an alternative to basic rice and potatoes.

For most of the Western world, wheat-based side dishes are the norm and even though it would seem that there are seemingly infinite varieties of pastas from all over the world, the variations seem to be mostly in the shaping and flavouring of the basic dough. I make this statement at the risk of angering cooks the world over. The dough that covers Chinese pot-sticker dumplings, perogies and ravioli are essentially the same. In fact most wheat based pasta is essentially the same regardless of where the recipe is from. This interesting quirk of human inventiveness makes recreating your particular favourite type of pasta a relatively easy task. Simply make up the basic noodle doughs in this chapter and turn them into the particular dish you crave.

Some side dishes which do not follow familiar approaches are spaetzle, couscous and Yorkshire pudding. This chapter contains great gluten-free replacements for these dishes to banish any feeling of deprivation. I hope this chapter makes preparing known side dishes easier for you, and that it adds some new and exciting flavours and textures to your meals.

Basic Buckwheat Kasha

This member of the rhubarb family, common in Russia and Japan, is a welcome addition to the gluten-free table and can be prepared using two different methods.

	Egg Method	
1 cup	kasha (whole toasted buckwheat groats)	250 ml
1	egg *or* egg white, well beaten	1
2 cups	water, stock *or* other flavourful liquid	500ml
¼ - ½ tsp	salt	2 - 3 ml

Instructions:

1. **Rinse and drain kasha** before combining with egg. Mix until fully combined. Let stand about 5 minutes so the egg will start to absorb into the kasha. The egg will create a partial barrier to the liquid, preventing the kasha from becoming overly mushy.

2. **Preheat a large skillet** over medium-high heat. Add the kasha mixture and cook, stirring constantly for 3 - 5 minutes until the grains are separate and toasted golden brown.

3. **Add liquid and salt** and stir to combine. Bring to a boil before reducing heat to low. Simmer covered about 15 minutes. Remove from heat and allow to stand 5 - 10 minutes before serving.

Yield: about 4 cups (875 ml)

Nutritional Information

Calculations based upon the basic recipe, excluding optional ingredients and variations.

Per 1 cup (250 ml) serving

energy	158 calories/661 kJ
protein	6g
fat	2 g
carbohydrate	31 g
sodium	155 mg
potassium	145 mg
calcium	16 mg
iron	1 mg

Oil Method

1 cup	kasha (whole toasted buckwheat groats)	250ml
1 tbsp	vegetable oil	15 ml
2 cups	stock *or* other flavourful liquid	500ml
¼ - ½ tsp	salt	2 - 3 ml

Instructions:

1. **Preheat a large skillet** over medium-high heat with the oil.

2. **Add kasha** and cook, stirring constantly for 3 - 5 minutes until the grains are toasted golden brown. The oil will create a partial barrier to the liquid, preventing the kasha from becoming overly mushy.

3. **Add liquid and salt** and stir to combine. Bring to a boil before reducing heat to low. Simmer covered about 15 minutes. Remove from heat and allow to stand 5 - 10 minutes before serving.

Yield: about 4 cups (875 ml)

Nutritional Information

Calculations based upon the basic recipe, excluding optional ingredients and variations.

Per 1 cup (250 ml) serving

energy	172 calories/720 kJ
protein	5 g
fat	5g
carbohydrate	31g
sodium	141mg
potassium	131 mg
calcium	10 mg
iron	1 mg

Basic Millet

This ancient grain of Africa and Asia is a nutritious gluten-free alternative to rice or potatoes. The toasted method results in a pleasant nutty taste. Untoasted millet can be served in place of rice or as a cooked breakfast cereal similar to oatmeal.

	Toasted Method	
1 cup	millet	250 ml
1 tbsp	vegetable oil	15 ml
2 cups	water, stock *or* other flavourful liquid	500 ml
¼ - ½ tsp	salt	2 - 3 ml

Instructions:

1. **Preheat a large skillet** over medium-high heat with the oil.
2. **Add millet** and cook, stirring constantly for about 3 - 5 minutes until the grains are toasted golden brown. From this point, follow the untoasted method below.

Yield: 4 cups (1 litre); serves about 4 - 6 as a side dish.

Nutritional Information

Calculations based upon the basic recipe, excluding optional ingredients and variations.
Per 1 cup (250 ml 0 serving

energy	219 calories/916 kJ
protein	6 g
fat	6 g
carbohydrate	36 g
sodium	139 mg
potassium	98 mg
calcium	7 mg
iron	2 mg

Untoasted Method

1 cup	millet	250 ml
2 ¼ cups	water, stock *or* other flavourful liquid	560 ml
¼ - ½ tsp	salt	2 – 3 ml

Instructions:

In the microwave:

1. **Microwave** the ingredients on high for 5 minutes in a covered 2 quart (2 litre) casserole dish, then on medium for another 15 minutes.
2. **Allow to stand** covered a further 5 - 10 minutes before serving. The result will be fluffy millet with no fuss, a great addition to a gluten-free dinner.

In the oven:

1. **Heat** liquid to a boil before adding other ingredients.
2. **Add** other ingredients to a 2 quart (2 litre) casserole dish and bake covered about 20 minutes at 350°F (180°C).
3. **Let stand** a further 5 - 10 minutes before serving.

On the stovetop:

1. **Add** an additional ¼ cup (60 ml) of liquid to the ingredients above and bring the liquid to a boil.
2. **Add millet** and stir only once when the millet is first added.
3. **Cook covered** on very low heat about 15 minutes without lifting the lid.
4. **Let stand** covered a further 5 - 10 minutes before serving.

Yield: 4 cups (1 litre); serves about 4 - 6 as a side dish.

Nutritional Information

Calculations based upon the basic recipe, excluding optional ingredients and variations.

Per 1 cup (250 ml) serving

energy	189 calories/791 kJ
protein	6 g
fat	2 g
carbohydrate	36 g
sodium	140 mg
potassium	98 mg
calcium	8 mg
iron	2 mg

Basic Quinoa

This ancient grain of the Andes is quick to cook, very nutritious and has a wonderful nutty taste when toasted. It can be substituted for rice or bulgur in pilaffs and salads.

1 cup	quinoa	250 ml
¼ - ½ tsp	salt	2 - 3 ml
2 cups	water, stock *or* other flavourful liquid	500ml

Instructions:

For best flavour, toast quinoa in a dry skillet over medium heat, shaking the pan frequently to allow the grains to toast evenly. When the grains have become golden brown and have a nutty aroma, they are ready for the next step, which can be completed three different ways.

In the microwave:

1. **Microwave** ingredients on high 5 minutes in a covered 2 quart (2 litre) casserole dish, then on medium 8 minutes more.
2. **Allow to stand** covered a further 5 - 10 minutes.
3. **Fluff with a fork** before serving.

In the oven:

1. **Heat** liquid to a boil before adding other ingredients.
2. **Add** other ingredients to a 2 quart (2 litre) casserole dish and bake covered for about 15 minutes at 350ºF (180ºC). Let stand a further 5 - 10 minutes.
3. **Fluff with a fork** before serving.

On the stovetop:

1. **Bring the liquid** to a boil.
2. **Add** quinoa and stir only once when the quinoa is first added.
3. **Cook covered** on very low heat for about 12 minutes without lifting the lid. Let stand covered a further 5 - 10 minutes.
4. **Fluff with a fork** before serving.

Yield: 3 ½ cups (875 ml); serves about 4 as a side dish.

Nutritional Information
Calculations based upon the basic recipe excluding
optional ingredients and variations.
Per 1 cup (250 ml) serving

energy	159calories/665 kJ
protein	6 g
fat	2 g
carbohydrate	29 g
sodium	146 mg
potassium	315 mg
calcium	29 mg
iron	4 mg

Variations:

This staple of the Incas is an extremely nutritious choice. Vary the liquids used and flavourings added to create many different variations.

- ✓ **Try apple cider, fruit juice or wine.** The amount of liquid used depends on the desired texture. More liquid makes for softer texture; less makes the quinoa firmer.
- ✓ Quinoa can be substituted for rice or bulgur in pilaffs and salads, served as a side dish or used to make stuffing for meat, fish or poultry.

Basic Risotto

*Combining creamy smoothness with a satisfyingly firm bite,
this hearty Italian rice is great as a side dish or a complete meal.*

6 - 7 cups	chicken stock *or* other flavourful liquid *(You may have some left when the risotto is finished, depending on the rice used)*	1 ¾ litres
2 tbsp	good olive oil (extra virgin)	30 ml
1	small onion, finely diced	1
2 cups	Italian short grain rice such as Arborio, Carnaroli, *or* Roma *(do not wash)*	500ml
	salt and pepper to taste	
½ cup	gluten-free grated Parmesan cheese *(optional)*	125ml

Instructions:

1. **Bring liquid to a simmer.**
2. **Sauté onion** in olive oil over medium heat in a separate medium-size saucepan until onion is translucent.
3. **Add rice to saucepan** and stir until it becomes translucent, leaving a white spot visible in each grain. Sauté about 2 minutes. This causes the fat to be absorbed into the grains of rice, preventing the absorption of too much liquid which would make the rice mushy.
4. **Add the simmering liquid** about 1 cup (250 ml) at a time (no more), stirring continuously. As the liquid is absorbed, add the next cup (250 ml), stirring until absorbed before adding the next, and so on. Continue until the rice is cooked, but still slightly firm in the centre of each grain. This should take no more than 20 minutes from the time the first liquid is added. The risotto should be creamy, but with all grains intact. It should be just thin enough to slowly flow back to level when pressed against the side of the pan.
5. **Stir in Parmesan cheese** (if using) and adjust seasoning with salt and pepper.
6. **Serve** as is for a tasty side dish, or dress it up with all manner of variations.

Yield: About 8 servings

Nutritional Information
Calculations based upon the basic recipe, excluding
optional ingredients and variations.
Per 1 cup (250 ml) serving

energy	217 calories/908 kJ
protein	4g
fat	4g
carbohydrate	38g
sodium	159mg
potassium	80 mg
calcium	4 mg
iron	1 mg

Variations:

Use the rice as a blank canvas and paint it with whatever suits you. Any pasta and sauce combination can be adapted to risotto. Here are a few variations to get you started:

✓ **Vary the liquid** with clam nectar, tomato sauce, fish stock, ham stock, vegetable stock, white or red wine, or any combination of these.

✓ **Stir in** diced cooked poultry, shellfish, anchovies, sausage and the like.

✓ **Try mushrooms, olives, tomatoes** or any other Mediterranean specialties.

✓ **Vary the herbs** used to complement the other ingredients.
   o Try lemon balm with seafood
   o Thyme with roasted poultry, or chives with red meats
   o Any combination of herbs and spices which suit your tastes can be used to bring life to this blank canvas.

✓ Do not be concerned with leftovers. Add 1 egg per 1 ½ cups (375 ml) cold leftover risotto, form into **pancake-shaped patties,** and fry with butter or olive oil over medium-low heat until crisp and brown on both sides. Many people like this variation better than the first time around.

Basic Teff

This tiny gluten-free grain, best known for its use in Ethiopian Injera bread, packs a lot of flavour, iron and fiber. The molasses-like taste is a wonderful complement to many dishes.

	Toasted Method	
1 cup	teff	250 ml
2 tbsp	vegetable oil	30 ml
2 cups	water, stock or other flavourful liquid	500 ml
¼-½ tsp	salt	2-3 ml

Instructions:

Preheat a large skillet with the oil over medium-high heat. Add teff and cook, stirring constantly for about 3 - 5 minutes until the grains are toasted and have a fragrant nutty aroma. Add liquid and salt, if desired, and continue cooking using your choice of the methods below.

In the microwave:

1. **Microwave** ingredients on high for 5 minutes in a covered 2 quart (2 litre) casserole dish, then on medium 12 minutes more.
2. **Allow to stand** covered a further 5 - 10 minutes before serving.

In the oven:

1. **Heat** liquid to a boil before adding other ingredients.
2. **Add** other ingredients to a 2 quart (2 litre) casserole dish and bake covered about 20 minutes at 350ºF (180ºC).
3. **Let stand** a further 5 - 10 minutes before serving.

On the stovetop:

1. **Add** an additional ¼ cup (60 ml) of liquid to the ingredients above and bring the liquid to a boil.
2. **Add** the teff and stir only once when the teff is first added.
3. **Cook covered** on very low heat for about 15 minutes without lifting the lid.
4. **Let stand** covered a further 5 - 10 minutes before serving

Yield: 4 cups (1 litre); serves about 4 as a side dish

Nutritional Information

Calculations based upon the basic recipe excluding optional ingredients and variations.

Per 1 cup (250 ml) serving

energy	271 calories/1134 kJ
protein	8 g
fat	8 g
carbohydrate	43 g
sodium	150 mg
potassium	0 mg
calcium	108 mg
iron	5 mg

Variations:

Try apple cider, fruit juice or wine. The amount of liquid depends on the desired texture. More liquid makes for porridge consistency; less makes the teff firmer.

Untoasted Method

1 cup	teff	250 ml
2 cups	water, stock *or* other flavourful liquid	500 ml
¼ - ½ tsp	salt	2 – 3 ml

Instructions:

Combine all ingredients in a suitable container for the cooking method you choose and follow the instructions above for microwave, oven or stovetop.

Nutritional Information

Calculations based upon the basic recipe excluding optional ingredients and variations.

Per 1 cup (250 ml) serving

energy	210 calories/879 kJ
protein	8 g
fat	1g
carbohydrate	43g
sodium	150 mg
potassium	0 mg
calcium	108 mg
iron	5 mg

Basic Wild Rice

The wonderful taste and chewy texture of this North American native rice is worth the extra cooking time and expense. Try combining wild rice with other gluten-free grains for visual appeal and flavour.

1 cup	wild rice (rinse to remove remaining husks)	250 ml
¼ - ½ tsp	salt	2 - 3 ml
3 cups or more	water, stock *or* other flavourful liquid (*see instructions for details*)	750 ml or more

Instructions:

Cooking times for wild rice can vary greatly, depending on the size of the grains and the processing used to remove the outer husk from the grain. The amount of liquid required depends on the desired texture. If the liquid is completely absorbed before the rice has softened sufficiently, add about ½ cup (60 ml) additional liquid at a time. Continue cooking until most of the grains have cracked open, showing their white interior. If any excess liquid remains when the grains are fully cooked simply pour it off. Basic wild rice can be prepared using a variety of methods:

In the microwave:

1. **Microwave** rice on high 5 minutes in a covered 2 litre (2 quart) casserole dish, then on medium-low 45 - 55 minutes more.
2. **Allow to stand** covered a further 5 - 10 minutes before serving.

In the oven:

1. **Heat liquid** to a boil before adding other ingredients.
2. **Add other ingredients** to a 2 quart (2 litre) casserole dish and bake covered about 45 - 55 minutes at 350°F (180° C).
3. **Allow to stand** a further 5 - 10 minutes before serving.

On the stovetop:

1. **Add** an additional ¼ cup (60 ml) of liquid to the ingredients above and bring the liquid to a boil.
2. **Cook covered** on very low heat about 45 - 55 minutes.
3. **Let stand** covered a further 5 - 10 minutes before serving.

Yield: 3 ½ cups (875 ml); serves about 4 as a side dish

Nutritional Information
Calculations based upon the basic recipe excluding
optional ingredients and variations.
Per 1 cup (250 ml) serving

energy	143 calories/598 kJ
protein	6 g
fat	trace
carbohydrate	30 g
sodium	141 mg
potassium	171 mg
calcium	13 mg
iron	1 mg

Variations:

This native North American grain is a delicious and nutritious addition to
anyone's diet, and better yet, it is gluten-free. Use it in:

✓ **Rice stuffing**
✓ **Salads**
✓ **Combinations of cooked grains** to add a touch of colour and flavour.

Pro-tip: Cooking times for wild rice tend to be inconsistent so for best results
cook it by itself before adding it into other dishes.

Egg Noodle Dough

Whether made into noodles or a variety of stuffed pastas, this dough allows you to enjoy these great ethnic specialties again.

1 ½ cups	sweet rice flour	375 ml
½ cup	tapioca starch	125 ml
1 tsp	xanthan gum	5 ml
¹/₄ tsp	salt	2 ml
5	eggs	5

Instructions:

1. **Combine first group of ingredients** in a heavy-duty mixer using the paddle attachment.
2. **Add eggs** and mix on low until smooth dough forms and pulls away from the sides of the bowl. If dough is a bit dry (differences in milling of the flour can cause variations), add water by the teaspoonful while mixing.
3. **At this point, dough is ready** to be made into any shape you wish.
Pro-tip: Take care to keep it from drying out by using a damp cloth to cover the portion you are not working with.
4. **Form the pasta** any way you wish.
Pro-tip: A light dusting of tapioca starch will make it easier to roll and cut.
5. You can make noodles by hand with a rolling pin and knife, or with a pasta rolling machine. The formed noodles can be kept fresh in the refrigerator for a few days or frozen for later use. This dough can also be made into all manner of stuffed pasta specialties; see variations below.

Yield: 2 - 3 portions as an entrée

Nutritional Information
Calculations based upon the basic recipe, excluding
optional ingredients and variations.
Per 1 cup (250 ml) serving

energy	399 calories/1669 kJ
protein	13 g
fat	8 g
carbohydrate	19g
sodium	274 mg
potassium	135 mg
calcium	44 mg
iron	2 mg

Pro-tip: One only needs to go down the pasta isle at the local market to see almost endless variations in pasta shapes. The good news is pasta rolling machines also have cutters which make all sorts of noodle shapes. A good rule of thumb is that the thinner the pasta, the thinner the sauce to go with it.

Variations: Stuffed Pasta

Many different types of stuffed pastas are enjoyed around the world. Here are a few ideas to get you started, but feel free to branch out and be creative.

Perogies

1. **Roll out dough** to about ¹/₈ inch (2 mm) thick and cut circles with the rim of a teacup.
2. **Fill dough** with a generous tablespoon of filling such as mashed potato (with bits of crisp fried bacon or onion or cheddar cheese) or dry cottage cheese.
3. **Brush edges** with beaten egg yolk. Fold over into crescent-shaped pockets and press edges well to seal.
4. **Boil** in plenty of salted water until perogies float; then boil 1 minute more.
5. **Toss** them with a bit of melted butter and eat immediately, or fry them until lightly browned.
6. **Serve** with sour cream and chopped scallions.

Ravioli

1. **Roll** out 2 sheets of dough to about ⅛ inch (2 mm) thick.
2. **Place a small amount of filling** of your choice in a grid pattern on one of the sheets.

Pro-tip: A common ravioli filling uses cooked chicken or veal, Parmesan cheese or alternate, Italian seasonings and a few gluten-free breadcrumbs, all combined and made into a paste in a food processor.

3. **Brush** areas between the filling spots with beaten egg yolk. Place the second sheet of dough on top. Press dough down between the spots of filling to seal the ravioli into individual pockets. They are now ready to be cut apart with a knife or fluted cutter wheel. You can cut into traditional squares, use cookie cutters, or design your own style. (For example, I once made lobster claw shaped ravioli with a lobster filling for a seafood festival.)
4. **Boil** in plenty of salted water until ravioli floats.
5. **Drizzle** with olive oil or butter, and top with a bit of Parmesan cheese or your favourite Italian sauce.

Tortellini

1. **Roll out dough** to about ⅛ inch (2 mm) thick and cut 1 ½ inch (3 - 4 cm) circles with a cutter or the rim of a small drinking glass.
2. **Fill circles** with about ½ tsp (3 ml) of filling (see ravioli mixture above).
3. **Brush edges** with beaten egg yolk. Fold over into crescent-shaped pockets and press edges well to seal. Fold the two ends of the crescent- shaped package toward each other across the flat edge and press to seal them together.
4. **Boil** in plenty of salted water until tortellini floats.
5. **Serve** in a tasty chicken broth topped with a bit of Parmesan cheese, or topped with your favourite Italian sauce.

Egg Free Pasta

Whether you can tolerate eggs or not, this easy to work dough will put fresh pasta back on the menu.

1 cup	brown rice flour	250 ml
1 cup	tapioca flour	250 ml
2 tsp	xanthan gum	10 ml
½ tsp	salt	3 ml
1 ½ tbsp	vegetable oil	22 ml
⅔ cup	water	165 ml

Instructions:

1. **Combine first group of ingredients** in a heavy-duty mixer using the paddle attachment and mix completely.
2. **Add oil and water,** and mix on low until smooth dough forms and pulls away from the sides of the bowl. If dough is a bit dry (differences in milling of the flour can cause variations) add water by the teaspoonful while mixing. Allow mixer to knead the dough 2 minutes on low.
3. **Form the pasta** any way you wish.

Pro-tip: Take care to keep dough from drying out by using a damp cloth to cover the portion you are not working with. A light dusting of tapioca starch will make it easier to roll and cut.

4. You can make noodles by hand with a rolling pin and knife, with a pasta rolling machine, or see variations *(p. 151)*. The formed noodles can be kept fresh in the refrigerator for a few days or frozen for later use.

Yield: 2 - 3 portions as an entrée

Nutritional Information

Calculations based upon the basic recipe, excluding optional ingredients.
Per 1 cup (250 ml) serving

energy	259calories/1084 kJ
protein	3 g
fat	3 g
carbohydrate	57 g
sodium	138 mg
potassium	114 mg
calcium	6 mg
iron	1 mg

Japanese Rice

Whether eaten hot or in sushi, this method will yield the staple of Japanese cooking. It can be scaled up to feed a Sumo!

1 cup	short or medium grain rice specified for use in Japanese cooking or sushi. *It is a different variety than regular short grain rice.*	250 ml
¼ tsp	salt	2 ml
1 ¼ cups	water	300 ml

Instructions:

In the microwave:

1. **Rinse rice** while stirring until water runs clear. Drain fully before continuing.
2. **Mix all ingredients** in a covered 2 quart (2 litre) casserole.
3. **Allow rice to sit** in the water for 10 minutes before continuing.
4. **Microwave rice** on high 5 minutes, then on medium 10 minutes more. Allow to stand covered a further 10 minutes before serving.

On the stovetop:

1. **Rinse the rice** while stirring until water runs clear. Drain fully before continuing.
2. **Mix all ingredients** in a pot with a tight fitting lid.
3. **Allow rice to sit** in the water for 10 minutes before continuing.
4. **Place pot over high heat** until it starts to boil vigorously (resist the urge to lift the lid to check; you can tell by escaping steam and the lid beginning to move).
5. **Turn heat down** to medium and cook a further 5 - 6 minutes until all water is absorbed. Let stand tightly covered a further 15 - 20 minutes before serving. Longer standing time makes the grains more tender.

Yield: 2 cups (500 ml); serves about 2 - 3 as a side dish, or 2 ½ - 3 sushi rolls

Nutritional Information
Calculations based upon the basic recipe, excluding
optional ingredients and variations.
Per ¾ cup (185 ml) serving

energy	227 calories/950 kJ
protein	4 g
fat	1 g
carbohydrate	52 g
sodium	187 mg
potassium	0 mg
calcium	3 mg
iron	trace

Variations:

Please refer to sushi rolls *(p. 72)*

Lazy Gnocchi

No need to miss Italian potato dumpling pasta anymore. The instant mashed potatoes make these lazy, and according to an Italian grandma I know, her kids can't tell the difference.

1	egg	1
2 cups	instant mashed potato flakes	500 ml
1 cup	boiling water	250 ml
½ cup	sweet rice flour	125 ml
½ cup	tapioca flour	125 ml
1 tsp	xanthan gum	5 ml
½ tsp	salt	3 ml

Instructions:

1. **Mix dry ingredients** fully in a heavy-duty mixer, using the paddle attachment.

2. **Pour in boiling water** while mixing on low speed. Mix until water has been incorporated.

3. **Add egg** and mix until a smooth, very firm dough has formed. This will take about 2 minutes. If too wet to handle easily, add a bit more sweet rice flour. If too dry, add water by the teaspoon.

4. **Separate into fist-sized clumps** and dust your work surface with a bit of sweet rice flour. Using your best play-dough skills (kids are great with this part), roll each clump into a ¾ inch (2 cm) thick rope.

5. **Cut the ropes** into ½ inch (1 cm) sections. If you really want to be lazy, you can stop here and cook the pieces as they are, or you can take the extra step to make them look truly authentic.

6. **Set each piece on one of the flat cut sides** across the back of a fork.

7. **Drag the pieces of dough,** allowing them to roll along the tines of the fork. With a bit of practice the gnocchi will resemble the classic oval shape with indented stripes.

8. **Boil the gnocchi** in lots of salted water until they float; then boil 1 minute more. Drain well and serve with your favorite pasta sauce (a rich meaty tomato sauce or pesto are traditional). Gnocchi can be kept fresh in the refrigerator for a few days. They also freeze well.

Yield: 2 generous dinner- sized portions, or 4 side dish portions

Nutritional Information

Calculations based upon the basic recipe, excluding optional ingredients and variations.

Per side dish serving (¹/₄ of recipe)

energy	207 calories/866 kJ
protein	4 g
fat	1 g
carbohydrate	33 g
sodium	176 mg
potassium	285 mg
calcium	15 mg
iron	1 mg

Variations:

✓ **Spinach Gnocchi**

Add 1 cup (250 ml) finely chopped, cooked spinach (with all the liquid pressed out) to the dough. You may need to add a little sweet rice flour to form a smooth firm dough.

✓ **Tomato Gnocchi**

Add ½ cup (125 ml) tomato paste to the dough. You may need to add a little sweet rice flour to keep the dough smooth and firm.

✓ **Herb Gnocchi**

Add herbs to the dough to suit the dish that will accompany the gnocchi. Basil, oregano, fennel seed or parsley are all great choices.

Polenta

This Italian corn meal mush is a great alternative to pasta, rice or potatoes. It can be served soft and warm, or allowed to cool, cut into pieces and grilled or fried for a crispier version.

2 cups	chicken stock *or* alternate	500 ml
1 tsp	butter *or* olive oil	5 ml
1	garlic clove, finely chopped	1
½ cup	corn meal *(coarse ground is best)*	125 ml
	salt and pepper to taste	
1 tbsp	grated Parmesan *or* other cheese *(optional)*	15 ml

Instructions:

1. **Bring first three ingredients to a rolling boil.**
2. **While stirring, pour the cornmeal** into the boiling liquid in a steady stream.
3. **Turn heat down** to a simmer and keep stirring regularly for about 10 minutes or until polenta thickens to the consistency of soft mashed potatoes.
4. **Adjust seasoning** with salt and pepper, and stir in the cheese *(if desired)*.
5. **Enjoy as is or spread out evenly** about ½ - ¾ inch (15 - 20 mm) thick on a greased baking sheet to cool (overnight in the refrigerator works well). When cool, it can be cut into portion-sized pieces (cookie cutters create a wide range of shapes) which can be grilled or pan-fried.

Yield: 2 cups (500 ml)

Nutritional Information

Calculations based upon the basic recipe, excluding optional ingredients and variations.

Per 1 cup (250 ml) serving

energy	186calories/778 kJ
protein	4g
fat	3 g
carbohydrate	32 g
sodium	220 mg
potassium	145 mg
calcium	7 mg
iron	3 mg

Variations:

With the addition of different herbs and spices, a huge range of variations can be created:

- ✓ Consider **pesto, sun-dried tomato, curry or even blue cheese**, to name just a few.
- ✓ For a **rustic Italian meal** serve polenta with grilled Italian sausage and a spinach salad
- ✓ **Grilled polenta** makes a great alternative to baked potatoes on the barbeque.

Potato Latkes

There is no reason why this Hanukkah favourite can't be enjoyed all year. Great as a side dish for grilled or roasted meats, it can be served in traditional style or dressed up with contemporary variations.

2 cups	baker potatoes, *peeled and coarsely grated*	500 ml
½	medium onion, finely chopped	½
1	egg, *beaten*	1
½ tsp	salt	3 ml
	peanut *or* canola oil for frying	

Instructions:

1. **Grate potatoes** and squeeze out as much of the excess water as possible.
   Pro-tip: Rolling the grated potatoes in a clean kitchen towel and twisting the ends works well for this purpose.
2. **Place potatoes, onions, egg and salt in a mixing bowl** and combine fully.
3. **Preheat frying pan** over medium heat with about ⅛ inch (3 mm) oil.
4. **Carefully place potato mixture** by large spoonfuls into the preheated pan.
   Pro-tip: An ice-cream scoop works well for this.
5. **Flatten** to roughly a 4 inch (10 cm) round pancake shape, about ¼ inch (5 mm) thick.
6. **Fry until golden brown** on both sides.
7. **Remove from pan** and set on paper towel for a moment to absorb excess oil. Serve while still warm.

Yield: about 8, 4 inch (10 cm) latkes

Nutritional Information

Calculations based upon the basic recipe, excluding optional ingredients and variations.

Per 1 latke serving

energy	141 calories/590 kJ
protein	2g
fat	10g
carbohydrate	12 g
sodium	154 mg
potassium	187 mg
calcium	11 mg
iron	1 mg

Variations:

- ✓ Latkes are **traditionally served warm**, topped with sour cream and / or applesauce.
- ✓ They are great as a **side dish** with roasted or grilled meats, poultry or fish.
- ✓ **A half and half mixture of baker potato and sweet potato** makes for a colourful and flavourful variation.
- ✓ **Add herbs** of your choice to match what you are serving it with.
- ✓ **Use latkes as a base for a variation on Eggs Benedict.** Top with back bacon or smoked salmon, a poached egg and some hollandaise for a fabulous brunch dish.
- ✓ **Stack two or three latkes alternately with grilled meats or fish fillets** for a great stand-up dinner presentation. Drizzle with an appropriate sauce and garnish with a few fresh herb sprigs to dress it up.
- ✓ Prepare the latkes in a **mini form** and use as a base for hot appetizers. Topped with smoked salmon, a few capers and a bit of sour cream, they are wonderful!

Rice "Couscous"

The parboiled, cracked wheat pasta from North Africa now has a gluten-free version. Enjoy all the Moroccan specialties with this staple side dish. The initial preparation is a bit labour-intensive, but once done it is a quick side dish to prepare.

Any amount	parboiled (instant) rice white or brown	Any amount

Instructions to prepare the "couscous" grains:

1. **Mill rice** so each grain is broken into 4 - 5 pieces, about $1/16$ inch (1 - 2 mm) in size.

Pro-tip: This can best be accomplished using a grain mill set on a very coarse setting. Alternatively, rice may be prepared in small batches in an electric coffee mill by 'pulsing' the grinder.

2. **Sift milled grains** to remove the rice flour dust.

Pro-tip: This dust can be kept for later use for such things as grainy breads or rice stuffing.

3. **Pan toast** the "couscous" over medium-high heat in a dry sauté pan until lightly golden brown, stirring or tossing regularly to allow even browning. When the desired colour has been attained, remove "couscous" from pan and spread on a baking sheet to cool and prevent continued browning. This toasting provides the grainy taste needed to emulate the flavour of the original.

4. **Reserve "couscous" for later use** in an airtight container, or prepare immediately as follows.

Instructions to cook the "couscous":

1 cup	prepared instant rice "couscous"	250 ml
1 cup	water *or* stock	250 ml
1 tsp	oil, butter, *or* non-dairy alternate	5 ml
pinch	salt	pinch

In the microwave

1. **Microwave** the ingredients on high 5 minutes in a covered 2 litre (2 quart) casserole dish.
2. **Allow** to stand covered a further 5 minutes before fluffing with a fork to separate the grains before serving.

On the stovetop

1. **Bring the liquid** to a boil.
2. **Add** the "couscous," stirring only once when the "couscous" is first added.
3. **Cook covered** on very low heat for about 5 minutes without lifting the lid.
4. **Let stand** covered a further 5 minutes before fluffing with a fork to separate the grains before serving.

Yield: 2 cups (500 ml); serves about 2 - 3 as a side dish

Nutritional Information

Calculations based upon the basic recipe, excluding
optional ingredients and variations.
Per 1 cup (250 ml) serving

energy	240 calories/1004 kJ
protein	4 g
fat	5 g
carbohydrate	43 g
sodium	146 mg
potassium	65 mg
calcium	39 mg
iron	2 mg

Variations:

✓ **Add spices or herbs** to suit the dish that will accompany the "couscous."
✓ **Add sautéed onions or garlic** before cooking the "couscous" to enhance the flavour.

Soba Noodles

These buckwheat noodles are just as tasty as the Japanese originals, without the wheat flour used in the commercial ones.

1 cup	light buckwheat flour *(dark buckwheat flour gives the soba a very strong taste)*	250 ml
¼ cup	sweet rice flour	60 ml
¼ cup	tapioca starch	60 ml
½ tsp	xanthan gum	3 ml
¼ tsp	salt	2 ml
¾ cup (give or take a little)	water	185 ml (give or take a little)

Instructions:

1. **Combine all the first group of ingredients** in a heavy duty mixer with the paddle attachment.
2. **Add water** and mix on low until smooth dough forms that pulls away from the sides of the bowl. If dough is a bit dry (differences in milling of the flour can cause variations in this,) add water by the teaspoonful while mixing and wait until incorporated and a smooth dough forms. If a bit too wet, add sweet rice flour by the teaspoonful until a smooth dough forms.
3. **At this point the dough is ready** to be made into any shape you wish.
Pro-tip: Take care to not allow the dough to dry out by keeping the portion you are not working with immediately covered with a damp cloth.
4. **Form the soba.** A light dusting of tapioca starch will make it easier to roll and cut. You can make noodles by hand with a rolling pin and a knife, or with a pasta rolling machine. Soba is traditionally cut into ⅛ inch (2-3 mm) square noodles, a bit like linguine. The formed noodles can be kept fresh for a few days in the refrigerator or frozen for later use.
5. **Cook the noodles in plenty of boiling water** until they float and then 1 minute more.
6. **Drain** the cooking water before serving in soups or stir-fry's.

Yield: 2 entree sized portions

Nutritional Information

Calculations based upon the basic recipe excluding optional ingredients and variations.

Per 1 cup (250 ml) serving

energy	205 calories/858 kJ
protein	6 g
fat	1 g
carbohydrate	37 g
sodium	185 mg
potassium	238 mg
calcium	20 mg
iron	2 mg

Variations:

Enjoy this gluten-free version of a classic Japanese noodle in:
- ✓ **Stir-fry's or soups** as traditionally served in Japan or,
- ✓ Try it in more novel ways such as **cold noodle salads or as a side dish** with stews.

This isn't just another bland noodle. The buckwheat gives soba a distinctive grainy taste all its own.

Spaetzle (Drop Noodles)

This has to be the world's easiest noodle to make and is a great accompaniment to goulash, stews, soups and roasted chicken.

½ cup	cornstarch	125 ml
⅓ cup	brown rice flour	85 ml
3 tbsp	tapioca starch	45 ml
1 tsp	xanthan gum	5 ml
pinch	salt *(optional)*	pinch
½ cup	water	125 ml
2 whole	eggs *or* egg white	2 whole
or		*or*
½ cup egg white		125 ml egg white

Instructions:

1. **Mix the first group of ingredients** together fully before adding the eggs and water. Continue mixing until a paste the texture of toothpaste has formed.
2. **Press through a *spaetzle machine* or a colander with large holes** so the resulting drops fall directly into boiling water.

Pro-tip: The spaetzle machine is a little gadget that looks like a dull cheese grater with a small sliding bin attached. It is made to sit across the top rim of a pot of boiling water to make spaetzle-making a very easy task. They are available quite inexpensively in most kitchenware shops.

3. **Allow to boil about 1 minute** or until all the noodles have begun to float.
4. **Drain off water** and rinse briefly in hot water.
5. **Use spaetzle** as is in soups or pasta salads, or toss it with melted butter or olive oil and serve immediately as a side dish. I know some people who think they are even better if toasted golden brown in a non- stick pan with a bit of butter.

Yield: about 2 cups (500 ml)

Nutritional Information

Calculations based upon the basic recipe excluding
optional ingredients and variations.

Per 1 cup (250 ml) serving

energy	321 calories/1343 kJ
protein	7 g
fat	5 g
carbohydrate	60 g
sodium	128 mg
potassium	130 mg
calcium	26 mg
iron	1 mg

Variations:

This classic European noodle has been claimed by many countries with corresponding names from each. All we really need to know is that this version is a great gluten-free alternative to pasta. Here are a few of the traditional variations for this recipe, but don't let them limit you, there are many more possible.

✓ **Herb Spaetzle**
Add 2 tsp (10 ml) fresh chopped parsley or other herb of your choice into the dough to add a dash of colour and flavour to this otherwise neutrally flavoured side dish.

✓ **Poppy Seed Spaetzle**
Add 2 tsp (10 ml) poppy seeds into the dough to add a dash of colour and a subtle grainy taste.

✓ **Hazelnut Spaetzle**
Add 1 - 2 tbsp (15 - 30ml) finely chopped toasted hazelnuts into the dough to produce a rich nutty taste. This variation is a perfect accompaniment to roast pork or duck.

✓ **Paprika Spaetzle**
Add 2 tsp (10 ml) paprika into the dough to add a great colour and flavour.

Yorkshire Pudding

While this classic accompaniment to roast beef isn't a dessert, it may make you want to skip dessert! A debate rages as to whether Yorkies should be low and somewhat doughy, or high and crisp. This recipe will keep everyone happy, with variations for both.

1 cup	brown rice flour	250 ml
²/₃ cup	corn starch	165 ml
¹/₃ cup	tapioca flour	85 ml
¾ tsp	xanthan gum	4 ml
¾ tsp	salt	4 ml
¼ tsp	nutmeg	1 ml
3	eggs	3
2 ½ – 3 cups	milk *or* non-dairy alternate (*this range allows for some customizing of the recipe. for low Yorkies use 2 ½ cups (625 ml); for high crisp ones, use 3 cups (750 ml)*)	625 - 750 ml
¾ cup	vegetable oil *or* beef drippings	180 ml

Instructions:

1. **Mix dry ingredients together;** then add the wet to form a smooth thin batter and set aside.

Pro-tip: I like to use a blender as the batter can then be easily poured after mixing. If not using a blender, put the batter into a pitcher for ease of pouring into muffin tins.

2. **Prepare a regular-sized muffin tin** by pouring about 1 tbsp (15 ml) vegetable oil or beef drippings into each of the cups.

3. **Place muffin tin** on a baking sheet large enough to catch any overflow.

4. **Preheat muffin tin** in a 450°F (230°C) oven until very hot (beginning to smoke).

5. **Working quickly to prevent the oil cooling,** pour batter into muffin cups, filling each one until the oil floating on top comes to the rim of the muffin cup. Return the pan to the oven.

6. **Bake at 450ºF (230ºC) for 15 - 20 minutes** until well-risen and a light golden brown color.

7. **Turn oven down to 250ºF (120ºC)** and continue baking another 15 - 20 minutes until Yorkies have crisped up enough to handle without deforming. For the recipe variation with more liquid, this may take a bit longer. These can be prepared ahead and reheated without loss of quality.

Yield: 12 standard muffin-sized portions

Nutritional Information
Calculations based upon the basic recipe, excluding optional ingredients and variations.
Per standard muffin sized serving

energy	247 calories/1033 kJ
protein	4 g
fat	16 g
carbohydrate	22 g
sodium	177 mg
potassium	139 mg
calcium	77 mg
iron	trace

Variations:

✓ Yorkshire puddings are traditionally served drenched with gravy together with roast beef and horseradish.

✓ Consider stuffing them with shaved roast beef as a variation to the open-faced hot beef sandwich.

✓ Make Yorkshire puddings in mini-muffin cups and stuff them with roast beef and Dijon mustard, or horseradish for a great hot appetizer.

Basic Pilaf

Made in traditional fashion with rice or using any gluten-free grains, the variations are unlimited and add a whole lot of flavour.

1 cup	gluten-free grain (e.g. rice, millet, teff, quinoa, amaranth)	250 ml
2 tbsp	butter *or* non-dairy alternate	30 ml
½ cup	onion, diced	125 ml
1	garlic clove, finely chopped (*optional*)	1
Use amounts for each grain as listed in basic recipes.	stock to suit the dish you are going to serve this with	Use amounts for each grain as listed in basic recipes.

Instructions:

1. **Sauté onions** in butter or alternate over medium heat until golden brown.
2. **Add grains** and garlic (if using), and continue to sauté 2 - 3 minutes.
3. From this point, **follow the instructions within the basic grains recipes.** Millet *(p. 140)*, Quinoa *(p. 142)*, Teff *(p. 146)*, Wild Rice *(p. 148)*, Buckwheat Kasha *(p. 138)*, Rice Couscous *(p. 162)*.

Yield: 3 ½ - 4 cups (875 - 1000ml); serves about 4 as a side dish

Nutritional Information
Due to the variations inherent in this recipe nutritional calculations are not possible.

Variations:

Try using chicken, beef, vegetable or seafood stocks to create a flavourful backdrop, then follow the basic recipe to cook the grains:

- ✓ For a **fruity flavour** add ¼ cup (60 ml) raisins or currants and 1 - 2 inch (2.5 - 5 cm) cinnamon stick or 2 whole star anise pods
- ✓ For a **fresh herbal flavour** add 1 tsp (5 ml) dried or 1 tbsp (15 ml) fresh herb of your choice
- ✓ For a **Mediterranean flavour,** add ¼ cup (60 ml) chopped sun-dried tomatoes and 2 tbsp (30 ml) toasted pine nuts.

Stocks and Soups

Stocks

Whether you call it stock, broth or bouillon; knowledge of this simple concept can change your meals from mundane to marvellous with very little effort or cost. The extra depth of flavour found in fine restaurant soups and entrees is usually due to the use of flavourful stocks in their preparation.

Stock is simply a liquid, usually water, which has had something flavourful simmered in it until the flavour is absorbed into the water. Sadly, in most home kitchens many of the ingredients for stocks are actually purchased and thrown away. The bones from a roast … the vegetable trimmings … the seafood shells… that last glass of wine that has oxidized in the bottle … they all form the basis for a great stock. Vegetables that are beginning to go soft, but are not yet spoiled, are perfect. Keep a container for these items in your freezer and collect the bits until you have the basis for a full flavoured stock. You will find it doesn't take long to accumulate enough for a batch. Simmer them and enjoy the flavour benefits. A slow-cooker is ideal for preparing stocks as it seems to have been deliberately built for this purpose.

Home-made stocks also have many benefits as compared to purchased ones. When you prepare the stock you control the amount of salt, fat, spice and ultimately the concentration of flavour. Please note that the stock recipes in this book do not have salt and strong spices added. This allows you to control the flavour of any dish containing the stock without concern for over-seasoning; after all, salt can always be added just before serving, if it is needed. With some great home-made stocks on hand, flavourful soups and sauces are just a step away.

Beef Stock

If there is a chef's secret to great beef soups,
gravies and sauces, this is it.

	raw and / or cooked beef bones (*or venison*) and / or trimmings	
	per 4 cups/1 litre of bones	
½ cup	equal parts onions, carrots and celery roughly chopped	125 ml
2 tbsp	tomato paste	30 ml
1	bay leaf	1
½ tsp	thyme	3 ml
2	whole cloves	2
1	garlic clove	1
	water to cover	

Instructions:

1. **Oven-roast bones**, vegetables and tomato paste at 450ºF (230ºC) until deeply browned.
2. **Transfer to a stock pot** and add the next group of ingredients. Simmer (*do not boil*) at least 4 hours, longer if the bones are large.

Pro-tip: This can also be done in a slow cooker set on low for 10 - 12 hours.

3. **Strain and reserve liquid**. Discard the rest.
4. **Remove fat** floating on the surface.

Pro-tip: The easiest method is to refrigerate the stock overnight. The fat will solidify and can be easily spooned off. Skimming the surface to remove the fat without wasting the stock takes considerable practice.
Alternately, you can pour the stock through a specially designed pitcher that takes the liquid from the bottom, leaving the floating fat behind.

5. **The stock can now be used** to make soups, sauces or whatever you choose. It will not keep more than a few days in the refrigerator so freezing is the best option. Freezing can be done as is, or the stock can be boiled down (reduced) to concentrate the flavour and reduce the space it requires in the freezer.

Pro tip: **The stock can be reduced** all the way down to a "glace" where a single ice cube-sized piece will equal 4 cups (1 litre) of stock. It will have a glue-like consistency when hot and turn rubbery when cold. I find freezing the stock "glace" in ice cube trays very handy and the results much better than the salty gluten-free bouillon cubes commercially available.

Please note: This recipe contains no salt or pepper which would become too strong when the stock is reduced. This enables the "glace" to be added to soups or sauces without fear of over-seasoning.

Yield: about 6 cups (1.5 litres) per recipe as above

Nutritional Information
Calculations based upon the basic recipe excluding optional ingredients and variations.
Per 1 cup (250 ml) serving

energy	110 calories/460 kJ
protein	22 g
fat	1 g
carbohydrate	3 g
sodium	114 mg
potassium	474 mg
calcium	42 mg
iron	3 mg

Variations:
This basic recipe is best left without too many variations which would only limit its versatility. Consider using it as a background flavour for soups, sauces, risotto or polenta. It also is the basis for all the rich beefy flavoured brown sauces and gravies you may be missing.

Brown Poultry Stock

Great poultry soups and gravies start here. By saving bones and trimmings in your freezer as they become available, this stock can be almost free to prepare.

	raw and / or cooked chicken *or* turkey *or* duck bones, trimmings, gizzards or necks, but **no** liver	
	per 4 cups/1 litre of bones	
½ cup	equal parts onions, carrots and celery roughly chopped	125 ml
1	bay leaf	1
½ tsp	thyme	3 ml
2	cloves	2
1	garlic clove	1
	water to cover	

Instructions:

1. **Oven-roast the bones** and vegetables at 450°F (230°C) until medium brown.
2. **Transfer to a stock pot** and add the next group of ingredients and simmer (*do **not** boil*) at least 2 hours.
Pro-tip: This can also be done in a slow cooker set on low for 4 - 6 hours.
3. **Strain and reserve the liquid.** Discard the rest.
4. **Remove the fat** floating on the surface.
Pro-tip: The easiest method is to refrigerate the stock overnight. The fat will solidify and can be easily spooned off. Skimming the surface to remove the fat without wasting the stock takes considerable practice.
Alternately, you can pour the stock through a specially designed pitcher that takes the liquid from the bottom, leaving the floating fat behind.
5. **The stock can now be used** to make soups, sauces or whatever you choose. It will not keep more than a few days in the refrigerator so freezing is the best option. Freezing can be done as is, or the stock can be boiled down (reduced) to concentrate the flavour and reduce the space it requires in the freezer.

Pro-tip: **The stock can be reduced** all the way down to a "glace" where a single ice cube-sized piece will equal 4 cups (1 litre) of stock. It will have a glue-like consistency when hot and turn rubbery when cold. I find freezing the stock "glace" in ice cube trays very handy and the results much better than the salty gluten-free bouillon cubes commercially available.

Please note: This recipe contains no salt or pepper which would become too strong when the stock is reduced. This enables the "glace" to be added into soups or sauces without fear of over-seasoning.

Yield: about 6 cups (1.5 litres) per recipe as above

Nutritional Information
Calculations based upon the basic recipe excluding optional ingredients and variations.
Per 1 cup (250 ml) serving

energy	74 calories/310 kJ
protein	9 g
fat	3 g
carbohydrate	2 g
sodium	46 mg
potassium	142 mg
calcium	28 mg
iron	1 mg

Variations:

This basic recipe is best left without too many variations which would only limit its versatility. Consider using it as a background flavour for soups, sauces, risotto or polenta. It also works well as a poaching liquid to add a bit of extra flavour to your poultry dishes.

Chicken Stock

If there is a chef's secret to great savoury dishes, this is it.
It is well worth the time and effort!

	raw and/or cooked chicken *or* turkey *or* duck bones, trimmings, gizzards or necks, but **no** liver	
	per 4 cups/1 litre of bones	
½ cup	equal parts onions, carrots and celery roughly chopped	125 ml
1	bay leaf	1
½ tsp	thyme	3 ml
2	cloves	2
1	garlic clove	1
	water to cover	

Instructions:

1. **Place all ingredients in a stockpot** and add just enough water to cover everything.
2. **Simmer** (*do not boil*) at least 1 ½ hours.
Pro-tip: This can also be done in a slow-cooker set on low for 4 - 6 hours.
3. **Strain and reserve liquid.** Discard the rest.
4. **Remove the fat** floating on the surface.
Pro-tip: The easiest method is to refrigerate the stock overnight. The fat will solidify and can be easily spooned off. Skimming the surface to remove the fat without wasting the stock takes considerable practice.
   Alternately, you can pour the stock through a specially designed pitcher that takes the liquid from the bottom, leaving the floating fat behind.
5. **The stock can now be used** to make soups, sauces or whatever you choose. It will not keep more than a few days in the refrigerator so freezing is the best option. Freezing can be done as is, or the stock can be boiled down (reduced) to concentrate the flavour and reduce the space it requires in the freezer.

Pro-tip: **The stock can be reduced** all the way down to a "glace" where a single ice cube-sized piece will equal 4 cups (1 litre) of stock. It will have a glue-like consistency when hot and turn rubbery when cold. I find freezing the stock "glace" in ice cube trays very handy and the results much better than the salty gluten-free bouillon cubes commercially available.

Please note: This recipe contains no salt or pepper which would become too strong when the stock is reduced. This enables the glace to be added into soups or sauces without fear of over-seasoning.

Yield: About 6 cups (1.5 litres) per recipe as above.

Nutritional Information
Calculations based upon the basic recipe excluding optional ingredients and variations.
Per 1 cup (250 ml) serving

energy	74 calories/310 kJ
protein	9 g
fat	3 g
carbohydrate	2 g
sodium	9 mg
potassium	142 mg
calcium	28 mg
iron	1 mg

Variations:
This basic recipe is best left without too many variations which would only limit its versatility. Consider using it as a background flavour for soups, sauces, risotto or polenta. It also works well as a poaching liquid to add a bit of extra flavour to your poultry dishes.

Fish Stock

A must-have for great fish and seafood dishes;
the added flavour is well worth the effort.

	fresh *or* frozen fish bones and heads without gills or skin; choose lean white fish such as cod, halibut, hake, flounder, or sole	
	per 4 cups/1 litre of bones	
½ cup	equal parts onions and celery roughly chopped	125 ml
1	bay leaf	1
½	lemon including peel	½
1	garlic clove	1
	water to cover	

Instructions:

1. **Place all ingredients in a stockpot** and add just enough water to cover everything.
2. **Simmer** (*do not boil*) at least 1 ½ hours.

Pro-tip: This can also be done in a slow cooker set on low for 3 - 4 hours.

3. **Strain and reserve liquid**. Discard the rest.
4. **Remove any fat** floating on the surface. With fish stock there is generally very little fat unless you have chosen oilier fish.

Pro-tip: Most fish oils will not solidify when refrigerated so you can either spoon the fat off the surface or pour the stock through a specially designed pitcher that takes the liquid from the bottom, leaving the floating fat behind.

5. **The stock can now be used** to make soups, sauces or whatever you choose. It will not keep more than a few days in the refrigerator so freezing is the best option. Freezing can be done as is, or the stock can be boiled down (reduced) to concentrate the flavour and reduce the space it requires in the freezer.

Pro-tip: **The stock can be reduced** all the way down to a "glace" where a single ice cube-sized piece will equal 4 cups (1 litre) of stock. It will have a glue-like consistency when hot and turn rubbery when cold. I find freezing the stock "glace" in ice cube trays very handy and the results much better than the salty gluten-free bouillon cubes commercially available.

Please note: This recipe contains no salt or pepper which would become too strong when the stock is reduced. This enables the "glace" to be added into soups or sauces without fear of over-seasoning.

Yield: about 6 cups (1.5 litres) per recipe as above

Nutritional Information
Calculations based upon the basic recipe excluding optional ingredients and variations.
Per 1 cup (250 ml) serving

energy	46 calories/192 kJ
protein	1 g
fat	1 g
carbohydrate	3 g
sodium	162 mg
potassium	118 mg
calcium	28 mg
iron	trace mg

Variations:

This basic recipe is best left without too many variations which would only limit its versatility. Consider using it as a background flavour for soups, sauces, risotto or polenta. It also works well as a poaching liquid to add a bit of extra flavour to your fish and seafood dishes.

Ham Stock

Whether you use it to make the classic split pea soup or anything else, this is well worth the time and effort.

	raw and / or cooked smoked ham bones and trimmings	
	per 4 cups/1 litre of bones	
½ cup	equal parts onions, carrots and celery roughly chopped	125 ml
1	bay leaf	1
½ tsp	thyme	3 ml
4	sprigs parsley (with stem)	4
	water to cover	

Instructions:

1. **Place all ingredients in a stockpot** and add just enough water to cover everything.

2. **Simmer** *(do not boil)* at least 3 hours.

Pro-tip: This can also be done in a slow cooker set on low for 6 - 8 hours.

3. **Strain and reserve liquid.** Discard the rest.

4. **Remove the fat** floating on the surface.

Pro-tip: The easiest method is to refrigerate the stock overnight. The fat will solidify and can be easily spooned off. Skimming the surface to remove the fat without wasting the stock takes considerable practice.
   Alternately, you can pour the stock through a specially designed pitcher that takes the liquid from the bottom, leaving the floating fat behind.

5. **The stock can now be used** to make soups, sauces or whatever you choose. It will not keep more than a few days in the refrigerator so freezing is the best option. Freezing can be done as is, or the stock can be boiled down (reduced) to concentrate the flavour and reduce the space it requires in the freezer.

Pro-tip: **The stock can be reduced** all the way down to a "glace" where a single ice cube-sized piece will equal 4 cups (1 litre) of stock. It will have a glue-like consistency when hot and turn rubbery when cold. I find freezing the stock "glace" in ice cube trays very handy and the results much better than the salty gluten-free bouillon cubes commercially available.

Please note: This recipe contains no salt or pepper which would become too strong when the stock is reduced. However, ham generally contains a lot of salt so care must be taken when adding it to soups or sauces to prevent them becoming over-seasoned.

Yield: about 6 cups (1.5 litres) per recipe as above

Nutritional Information
Calculations based upon the basic recipe excluding optional ingredients and variations.
Per 1 cup (250 ml) serving

energy	182 calories/761 kJ
protein	36 g
fat	2 g
carbohydrate	3 g
sodium	123 mg
potassium	676 mg
calcium	153 mg
iron	3 mg

Variations:
This basic recipe is best left without too many variations which would only limit its versatility. Consider using it as a background flavour for soups, sauces, risotto or polenta. It also works well as a poaching liquid to add a bit of extra flavour to vegetables or potatoes.

Roasted Vegetable Stock

With all the different vegetables available a myriad of flavours are possible, making it well worth the time and effort.

	vegetables that are clean, but not necessarily peeled *Pro-tip:* If they are beginning to wilt, but are not yet rotting, they are perfect candidates. *(see variations below for types)*	

	per 4 cups/1 litre of coarsely chopped vegetables *Pro-tip:* Measure before roasting as they shrink a great deal during roasting.	
1	bay leaf	1
½ tsp	thyme *or* other herb of your choice	3 ml
2	cloves	2
1	garlic clove	1
	water to cover	

Instructions:

1. **Chop the vegetables** coarsely before oven-roasting at 400ºF (200ºC) until tender and flavourful. The roasting time varies depending on the vegetables chosen.

Pro-tip: I use a baking sheet lined with bakers' parchment and place the parchment into the stockpot to get all the flavour from the drippings.

2. **Transfer all ingredients to a stockpot**. Add water to just cover everything.

3. **Simmer** *(do not boil)* at least 1 ½ hours.

Pro-tip: This can also be done in a slow cooker set on low for 3 - 4 hours.

4. **Strain and reserve liquid**. Discard the rest.

5. **The stock can now be used** to make soups, sauces or whatever you choose. It will not keep more than a few days in the refrigerator so freezing is the best option. Freezing can be done as is, or the stock can be boiled down (reduced) to concentrate the flavour and reduce the space it requires in the freezer.

Pro-tip: **The stock can be reduced** all the way down to a "glace" where a single ice cube-sized piece will equal 4 cups (1 litre) of stock. I find freezing the stock "glace" in ice cube trays very handy and the results much better than the salty gluten free bouillon cubes commercially available.

Please note: This recipe contains no salt or pepper which would become too strong when the stock is reduced. This enables the "glace" to be added into soups or sauces without fear of over seasoning.

Yield: About 6 cups (1.5 litres) per recipe as above.

Nutritional Information
Due to the variations inherent in this recipe
nutritional calculations are not possible.

Variations:
Your choice of vegetables will create very full flavours representative of the ingredients chosen. You can make a stock entirely from one type of vegetable, or mix and match to suit yourself. If you store the extra half of that unused pepper or onion in the freezer, you will have the basis for some stock in no time. The leftover vegetables in many refrigerators tend to be forgotten and wasted. This will put them to good use.

Some of the best vegetables for roasting are:
- ✓ **Sweet peppers**
- ✓ **Tomatoes**
- ✓ **Onions**
- ✓ **Garlic**
- ✓ **Beets**
- ✓ **Corn**
- ✓ **Carrots**
- ✓ **Parsnip**
- ✓ **Fennel**

Consider using your roasted vegetable stock as a background flavour for soups, sauces, risotto or polenta. It also works well as a poaching liquid for poultry or meats to add a bit of extra flavour.

Vegetable Stock

This fat-free flavour booster will add that little extra to whatever you use it in. It is well worth the time and effort.

	vegetables that are clean, but not necessarily peeled *Pro-tip:* If they are beginning to wilt, but are not yet rotting, they are perfect candidates. *(see variations below for types)*	

	per 4 cups/1 litre *of coarsely chopped vegetables*	
1	bay leaf	1
½ tsp	thyme *or* other herb of your choice	3 ml
2	cloves	2
1	garlic clove	1
	water to cover	

Instructions:

1. **Chop vegetables** coarsely and place them in a stock pot with just enough water to cover everything.
2. **Simmer** *(do not boil)* at least 1 ½ hours.

Pro-tip: This can also be done in a slow cooker set on low for 3 - 4 hours.

3. **Strain and reserve liquid**. Discard the rest.
4. **The stock can now be used** to make soups, sauces or whatever you choose. It will not keep more than a few days in the refrigerator so freezing is the best option. Freezing can be done as is, or the stock can be boiled down (reduced to concentrate the flavour and reduce the space it requires in the freezer.

Pro-tip: **The stock can be reduced** all the way down to a "glace" where a single ice cube-sized piece will equal 4 cups (1 litre) of stock. I find freezing the stock "glace" in ice cube trays very handy and the results much better than the salty gluten free bouillon cubes commercially available.

Please note: This recipe contains no salt or pepper which would become too strong when the stock is reduced. This enables the "glace" to be added into soups or sauces without fear of over seasoning.

Yield: about 6 cups (1.5 litres) per recipe, as above

Nutritional Information
Due to the variations inherent in this recipe
nutritional calculations are not possible.

Variations:

Your choice of vegetables will create very full flavours representative of the ingredients chosen. You can make a stock entirely from one type of vegetable or mix and match to suit yourself. If you store the extra half of that unused pepper or onion in the freezer, you will have the basis for some stock in no time. The leftover vegetables in many refrigerators tend to be forgotten and wasted. This will put them to good use.

Some of the best vegetables for stock are:
- ✓ **Sweet peppers**
- ✓ **Tomatoes**
- ✓ **Onions**
- ✓ **Garlic**
- ✓ **Beets**
- ✓ **Corn**
- ✓ **Carrots**
- ✓ **Parsnip**
- ✓ **Fennel**
- ✓ **Mushrooms**
- ✓ **Celery**

Consider using your vegetable stock as a background flavour for soups, sauces, risotto or polenta. It also works well as a poaching liquid for poultry, meats, seafood or potatoes to add a bit of extra flavour.

Soups

Soups are a basic staple of almost every cuisine in the world. They are the ultimate comfort food on cold dreary days, yet can also be an integral part of the most elegant banquet. They can be a light appetizer or a hearty meal. In short, soup is a nourishing necessity that cannot be overlooked in a gluten-free diet.

Unfortunately, the vast majority of commercially prepared soups are loaded with fat and sodium, as well as gluten based thickeners, stabilizers or hydrolyzed vegetable protein flavourings. Don't let this discourage you. In fact, soups are among the easiest things to prepare. Any chef could tell you, but probably wouldn't, that soup is the best way to give your leftovers an appetizing second life. Any leftover gluten-free grains, pastas, vegetables, meats or seafood can be simmered in liquid and flavoured in as many different ways as there are cooks in the world.

In this book I could not possibly list even a small percentage of all the soups made around the world. I have not included many clear soups simply because they require little more than a reminder to check that all ingredients are gluten-free. Cream soups, chowders and the like require more complex changes to achieve the best gluten-free results, and that is what I have included here.

The recipes included in this section are all basic templates and the nutritional analysis for each reflects this. Your completed soups seasoned to your tastes will vary from the basic recipes, but the nutritional information provided is intended to give you an idea of the nutritional values possible. Please note the nutritional analysis was calculated using unsalted homemade stocks.

I encourage you to use these basic recipes as an outlet for your imagination and your leftovers. Who knows, with a thermos full of great soup for lunch your friends at work may envy your meals for a change.

Avgolemono

A quick and easy version of the classic Greek lemon soup

6 cups	chicken stock	1.5 litres
½ cup	uncooked rice	125 ml
2 - 3 tbsp	fresh squeezed lemon juice	30 - 45 ml
½ tsp	lemon zest	3 ml
4	whole eggs	4
pinch	nutmeg	pinch
1 cup	diced cooked chicken (*optional*)	250 ml
	salt and pepper to taste	

Instructions:

1. **Bring 6 cups (1.5 litres) of chicken stock to a boil** and cook rice in stock until tender. Reduce heat to a simmer.

2. **Whisk together next group of ingredients** with remaining (cold) stock. Whisk them into the hot stock and rice mixture. Bring back to a simmer, being careful not to boil the soup (this would cause it to curdle).

3. **If using chicken**, add it at this point. After a few minutes, the soup will thicken to a velvety smooth texture. Further cooking is not advisable as the soup will continue to thicken and turn pasty.

4. **Adjust the seasoning** with salt and pepper. Enjoy immediately for best texture. Reheating requires the addition of more stock (to adjust for the rice absorbing more of the liquid). Care must be taken in reheating to prevent curdling.

Yield: about 7 cups (1.75 litres)

Nutritional Information

Calculations based upon the basic recipe excluding
optional ingredients and variations.

Per 1 cup (250 ml) serving

energy	93 calories/389 kJ
protein	4 g
fat	2 g
carbohydrate	11 g
sodium	178 mg
potassium	110 mg
calcium	16 mg
iron	2 mg

Serving suggestions:

This classic soup needs no extra help to be delicious. Serve with a side salad and some crusty bread like the French Bread *(p.124)*.

Basic Cream Soup

With this recipe you can prepare any type of cream soup you wish

1 cup	diced onion	250 ml
¼ cup	butter *or* alternate	60 ml
3 - 4 cups total	additions (*see below*)	750 - 1000 ml
¼ cup	sweet rice flour	60 ml
1 cup	chicken stock *or* alternate	250 ml
6 cups	milk *or* non-dairy alternate	1.5 L
½ cup	heavy cream *or* non-dairy alternate	125 ml
	salt and pepper to taste	

Instructions:

1. **Sauté onion** in butter or alternate over medium heat until onion becomes translucent. If using fresh vegetables for the soup (except leaves such as spinach, watercress or sorrel), add them at this point and allow them to sauté and soften.
2. **Stir in sweet rice flour** until no more spots of dry flour can be seen.
3. **Add in stock** or alternate and milk, and bring to a gentle simmer.
4. **If using leaf vegetables** such as those listed above, add them at this point.
5. **Adjust seasoning** with salt and pepper. The soup is ready to serve if the additions are fully cooked. You can choose to serve the soup chunky or use a blender to puree it.

Pro-tip: I like to use an immersion type blender for this purpose.

Yield: 8 cups (2 litres)

Nutritional Information

Calculations based upon the basic recipe excluding
optional ingredients and variations.
Per 1 cup (250 ml) serving

energy	203 calories/849 kJ
protein	7 g
fat	13 g
carbohydrate	11 g
sodium	182 mg
potassium	344g
calcium	241 mg
iron	trace

Variations:

Chefs the world over know that soup is a great way to give leftovers a tasty second life. Raid the refrigerator of all the little bits and enjoy the possibilities. Make sure the items are pre-cut to a reasonable spoon size if you do not wish to puree the soup. You can use 3 - 4 cups (750 – 1000 ml) of anything you wish to add, alone or in any combination. The options are limited only by your imagination. Here are just a few ideas which make use of this recipe:

- ✓ **Poultry or Seafood** - Use up leftover chicken, turkey, shrimp, fish and shellfish.
- ✓ **Root Vegetables** - Try carrots, celery root, parsnips, turnips, onions and leeks.
- ✓ **Stalk Vegetables** - Try celery, fennel or asparagus.
- ✓ **Leafy Vegetables** - Try spinach, sorrel, watercress, kale or Swiss chard.
- ✓ **Legumes** - Try fresh green or yellow beans, chick peas, dried beans or lentils.
- ✓ **Mushrooms** - Try store bought or wild varieties, fresh or dried.
- ✓ **Rice** - Enjoy the flavour variations of wild, brown and white rice. Some interesting rice types such as Thai red or sweet black can provide great taste and a great looking soup too.
- ✓ **Pasta** - Try any gluten-free noodles you can buy, or make your own. The spaetzle *(p. 166)* are particularly good in soups.

Basic Red Chowder

If you like your chowders tomato based, this is for you.
By changing the spices, flavourings and additions,
the possibilities are almost limitless.

3 strips	strips bacon *or* smoked tofu diced	3
	(*or* 1 tbsp butter *or* non-dairy alternate)	
1	medium onion, diced	1
2	stalks celery, diced	2
1	small red *or* yellow bell pepper	1
3 cups	crushed tomatoes	750 ml
3 cups	diced potato (red *or* yellow)	750 ml
½ tsp	thyme leaves	3 ml
2	bay leaves	2
2 tbsp	sweet rice flour	30 ml
½ tsp	gluten-free Worcestershire sauce	3 ml
	(*optional*)	
3 cups	clams *or ... (see variations)*,	750 ml
	with juice or stock, just enough to cover	
	salt and pepper to taste	

Instructions:

1. **Fry bacon** or alternate over medium heat until crisp and brown. Discard drippings.
2. **Add next group of ingredients** and sauté them until they have become soft and translucent.
    - ✓ If not using bacon, just sauté onions and celery in butter or alternate.
    - ✓ If using precooked meats (like leftover turkey), you can add them now as the simmering will only make them more tender.
    - ✓ If using seafood, refer to steps 3 and 4.
3. **Add the third group of ingredients**, taking care to stir in the sweet rice flour before it comes to a simmer again. Simmer about 20 minutes, stirring occasionally until the potatoes have become tender.

- ✓ If using clams or other seafood they are best added close to the end of cooking to prevent them from toughening up

4. **Adjust seasoning** with salt and pepper and serve. This chowder will keep a few days in the refrigerator or freezes well.

Yield: 8 cups (2 litres)

Nutritional Information

Calculations based upon the basic recipe excluding optional ingredients and variations.

Per 1 cup (250 ml) serving

energy	194 calories/812 kJ
protein	19 g
fat	3 g
carbohydrate	22 g
sodium	239 mg
potassium	1042 mg
calcium	101 mg
iron	19 mg

Variations:

Many different types of chowders are possible. Here are a few ideas to get you started.

- ✓ **Clam or Seafood Chowder**
  Clam chowder is the best known by far, but mussels, oysters, shrimp and scallops are all great variations. Any firm-fleshed fish also makes a great choice.
- ✓ **Chicken or Turkey Chowder**
  Turn leftover chicken or turkey into an easy one-dish meal.
- ✓ **Roasted Pepper Chowder**
  Whether you choose to roast and peel your own peppers, or use one of the many types available in Mediterranean markets, this is sure to be a flavourful variation.
- ✓ **Spicy Sausage Chowder**
  Spicy sausage such as spicy Italian, Cajun or Chorizo can really add some flavour to basic chowder.

Basic White Chowder

No matter what you add to it, this is a great chowder that can be frozen for later use. By changing the spices, flavourings and additions, the possibilities are almost limitless.

3 strips	strips bacon *or* smoked tofu diced (*or* 1 tbsp butter *or* non-dairy alternate)	3
1	medium onion, diced	1
2	stalks celery, diced	2
1	small red *or* yellow bell pepper	1
3 cups	milk *or* non-dairy alternate	750 ml
3 cups	diced potato (red *or* yellow)	750 ml
½ tsp	thyme leaves	3 ml
2	bay leaves	2
2 tbsp	sweet rice flour	30 ml
¼ tsp	gluten-free Worcestershire sauce (*optional*)	2 ml
3 cups	clams *or* … with juice or stock, just enough to cover	750 ml
	salt and pepper to taste	

Instructions:

1. **Fry bacon** or alternate over medium heat until crisp and brown. Discard drippings.
2. **Add next group of ingredients** and sauté them until they have become soft and translucent.
   - ✓ If not using bacon, just sauté onions and celery in butter or alternate.
   - ✓ If using precooked meats (like leftover turkey), add them now as the simmering will only make them more tender.
   - ✓ If using seafood, refer to steps 3 and 4.
3. **Add third group of ingredients**, taking care to stir in the sweet rice flour before it comes to a simmer again. Simmer about 20 minutes, stirring occasionally until the potatoes have become tender.

✓ If using clams or other seafood they are best added close to the end of cooking to prevent them from toughening up

4. **Adjust seasoning** with salt and pepper and serve. This chowder will keep a few days in the refrigerator or freezes well.

Yield: 8 cups (2 litres)

Nutritional Information

Calculations based upon the basic recipe excluding optional ingredients and variations.
Per 1 cup (250 ml) serving

energy	204 calories/854 kJ
protein	21 g
fat	3 g
carbohydrate	20 g
sodium	164 mg
potassium	917 mg
calcium	182 mg
iron	18 mg

Variations:

Many different types of chowders are possible. Here are a few ideas to get you started.

✓ **Clam or Seafood Chowder**
Clam chowder is the best known by far but, mussels, oysters, shrimp and scallops are all great variations.

✓ **Chicken or Turkey Chowder**
Turn leftover chicken or turkey into an easy one-dish meal.

✓ **Corn Chowder**
For a great vegetarian variation and a richer flavour try roasting the corn or toasting the kernels in a skillet until they brown slightly.

✓ **Spicy Sausage Chowder**
Spicy sausage such as spicy Italian, Cajun or Chorizo can really add some flavour to basic chowder.

Cream of Tomato Soup

With this recipe you can prepare the rainy day classic.

1 cup	onion, diced	250 ml
¼ cup	butter *or* non-dairy alternate	60 ml
3 - 4 cups	chopped fresh tomato, *or* crushed canned tomato	750 - 1000 ml
¼ cup	sweet rice flour	60 ml
2 tsp	white sugar *(only required if the tomatoes are not very sweet)*	10 ml
1 cup	chicken stock *or* alternate	250 ml
6 cups	milk *or* non dairy alternate	1.5 litres
½ cup	heavy cream *or* non-dairy alternate *(optional)*	125 ml
	salt and pepper to taste	

Instructions:

1. **Sauté onion** and butter or alternate over medium heat until the onion becomes translucent. (If adding any of the variations below which require cooking time to soften, add them at this stage.)
2. **Add tomatoes** at this point and allow them to sauté and soften.
3. **Stir sweet rice flour** into milk and stock, or alternate.
4. **Add stock,** or alternate, and milk to the tomato mixture.
5. **Bring to a gentle simmer,** stirring occasionally. If using leafy vegetables for the soup such as spinach, watercress or sorrel), add them at this point and allow them to sauté and soften.
6. **Adjust seasoning** with salt and pepper. At this point the soup is ready to serve. You can choose to serve the soup chunky or use a blender to puree it and strain out the seeds, etc.

Pro-tip: I like to use an immersion type blender for this purpose.

Yield: about 8 cups (2 litres)

Nutritional Information

Calculations based upon the basic recipe excluding
optional ingredients and variations.
Per 1 cup (250 ml) serving

energy	190 calories/795 kJ
protein	8 g
fat	8 g
carbohydrate	19 g
sodium	318 mg
potassium	645 mg
calcium	268 mg
iron	2 mg

Variations:

There are as many variations of tomato soup as there are cooks. A myriad of additions can be made. Make sure the items are pre-cut to a reasonable spoon size if you do not wish to puree the soup. You can use 3 - 4 cups (750 – 1000 ml) of anything you wish to add to your tomato soup. The options are limited only by your imagination. Here are just a few ideas to make use of this recipe:

- ✓ **Poultry or Seafood** - Use up leftover chicken, turkey, shrimp, fish and shellfish.
- ✓ **Root Vegetables** - Try carrots, celery root, parsnips, turnips, onions and leeks.
- ✓ **Stalk Vegetable** - Try celery, fennel, or asparagus.
- ✓ **Leafy Vegetables** - Try spinach, sorrel, watercress, kale or Swiss chard.
- ✓ **Legumes** - Try fresh green or yellow beans, chick peas, dried beans or lentils.
- ✓ **Mushrooms** - Try store bought or wild varieties, fresh or dried.
- ✓ **Rice** - Enjoy the flavour variations of wild, brown and white rice. Some interesting rice types such as Thai red or sweet black can provide great taste and great looking soup too.
- ✓ **Pasta** - Try any gluten-free noodles you can buy, or make your own. The spaetzle *(p. 166)* is particularly good in soups.

French Onion

Enjoy the classic in gluten-free fashion or update the common restaurant version by eliminating the bread on top.

8 cups	thinly sliced onions	2 litres
	Pro-tip: I use a slicing disk on my food processor for this purpose.	
	Pro-tip: Adding different types of onions enhances the depth of flavor.	
½ tsp	thyme leaves	3 ml
2	bay leaves	2
¼ cup	brandy, *or* ½ cup (125 ml) wine, dry cider, *or* gluten-free beer	60 ml
8 cups	beef stock, *or* water and bouillon	2 litres
	salt and pepper to taste	
1 cup	shredded cheese of your choice	250 ml
	toasted gluten-free bread cut to the shape of the surface of the serving bowls *or* thinly sliced apple or pear to cover the surface of the serving bowls	

Instructions:

1. **Sauté onions** on medium-high heat in a heavy-bottomed pot. No added fat or liquid is required because the natural juices in the onions will suffice. Ensure the pot has a holding capacity of at least 12 cups (3 litres).

2. **Continue cooking** until the onions are soft and medium brown, stirring occasionally.

Pro-tip: Do not be alarmed if the juices burn slightly to the pot. Onions are one of the few foods that do not taste bad when burnt. This dark brown / black glaze on the bottom of the pot gives the soup its rich colour.

3. **Add brandy, wine or alternate** while scraping the glaze with a wooden spoon (no metal) in order to get this colour into the soup. Before the liquid

has a chance to boil away completely add the stock, bay leaves and thyme. Simmer 30 minutes.

4. **Adjust seasoning** with salt and pepper.

5. If making the traditional recipe, **pour the hot soup** into ovenproof bowls, cover with a toasted gluten-free bread crouton and top with Swiss cheese. A few minutes under the broiler to melt the cheese completes the dish.

Yield: about 10 cups (2.5 litres)

Nutritional Information

Calculations based upon the basic recipe excluding optional ingredients and variations.
Per 1 cup (250 ml) serving

energy	80 calories /335 kJ
protein	2 g
fat	trace g
carbohydrate	12 g
sodium	164 mg
potassium	269 mg
calcium	29 mg
iron	2 mg

Variations:

This classic soup can be the host to many variations; try some of the ones below to update this old standard.

✓ **Cheese Variations**

Change the cheese for a tasty twist. Try an old Cheddar, Asiago, Parmesan or even Blue. The options are limitless.

✓ **Apple/Pear Crouton**

I created another more updated version to please the frequent requests for onion soup without the "soggy bread" common on restaurant menus. Place thin strips of apple or pear on the surface of the hot soup in the serving bowls and top with the cheese of your choice. Serve as is, or broil to melt the cheese. The savory soup with the tartness of the apple or pear, and the nip of a strong cheese makes a wonderful trinity of flavors.

Mulligatawny Soup

This perennial favourite can't miss with curry, rice and apples flavouring a rich cream of chicken soup.

1 cup	onion, diced	250 ml
1 cup	apples, diced	250 ml
¼ cup	butter *or* non-dairy alternate	60 ml
1 - 3 tbsp	curry powder (depending on your tastes. Make sure yours is gluten-free)	15 - 45 ml
¼ cup	sweet rice flour	60 ml
3 cups	chicken stock *or* alternate	750 ml
3 cups	milk *or* non-dairy alternate	750 ml
1 cup	cooked rice	250 ml
1 cup	cooked diced chicken	250 ml
1 cup	heavy cream *or* coconut milk *(optional)*	250 ml
	salt and pepper to taste	

Instructions:

1. **Sauté first group of ingredients** over medium heat until the onion becomes translucent.
2. **Stir in sweet rice flour** until no more spots of dry flour can be seen.
3. **Add in stock or alternate,** and milk or alternate
4. **Bring to a gentle simmer**. At this point add the rice and chicken.
5. **Adjust seasoning** with salt and pepper. The soup is ready to serve. If you choose to enrich the soup with cream or coconut milk, add it just before serving.

Yield: about 8 cups (2 litres)

Nutritional Information

Calculations based upon the basic recipe excluding
optional ingredients and variations.
Per 1 cup (250 ml) serving

energy	210 calories/879 kJ
protein	10 g
fat	10 g
carbohydrate	16 g
sodium	194 mg
potassium	299 mg
calcium	130 mg
iron	1 mg

Variations:

Flavour variations in curries from around the world make this recipe very easy to customize to suit your tastes. From fiery, to mild and savoury, the options are numerous. The sweet rice thickener in this soup makes it freeze / thaw stable so make a bit extra and have some on hand for a quick meal.

✓ **Fruit Variation**

Replace the apple with pear, mango, or pineapple for an interesting twist.

✓ **Fennel Variation**

Replace the onion with fennel bulb for a fresh anise flavour.

✓ **Seafood Variation**

Replace the chicken and chicken stock with seafood and fish stock. Shrimp, clams, mussels and scallops all make flavourful variations.

Roasted Squash Soup

This simple soup, full of flavour and nutrition, is surprisingly easy to make even though the instructions seem long. The starchiness of the squash naturally thickens the soup so no added thickeners are needed.

any amount you wish	shelled squash such as butternut, banana, acorn *or* pumpkin	any amount you wish
about ¹/₁₀ the amount of the squash	onion peeled and coarsely chopped	about ¹/₁₀ the amount of the squash
about ¹/₁₀ the amount of the squash	celery coarsely chopped	about ¹/₁₀ the amount of the squash
as required to dilute the puree to the desired consistency	water, stock, *or* other flavourful liquid	as required to dilute the puree to the desired consistency
	spices *see variations below*	
as desired	cream, non-dairy alternate *or* coconut milk *(optional)*	as desired
to taste	salt and pepper	to taste

Instructions:

1. **Peel, remove seeds and coarsely chop** squash, onions and celery. Roast vegetables until fully softened. Do not be concerned if there is a bit of browning as this will only add to the flavour.

Pro-tip: If possible, use a soup pot that can be placed in the oven so none of the flavourful roasted juices will be lost in the transfer to another container.

Alternately, **roast squash whole** on a baking sheet after poking a few holes in it to allow the steam to escape. Roast until squash starts to soften before adding the onions and celery. Continue roasting until the squash softens to the point where it slumps and loses its shape. Cut the squash open end to end, and use a large spoon to scoop out the seeds and discard them. Then scoop all the softened squash out of the shell / skin. This method is a bit messier, but it is also less work. Be sure to keep all juices from the roasting pan to return them to the soup.

2. **Puree roasted squash pulp, onion and celery** in a blender.
Alternately, this can be done in the soup pot with an immersion blender.

3. **Dilute puree** to desired consistency with water, stock or other flavourful liquid. The amount of liquid required varies widely with different types of squash. Bring the soup back to a simmer before continuing.

4. **Add cream or alternates,** if desired

5. **Spice and season** to taste with salt and pepper.

Yield: varies depending on ingredients chosen.

Nutritional Information
Due to the variations inherent in this recipe
nutritional calculations are not possible.

Variations:
This basic concept has many possible variations. By using different types of squash, seasonings, and cream or alternates, many options are possible. Here are just a few ideas to get you started.

✓ **Curried Squash Soup**
   Try seasoning the soup with curry, and enrich the soup with coconut milk for an interesting variation.

✓ **South-Western Squash Soup**
   Try seasoning the soup south-west style with chillies, cilantro, garlic and cumin. Add some black beans, corn and bell pepper to make a spicy and hearty version.

✓ **Savoury Squash Soup**
   Season the soup with a little thyme and rosemary, and enrich with a bit of cream for a savoury soup perfect for winter meals.

✓ **Roasted Yam Soup**
   Replace the squash with yams or sweet potato for another variation to this concept

Stracciatella

This classic Italian egg-drop soup is
super quick and easy to prepare.

6	eggs	6
3 tbsp	cornstarch	45 ml
2 tbsp	brown rice flour	30 ml
1 tbsp	tapioca starch	15 ml
½ cup	grated Parmesan *or* Asiago *or* Romano cheese	125 ml
1 ½ tsp	chopped Italian flat leaf parsley	8 ml
pinch	nutmeg	pinch
7 cups	chicken stock *or* alternate	1.75 litres
	salt and pepper to taste	
	additional grated cheese (*optional*)	

Instructions:

1. **Mix together first group of ingredients** and set aside.
2. **Bring stock to a boil** and whisk the reserved mixture into the boiling stock.
3. **Turn heat down to a simmer** and continue to whisk periodically for the next 3 minutes.
4. **Adjust seasoning** with salt and pepper. Enjoy it topped with more grated cheese, if desired.

Yield: about 8 cups (2 litres)

Nutritional Information

Calculations based upon the basic recipe excluding
optional ingredients and variations.
Per 1 cup (250 ml) serving

energy	116 calories/485 kJ
protein	7 g
fat	5 g
carbohydrate	7 g
sodium	310 mg
potassium	129 mg
calcium	88 mg
iron	2 mg

Variations:

This classic Italian soup makes a tasty light lunch when served with a salad.
Egg drop soups are made the world over with a great variety of flavours. Here
are just a few to try:

✓ **Asian Style**

Prepare the soup without the cheese, and flavour the broth with green
onion, ginger, sesame oil and tamari.

✓ **Mexican Style**

Prepare the soup with a cheese such as Monterey or even cheddar, and
flavour the broth with green onion, cilantro, tomato and chillies. Add
some crumbled corn chips to give the soup a bit more body.

✓ **Greek Style**

Prepare the soup with finely grated feta cheese, and flavour the broth
with lemon, oregano and garlic.

Leek and Potato Soup

A classic served hot, or cold as Vichyssoise

3 cups	leeks, sliced (white and tender green parts only)	750 ml
3 cups	baking potatoes, peeled and chopped	750 ml
6 cups	chicken stock *or* water	1.5 litres
	salt and pepper to taste	
½ cup	sour cream *or* yogurt *or* non-dairy alternate *(optional)*	125 ml

Instructions:

1. **Simmer leeks and potatoes** in stock for 20 - 30 minutes until tender. Serve as is for a rustic style soup or puree.

   Pro-tip: An immersion blender works well for a producing a more refined texture.

2. **Adjust seasoning** with salt and pepper. If using sour cream, stir it in just before serving. Garnish with fresh chives if you wish.

Yield*: about 8 cups (2 litres)

Nutritional Information

Calculations based upon the basic recipe excluding optional ingredients and variations.

Per 1 cup (250 ml) serving

energy	81 calories/469 kJ
protein	2 g
fat	trace g
carbohydrate	15 g
sodium	160 mg
potassium	429 mg
calcium	25 mg
iron	2 mg

Variations:

✓ **Add fresh herbs** of your choice close to the end of cooking.
✓ **Serve cold as Vichyssoise.**

Bean and Bacon Soup

Warm, hearty and full of protein

2, 19 oz cans	beans of your choice (a medley is tasty)	2, 540 ml cans
¼ lb (4 strips)	bacon, ham, or smoked tofu, cut into small pieces	100 g
1	medium onion, finely chopped	1
2	celery stalks, finely chopped	2
4 cups	chicken stock or water	1 L
1 pinch	thyme leaves	1 pinch
	salt and pepper to taste	

Instructions:

1. **Prepare bacon or alternate**, onion and celery as listed above.
2. **Fry bacon or alternate** until crisp on medium-high heat in a heavy bottomed pot of at least 3 quarts (3 litres) capacity. Discard drippings.
3. **Add in onion and celery,** and cook until the onion has become soft and translucent.
4. **Add stock, thyme and beans**, and simmer 10 minutes.
5. **Adjust seasoning** with salt and pepper.

Yield: about 8 cups (2 litres)

Nutritional Information

Calculations based upon the basic recipe excluding optional ingredients and variations.

Per 1 cup (250 ml) serving

energy	252 calories/1054 kJ
protein	15 g
fat	8 g
carbohydrate	30 g
sodium	939 mg
potassium	550 mg
calcium	73 mg
iron	4 mg

Sauces

Sauces are undoubtedly the single most important component in making delicious entrees. A multitude of small errors and oversights in cooking can be repaired by a great sauce. This is witnessed by the fact that in most commercial kitchens the saucier, the person who makes the sauces, is usually one of the highest ranking members of the team.

A sauce moistens the mouth and carries flavours which greatly enrich the sensation of eating. Eat a plain roast chicken or steak with boiled potatoes and steamed broccoli, and you will discover very quickly that you probably agree with the previous statement. Unfortunately, many sauces have traditionally been thickened with wheat flour, a practice often used in prepared foods and in many restaurants. Many sauces have also been given a great deal of bad press due to their high fat and salt content. By making your own sauces you control all of the ingredients and need not do without.

Fortunately, sauces are generally quite easy to make. Also, many of the sauces in this chapter can be made in larger quantities and frozen to have on hand for later use. You will find that the majority of your best loved entree recipes, those containing gluten and those without, are actually sauce recipes which include other items. Pot pies, pastas, stews, stir-fries, roasted meats and poultry are all examples where the sauce is the essence of the dish. Make your sauces to suit your tastes, and enjoy all the flavour possible from your meals.

Asian Sweet and Sour Sauce

Pair this quick and easy sauce with chicken, pork,
meatballs or shrimp for a quick and tasty entrée.

1 cup	orange *or* pineapple juice	250 ml
1 cup	sugar	250 ml
½ cup	vinegar *(rice vinegar is best, but not absolutely necessary)*	125 ml
½ cup	ketchup	125 ml
¼ cup	gluten-free soy sauce (tamari)	60 ml
1 tsp	ginger (fresh *or* powdered)	5 ml
2 - 3 tbsp	sweet rice flour *(slightly more or less depending on desired thickness)*	30 - 45 ml
	salt and pepper to taste	

Instructions:

There are two ways to make use of this recipe; as a side sauce or made together with meat or seafood. The later method saves time and dishes. Regardless of how it is prepared, this sauce can also be frozen without separating.

Side Sauce

1. **Mix all ingredients together** cold in a saucepan.
2. **Bring to a low boil** stirring frequently.
3. **It is finished cooking** once the sauce has come to a boil.
4. **Adjust the seasoning** with salt and pepper and it is ready to serve.

Yield: 2 ½ cups (625 ml)

Time Saver

1. **Mix all ingredients together** in a container with a tight fitting lid. A 3 cup (750 g) yogurt container works well. Hold the lid and shake to mix.
2. **Pour over seared meat or seafood** in the pan in which it was seared. Simmer meats until tender.

Pro-tip: For shrimp or scallops, bring sauce just to a boil before removing from heat to prevent the seafood from becoming rubbery.

3. **Adjust the seasoning** with salt and pepper and it is ready to serve.

Yield: 2 ½ cups (625 ml)

Nutritional Information
Calculations based upon the basic recipe excluding
optional ingredients and variations.
Per ½ cup (125 ml) serving

energy	229 calories/958 kJ
protein	3 g
fat	trace g
carbohydrate	54 g
sodium	1091 mg
potassium	278 mg
calcium	16 mg
iron	1 mg

Variations:

This recipe is very basic and a great place to start when making any sweet and sour dish. Feel free to add other flavours that appeal to you. Try adding:
- ✓ **Chillies** for a bit of heat
- ✓ **Garlic** for some pungency
- ✓ **Chinese Five Spice** powder for more complexity

With steamed rice and vegetables this could be a quick and easy meal.

Basic Cream Sauce

*With this as a starting point you can make hundreds
of different cream sauce variations.*

½ cup	white wine	125 ml
½	small onion diced fine	½
2 - 3 tbsp	sweet rice flour *(slightly more or less depending on desired thickness)*	30 - 45 ml
1 cup	chicken stock	250 ml
1 cup	heavy cream *or* non-dairy alternate	250 ml
	salt and white pepper to taste	

Instructions:

1. **Sauté onion** in the white wine until translucent.
2. **Whisk together** remaining ingredients except cream or alternate, and bring to a simmer.
3. **When mixture has thickened**, stir in cream or alternate.
4. **Season to taste** with salt and white pepper. At this point, the addition of flavours or seasonings can make this sauce very versatile.

See variations below

Yield: 2 ½ cups (625 ml)

Nutritional Information
Calculations based upon the basic recipe excluding
optional ingredients and variations.
Per 1 cup (250 ml) serving

energy	426 calories/1782 kJ
protein	4 g
fat	37 g
carbohydrate	7 g
sodium	125 mg
potassium	208 mg
calcium	77 mg
Iron	1 mg

Variations:

In many restaurant kitchens a basic cream sauce is kept on hand and finished with various ingredients when the patron orders it. The use of sweet rice flour makes this sauce freezer stable so you can prepare some ahead and make a quick sauce, or variety of dishes, in just a few minutes. The possible combinations are limited only by your creativity. Here are just a few ideas to get you started:

- ✓ **Herb Cream Sauce**
  Stir in any fresh or dried herb you choose to suit your dish. Allow a few minutes for the flavour to develop fully before serving. This sauce is great served with fish, seafood, poultry and pasta.

- ✓ **Alfredo Sauce**
  Stir in crushed garlic and Parmesan cheese to the hot sauce. Allow a few minutes for the flavour to develop fully. Toss with some gluten-free pasta for a classic Italian meal.

- ✓ **Mushroom Sauce**
  Stir in sliced, sautéed mushrooms for a great accompaniment to poultry. Combining this sauce with leftover turkey or chicken makes a great entrée that doesn't taste like leftovers. Serve over rice or pasta.

- ✓ **Seafood Sauce**
  Stir in seafood such as shrimp, lobster meat, clams or mussels. Serve over rice or pasta for a quick and easy meal.

Basic Velouté Sauce

This classic stock-based sauce finds its way into a huge variety of dishes. With the addition of different flavouring elements it has almost unlimited possibilities. The lack of cream also makes this savoury sauce low in fat.

½	diced medium onion	½
1 tbsp	butter *or* non-dairy alternate	15 ml
2 cups	meat, vegetable *or* fish stock *(Make your own, pgs.171-184. Canned broth or gluten-free bouillon cubes will also work, but will not taste as good.)*	500 ml
2 - 3 tbsp	sweet rice flour *(depending upon how thick you wish your finished sauce to be)*	30 - 45 ml
	herbs and spices of your choice *(see variations below)*	
	salt and pepper to taste	

Instructions:

1. **Sauté onion** with butter or alternate until translucent.
2. **Combine all other ingredients cold** to prevent lumps from forming or mix the sweet rice flour with about ½ a cup (125ml) of your stock or water cold before adding it in. Then add to the onions. Bring to a simmer for 15 - 20 minutes to allow the flavours to develop. Stir frequently to prevent burning.
Alternately, this can be made over a double boiler to prevent burning.
3. **Strain** to remove the spices and onion.
4. **Adjust seasoning** with salt and pepper.

Yield: 2 cups (500 ml)

Nutritional Information

Calculations based upon the basic recipe excluding
optional ingredients and variations.

Per ½ cup (125 ml) serving

energy	61 calories/255 kJ
protein	1 g
fat	2 g
carbohydrate	2 g
sodium	130 mg
potassium	78 mg
calcium	7 mg
iron	1 mg

Variations:

In many restaurant kitchens a basic Veloute sauce is kept on hand and finished with various ingredients when the patron orders it. The use of sweet rice flour makes this sauce freezer stable so you can prepare some ahead and make a quick sauce for meats or seafood in just a few minutes. The variations possible are limited only by your imagination. Here are just a few ideas to get you started:

✓ **Herb Veloute Sauce**

Stir in any fresh or dried herb you choose to suit your dish. Allow a few minutes for the flavour to fully develop before serving. This sauce is great served with fish, seafood, poultry and pasta.

✓ **Mushroom Veloute**

Stir in sliced, sautéed mushrooms for a great accompaniment to poultry. Pairing this sauce with leftover turkey or chicken makes a great entrée that doesn't taste like leftovers. Serve over rice or pasta.

✓ **Seafood Veloute**

Stir in seafood such as shrimp, lobster meat, clams or mussels. Serve over rice or pasta for a quick and easy meal.

✓ **Pot Pies**

Stir cooked meats, vegetables, and / or seafood into a thick, suitably flavoured Veloute to make a filling for a pot pie. Just place it in a pie shell and bake for a great one dish meal.

Basic White Wine Butter Sauce
(Beurre Blanc)

This rich and decadent sauce will make even the plainest poached fish or poultry into a fine meal. This method is much easier to make than the original as there is no worry of the butter separating. With the variations listed below, this can be a very quick and versatile recipe.

4	shallots *or* ½ cup onion finely chopped	4
¼ cup	white wine	60 ml
¼ cup	white wine vinegar	60 ml
½ lb	cold butter *or* non-dairy alternate cut in small pieces	225 g
1 tsp	sweet rice flour	5 ml
	salt and pepper to taste	

Instructions:

1. **Combine first group of ingredients** in a saucepan and boil to reduce the volume by about half.
2. **Mix sweet rice flour into the cut pieces of butter** or non dairy alternate to coat them.
3. **Add butter** or non dairy alternate a little at a time to boiling liquid, stirring constantly until all butter or non dairy alternate has been absorbed and sauce has boiled for 1 minute.
4. **Season to taste** with salt and pepper.
5. **Serve as is or strain** to remove the pieces of onion or shallot.

See variations below

Yield: about 1 cup (250 ml)

Nutritional Information

Calculations based upon the basic recipe excluding
optional ingredients and variations.

Per 2 tbsp (30 ml) serving

energy	214 calories/895 kJ
protein	trace g
fat	23 g
carbohydrate	1 g
sodium	235 mg
potassium	38 mg
calcium	10 mg
iron	trace mg

Variations:

Any flavourful acidic liquid can be used to replace the white wine and vinegar.
See below for some ideas:

✓ **Citrus Butter Sauce**
Replace the white wine and white wine vinegar with ½ cup (125 ml)
orange juice and 2 tbsp (30 ml) fresh lemon juice.

✓ **Red Wine Butter Sauce**
Replace the white wine and white wine vinegar with ¼ cup (60 ml) red
wine and ¼ cup (60 ml) red wine vinegar.

✓ **Cranberry Butter Sauce**
Replace the white wine and white wine vinegar with ½ cup (125 ml)
cranberry juice and 2 tbsp (30 ml) red wine vinegar.

Any herb or spice of your choice can be added to further enhance the flavour.
The following are some suggestions to get you started:

✓ **Chives**
✓ **Tarragon**
✓ **Oregano**
✓ **Chervil**

Béchamel Sauce

This classic milk-based sauce finds its way into a huge variety of dishes, and is a lower fat alternative to cream sauces.

2 cups	milk *or* non dairy alternate	500 ml
½	small onion left	½
1	bay leaf	1
4	whole cloves *or* ¼ tsp (3 ml) nutmeg	4
2 tbsp	butter *or* non-dairy alternate	30 ml
3 tbsp	sweet rice flour *(slightly more or less depending on desired thickness)*	45 ml
	salt and white pepper to taste	

Instructions:

1. **Combine all ingredients cold;** then bring to a simmer for 15 - 20 minutes to allow the flavours to develop. Stir frequently to prevent burning.
Alternately, this can be made over a double boiler to prevent burning.
2. **Strain** to remove the spices and onion.
3. **Adjust seasoning** with salt and pepper.

Yield: 2 cups (500 ml)

Nutritional Information

Calculations based upon the basic recipe excluding optional ingredients and variations.
Per 1 cup (250 ml) serving

energy	351 calories/1469 kJ
protein	10 g
fat	22 g
carbohydrate	23 g
sodium	271 mg
potassium	590 mg
calcium	390 mg
iron	2 mg

Variations:

Béchamel is one of the essential "mother" sauces in classical cooking; it has a whole family of sauces derived from it. It can be used in the same way as any cream sauce but is much lower in fat. Here are just a few ideas to get you started:

✓ **Cheese Sauce**
   Stir in about 1 cup (250 ml) grated cheese of your choice such as cheddar or Swiss, together with small pinch of cayenne pepper for a great accompaniment to vegetables such as cauliflower or broccoli.

✓ **Dijon Sauce**
   Stir in a 1 tbsp (15 ml) or more of Dijon mustard with a few chopped chives. Serve with ham, poultry or fish.

✓ **Herb Sauce**
   Stir in any fresh or dried herb you choose to suit your dish. Allow a few minutes for the flavour to fully develop before serving. This sauce is great served with fish, seafood, poultry and pasta.

✓ **Lower Fat Alfredo Sauce**
   For a lower fat version of the creamier original, stir in crushed garlic and Parmesan cheese to the hot sauce. Allow a few minutes for the flavour to develop fully. Toss with some gluten-free pasta for a classic Italian meal.

✓ **Mushroom Sauce**
   Stir in sliced, sautéed mushrooms for a great accompaniment to poultry. Combining this sauce with leftover turkey or chicken makes a great entrée that doesn't taste like leftovers. Serve over rice or pasta.

✓ **Seafood Sauce**
   Stir in seafood such as shrimp, lobster meat, clams or mussels. Serve over rice or pasta for a quick and easy meal.

✓ **White Wine Sauce**
   Stir in a flavourful white wine to a slightly thicker version of this sauce and simmer a few minutes to allow the alcohol to cook out. The fruity acidity and aroma of this sauce goes well with fish or poultry.

✓ **Florentine Sauce**
   Stir in about 1 cup (250 ml) chopped spinach and cook until the spinach has just become softened, but no longer. As a low fat variation to Eggs Benedict, try Florentine sauce over your poached eggs on English muffins *(p. 64)*. It makes a great brunch dish that you needn't feel guilty about.

Basic Brown Sauce

This classic stock-based sauce finds its way into a huge variety of meat dishes. With the addition of different flavourings, it has almost unlimited possibilities.

½	diced medium onion	½
1 tbsp	vegetable oil	15 ml
2 tbsp	tomato paste	30 ml
2 - 3 tbsp	sweet rice flour *(depending upon how thick you wish your finished sauce to be)*	30 - 45 ml
2 cups	beef *or* venison stock	500 ml
½ cup	red wine *(optional)*	125 ml
	herbs and spices of your choice *(see variations below)*	
	salt and black pepper to taste	

Instructions:

1. **Sauté onion** with vegetable oil until thoroughly browned before adding tomato paste. Continue cooking about 5 minutes until tomato paste has also begun to brown slightly.

2. **Combine all other ingredients cold** and add to onions and tomato paste. Bring to a simmer for 15 - 20 minutes to allow the flavours to develop. Stir frequently to prevent burning.

3. **Strain** to remove the spices and onion.

4. **Adjust seasoning** with salt and pepper.

Yield: 2 cups (500 ml)

Nutritional Information

Calculations based upon the basic recipe excluding
optional ingredients and variations.
Per ⅓ cup (85 ml) serving

energy	48 calories/201 kJ
protein	1 g
fat	2 g
carbohydrate	2 g
sodium	110 mg
potassium	103 mg
calcium	6 mg
iron	1 mg

Variations:

In many restaurant kitchens, a basic brown sauce is kept on hand and finished with various ingredients when the patron orders it. The use of sweet rice flour makes this sauce freezer stable so you can prepare some ahead and make a quick sauce for meat dishes in just a few minutes. The variations possible are limited only by your creativity. Here are just a few ideas to get you started:

✓ **Wine and Herb Sauce**

Stir in any fresh or dried herb you choose to suit your dish. Add 1 cup (250 ml) red wine and reduce by boiling until the sauce has returned to the same amount it was before the wine was added.

✓ **Demi Glace**

Mix equal parts brown sauce with beef stock and reduce by boiling until the sauce has returned to the same amount it was before the stock was added. This version of the sauce really packs a lot of rich beefy flavour.

✓ **Beef Stew**

Stir in root vegetables, potatoes, cubes of seared beef and your favourite seasonings. Simmer until tender. Serve as is or bake with a covering of buttermilk biscuits for a quick and easy meal.

✓ **Pot Pies**

Stir cooked meats and vegetables into a thick, suitably flavoured brown sauce to make a filling for a pot pie. Just place it in a pie shell and bake for a great one dish meal.

Easy Coconut Curry Sauce

A quick, easy and tasty way to simmer
chicken or seafood into a great entrée.

1 can (14 oz)	coconut milk	1 can (398 ml)
1 cup	chicken stock *or* water	250 ml
2 tbsp	sweet rice flour	30 ml
½	small onion (finely diced)	½
2 tbsp	mild to medium curry paste *or* powder *(check to see that yours is gluten free)*	
1 tbsp	sugar	15 ml
3 - 4	lime leaves *(optional - available in Asian markets)*	3 - 4
	salt and pepper to taste	

Instructions:

There are two ways to make use of this recipe; as a side sauce or made together with meat or seafood to save time and dishes. Regardless of how it is prepared, this sauce can also be frozen without separating.

Side Sauce

1. **Mix all ingredients together** cold in a saucepan.
2. **Bring to a low boil** stirring frequently.
3. **Once sauce has come to a boil**, turn down the heat to a low simmer for about 15 minutes.
4. **Adjust seasoning** with salt and pepper and the sauce is ready to serve.

Time Saver

1. **Mix all ingredients together** in a container with a tight fitting lid
Pro-tip: I use a 3 cup (750 ml) yogurt container and shake it while holding the lid.
2. **Pour over seared meat** and simmer until tender.
Pro-tip: Simmering seafood tends to make many of them tough so add them into the prepared sauce just a few moments before serving.
3. **Adjust seasoning** with salt and pepper.

Yield: about 2 ½ cups (625 ml)

Nutritional Information

Calculations based upon the basic recipe excluding
optional ingredients and variations.

Per ⅓ cup (85 ml) serving

energy	154 calories/646 kJ
protein	2 g
fat	13 g
carbohydrate	7 g
sodium	38 mg
potassium	203 mg
calcium	20 mg
iron	2 mg

Variations:

All the flavour variations available in curries from many different countries make this recipe very easy to customize to suit your tastes. From fiery, to mild and savoury, the options are numerous. The sweet rice thickener in this sauce makes it freeze / thaw stable so make a bit extra and have some on hand for a quick meal. Simply heat and stir in some cooked chicken or shrimp for the basis of a great meal when served over rice with a few fresh vegetables.

Lazy Hollandaise

This classic Dutch butter sauce is the key to Eggs Benedict,
but with a few alterations it can dress up many dishes.
This sauce can be prepared in about five minutes.

½ lb	butter *or* non-dairy alternate	225 g
⅓ cup	juice of 1 lemon	85 ml
3	egg yolks	3
	salt to taste	
	(If using regular salted butter this will	
	probably be unnecessary.)	
1 - 2 drops	hot pepper sauce (e.g. Tabasco)	1 - 2 drops

Instructions:

1. **Heat butter** *or* non-dairy alternate to a boil, but do not allow it to brown.
2. **While butter** *or* non-dairy alternate **is heating,** separate egg yolks and place them and the lemon juice into a blender or in tall narrow container for use with an immersion blender.
3. **Whip egg yolks and lemon juice** in the blender for a few seconds until mixed.
4. **Add hot butter** *or* non-dairy alternate in a steady stream with the blender running (this should take about 10 seconds). The heat of the butter *or* non-dairy alternate will coagulate the egg yolk and thicken the sauce to a consistency similar to mayonnaise.
5. **Adjust seasoning** with salt and hot pepper sauce.
6. **If desired, you can thin the consistency of the sauce** by blending in a little hot water.
7. **Serve immediately or keep for a short time** by immersing the container in a warm water bath.

Pro-tip: The water bath temperature should be no warmer than you could tolerate as a bath for yourself. Do **not** overheat the sauce or it will separate.

Pro-tip: **Do not attempt to make a smaller batch** of this recipe; the decreased amount of butter or non-dairy alternate will not have sufficient heat to cook the egg yolks.

Pro-tip: **If the sauce separates**, heat or cool the sauce as required to return it to about 110°F (35°C). Place 1 tbsp (15 ml) boiling water in the blender and slowly pour in the broken sauce while the blender is running, and allow the sauce to recombine. If you have excess sauce, refrigerate it. To revive the sauce, gently bring it back up to bath water warm; then follow the directions above for separated sauce.

Yield: about 1 cup (250 ml)

Nutritional Information

Calculations based upon the basic recipe excluding optional ingredients and variations.
Per 1 tablespoon (15 ml) serving

energy	114 calories/477 kJ
protein	1 g
fat	12 g
carbohydrate	1 g
sodium	119 mg
potassium	13 mg
calcium	8 mg
iron	Trace

Variations:

The lazy part comes from the fact that the butter doesn't need to be clarified, there is no tedious whisking, and the reduction of vinegar and wine is replaced by fresh lemon juice. This sauce is not quite as fluffy as the hand-beaten original, but it is just as tasty. To vary the taste and possible uses of this recipe, try any of the following, or branch out and paint this blank canvas with your own style.

✓ **Orange Hollandaise**
Replace the lemon juice with 2 tbsp (30 ml) orange juice concentrate and 3 tbsp (45 ml) white wine vinegar.

✓ **Fruity Hollandaise**
Replace the lemon juice with 3 tbsp (45 ml) warm fruit preserves (e.g. blackberry, blueberry, raspberry, marmalade) and 3 tbsp (45 ml) red or white wine vinegar.

Reduction Sauce

This sauce couldn't be easier and the depth of flavour it offers is unmatched by any other method. This is definitely one of the great secrets used by professional chefs to give meals a robust flavour. Almost any flavourful liquid can become a concentrated burst of flavour.

Begin with 4 - 5 times the amount of liquid you wish to end up with. About 1 tbsp (15 ml) completed reduction is a reasonable portion.	flavourful liquid such as stock, cider, wine *or* flavoured vinegar ***Pro-tips:*** Avoid using any liquid with a lot of pulp, salt, or seasonings such as pepper. Do not attempt this with purchased bouillon because it will become too salty to be usable. *(see variations for ideas)*	Begin with 4 - 5 times the amount of liquid you wish to end up with. About 1 tbsp (15 ml) completed reduction is a reasonable portion.
to taste	salt and pepper *or* sugar *(if desired)*	to taste

Instructions:

1. **Place liquid in a sauté pan or other pot with a large surface area**. This aids the evaporation of unwanted water and prevents boiling over during the early stages of the process.
2. **Boil to reduce volume** until the liquid starts to take on a syrupy consistency. This generally starts to happen when it has reduced to ¼ - ⅕ of the original volume.
3. **Adjust seasoning** if desired with salt, pepper, or sometimes sugar if you are working with a very acidic liquid.

Yield: varies depending upon ingredients used

Nutritional Information
Due to the variations inherent in the recipe nutritional calculations are not possible.

Variations:

Whether you choose to make a reduction from a good bottle of wine for a special occasion; or use leftover wine, stock or cider, this recipe concept is sure to add some flavour to your meals. It also is a great way to make these items easier to store and prevent them from spoiling. You can enrich and extend the reductions by whisking in a little butter or oil. Here are just a few ideas to get you started:

- ✓ **Cider Reduction**

  Dry apple, pear or peach ciders make great reductions to pair with pork or poultry. Try adding spices such as cinnamon or cardamom just shortly before the reduction is complete to add another layer of flavour. Sweet cider reductions are great on desserts.

- ✓ **Wine Reduction**

  That extra glass of oxidized wine left in the bottle is great for reductions because the reduction process oxidizes it anyway. Red wine reductions are terrific with red meats, but can also really help out poultry. White wine reductions are best with seafood or poultry. Try adding fresh cracked pepper or fresh herbs shortly before the reduction is complete to add another layer of flavour.

- ✓ **Vinegar Reduction**

  The huge variety of flavoured vinegars available in the markets gives us countless possibilities. The reduction process tends to mellow the acids somewhat, leaving behind the robust underlying flavour. Balsamic vinegar reduction with sautéed mushrooms and steak is a fabulous combination. Tarragon vinegar reduction is great to flavour fish, and raspberry vinegar reduction is a perfect compliment to roast chicken. Be sure to avoid malt vinegar as it isn't gluten-free.

- ✓ **Stock Reduction**

  The savoury flavours of stocks become irresistibly powerful when reduced. This is simply a seasoned version of the "glace" discussed in the, "Stocks" recipes *(pgs. 171-184)*. Pair stocks with their corresponding meats or fish to add some intensity of flavour. Vegetable stock reductions are fabulous to sauté vegetables and add flavour without fat or added salt.

Stir Fry Sauce

With the addition of some vegetables, and meat or seafood,
you have a quick and tasty way to a one pot/wok meal.

½ cup	ketchup	60 ml
¼ cup	Thai fish sauce	30 ml
2 tbsp	sesame oil	15 ml
¼ cup	gluten-free soy sauce (tamari)	30 ml
¼ cup	sugar	60 ml
1 tbsp	fresh grated ginger	8 ml
¼ tsp	chilli flakes (*optional*)	1 ml

Instructions:

There are two ways to make use of this recipe; as a side sauce, or made together with the meat or seafood to save time and dishes. This sauce can also be frozen without separating.

Side Sauce

1. **Mix all ingredients together** cold in a saucepan.
2. **Bring to a low boil** stirring frequently.
3. **It is finished cooking** once the sauce has come to a boil.
4. **Adjust seasoning** with salt and pepper, and it is ready to serve.

Yield: 1 ⅓ cups (335 ml)

Time Saver

1. **Mix all ingredients together** in a container with a tight fitting lid. A 3 cup (750 ml) yogurt container works well. Hold the lid and just shake it to mix.
2. **Pour over seared meat or seafood and vegetables** that are almost cooked, leaving them in the pan or wok in which they were seared. Bring sauce just to a boil before removing from heat.
3. **Adjust seasoning** with salt and pepper and it is ready to serve.

Yield: 1 ⅓ cups (335 ml)

Did you know? If you are surprised to see ketchup in an Asian style stir fry, consider that the original idea for ketchup came from Indonesia.

Nutritional Information

Calculations based upon the basic recipe excluding
optional ingredients and variations.
Per ⅓ cup (85 ml) serving

energy	155 calories/648 kJ
protein	2 g
fat	7 g
carbohydrate	22 g
sodium	1362 mg
potassium	191 mg
calcium	10 mg
iron	trace

Variations:

This recipe is very basic and a great place to start when making a stir fry dish.
Feel free to add other flavours that appeal to you. Some ideas to get you started
are:

- ✓ **Lime leaf or lemon grass** provides more flavour.
- ✓ **Garlic** offers some pungency.
- ✓ **Chinese Five Spice powder** creates more complexity.

With some steamed rice or gluten-free Asian noodles, this could be a quick and
easy meal.

Batters and Coatings

Crispy crunchy coatings on fried or baked foods are a texture most have come to enjoy. In fact, I have written this chapter because of the huge demand for these types of recipes from people living gluten-free. We all know that they aren't exactly good for us, but if we choose to enjoy these treats only once in a while we can have those familiar foods and enjoy them without the worries of gluten ingestion.

Familiar recipes often call for items to be dredged, coated or battered. Generally all these terms refer to some sort of protective coating placed on vegetables, fish, seafood, meats and poultry to prevent them from drying out or falling apart. Onion rings, fish and chips, fried chicken and shrimp tempura are all good examples. Traditionally, all of the above are laden with gluten, but gluten-free alternates are possible.

In this chapter gluten-free substitutes for most common coatings and batters are covered, but some novel approaches are also suggested. Try some of these new ideas and you may find they are more flavourful than the gluten based originals. Coatings are usually deep fried or pan fried, but in many cases this is unnecessary. Try placing the coated items on a wire rack that allows hot air to circulate, and bake in a hot oven until nicely browned. They will be crunchy without all the extra fat. The choice is yours; you can indulge your craving for the deep fried version or be 'good' with the lower fat version.

The batters and coatings which bring that crunchy sensation back into our meals are a great way to both liven up some fairly dull items, and extend some fairly pricey ones. The lowly onion can be transformed with a light crispy batter into the perfect accompaniment to a steak or burger. Onion rings are surprisingly high on the, "I really miss," lists of many people I have spoken with. Another traditional use of coatings has been to extend the value of expensive items like veal and seafood. The classics such as Wiener schnitzel and chicken Cordon Bleu are just clever examples of making small expensive cuts of meat into filling meals.

Whether you choose to use coatings to liven up basic foods or to bulk up expensive ones, I hope these recipes will put many old favourites back on your menu.

Fish n' Chip Batter

That craving for fish and chips has just been fulfilled. Fry it up and wrap it in newspaper for a taste of this Maritime classic that is crisp without being too oily.

1 cup	potato starch	310 ml
½ cup	sweet rice flour	30 ml
¾ tsp	salt	5 ml
½ tsp	xanthan gum	3 ml
1 tbsp	baking powder	15 ml
1 ½ tsp	paprika	8 ml
2	eggs	2
³/₄ cup (give or take a little)	soda water	185 ml (give or take a little)
to dredge	sweet rice flour	to dredge

Instructions:

1. **Mix dry ingredients together fully;** then add eggs and soda water. Mix to form a smooth batter.
2. **Preheat deep fryer to 375ºF (190ºC).**

Pro-tip: Any lower temperature will result in more of the oil being absorbed into the batter.

3. **Dredge the items to be battered** in the sweet rice flour.
4. **Dip items to be battered** into the batter. Allow the excess to drip off, leaving a thin coating of batter behind.

Pro-tip: For best results be sure the pieces are no more than ¼ inch (6 mm) thick before battering.

5. **Very carefully place the battered items into the fryer** a few at a time, allowing room between each to fry.
6. **Turn each piece over** as the bottom becomes brown to allow the other side to cook. When the batter has become a light golden brown the fish inside will be fully cooked and tasty.

Yield: enough batter to coat 4 – 6, 2 piece portions of fish fillets

Superlight Tempura Batter

This ultra crisp light batter is my absolute favourite for onion rings, but is great on just about anything else you might try.

½ cup	cornstarch	125 ml
½ tsp	paprika	3 ml
½ tsp	salt	3 ml
4	egg whites	4

	cornstarch for dredging	

Instructions:

1. **Mix dry ingredients together fully.**
2. **Beat the egg whites** lightly and mix into the dry ingredients.
3. **Preheat deep fryer to 375ºF (190ºC).**
Pro-tip: Any lower temperature will result in more of the oil being absorbed into the batter.
4. **Dredge the items to be battered** in cornstarch.
5. **Dip items to be battered** into the batter. Allow the excess to drip off leaving a thin coating of batter behind.
Pro-tip: For best results, be sure the pieces are no more than ¼ inch (6 mm) thick before battering.
6. **Very carefully place the battered items into the fryer** a few at a time, allowing room between each to fry.
7. **Turn each piece over** as the bottom becomes brown to allow the other side to cook. When the batter has become a light golden brown, it is done.

Yield: enough batter to coat three dozen large shrimp or cut vegetable pieces or a much bigger pile of onion rings than I will admit to eating.

Nutritional Information
Due to the variations inherent in this recipe,
nutritional calculations are not possible.

Parmesan Egg Batter

This batter on veal or chicken scaloppini beats breaded veal hands down. With the addition of gluten-free pasta and a small green salad, it makes a wonderful dinner.

4 whole *or* 1 cup egg white	eggs *or* egg white	4 whole *or* 250 ml egg white
½ cup	finely grated Parmesan cheese	125 ml
½ cup (give or take a little)	sweet rice flour for dredging cutlets	125 ml (give or take a little)
to season cutlets	salt and pepper	to season cutlets

Instructions:

1. **Mix together the eggs and cheese** in a relatively flat container to make coating the scaloppini / cutlets easier.

Pro-tip: No seasoning is needed in the batter because of the inherent saltiness of the cheese.

2. **Dredge the item to be coated** with sweet rice flour and season if desired. *See variations below for ideas.*

Pro-tip: The sweet rice flour enables the batter to stick to the scaloppini.

3. **Coat the dredged scaloppini** with the batter, one at a time, before placing them in a preheated, lightly greased skillet over medium low heat. Cook until lightly browned on both sides.

Yield: enough batter to coat 8, 2 ounce (60 g) scaloppini (4 dinner portions)

Nutritional Information

Calculations based upon the basic recipe excluding
optional ingredients and variations.

Per 2 cutlet serving

Note: Nutritional information reflects coating only.

energy	167 calories/699 kJ
protein	11 g
fat	7 g
carbohydrate	1 g
sodium	243 mg
potassium	75 mg
calcium	161 mg
iron	1 mg

Variations:

Frequently batters and coatings serve to extend expensive items such as meat or fish, as well as to protect them from drying out. This Italian batter dresses up a small amount of meat in a flavourful coating to create a great dish. Top it with a little tomato sauce or lemon juice, and serve with a side of gluten-free pasta and a green salad. It is traditionally made with veal, but pork or chicken breasts are equally delicious. Lean white fish such as sole also work well.

You can have your butcher prepare the scaloppini for you or follow the directions below.

How to prepare scaloppini:

1. **Cut 2 ounce** (60 g) slices of lean veal, chicken or pork across the grain.
2. **Place the meat** between two layers of heavy plastic and pound the meat with a meat mallet or the bottom of small heavy saucepan to about 1/8 inch (3 mm) thick. This flattening process breaks up the muscle fibres in the meat, making it more tender and ensuring quick even cooking.

Pro-tip: Be sure to flatten the meat fully. If this is not done, the meat inside the batter will not be cooked by the time the batter on the outside is done. This is especially important if using chicken.

Yield: 2 scaloppini prepared with this batter make a great portion for dinner

Three Part Coatings

This is a lot more than just "breaded." You can have those breaded favourites gluten-free, but you can also have a lot more flavour and crunch than the regular breading for fried or baked chicken, fish or seafood.

	dredging	
½ cup	sweet rice flour	125 ml
	seasoning as desired	

	egg wash	
¼ cup	milk *or* non-dairy alternate	125 ml
1	egg	1

	outer coating	
¾ cup	(see variations below)	185 ml
	seasoning as desired	

Instructions:

1. **Place the sweet rice flour in a heavy plastic bag** such as a large zip top bag or bread bag.

Pro-tip: Using the bag means you need less of the sweet rice flour to complete this process.

2. **In a separate container, mix the milk or alternate and the egg.**

3. **In a third container,** place the outer coating material. Another heavy plastic bag works well for this.

4. **All three steps are now ready** to proceed.

5. **Dredge the items to be coated** in the sweet rice flour. This is easily accomplished by closing the bag and shaking vigorously. If the items to be coated are particularly wet, dry them first or use a bit more sweet rice flour so they are completely covered.

6. **Remove the items to be coated** from the sweet rice flour bag, allowing any excess flour not adhering to the items to fall back into the bag.

7. **Place the sweet rice flour-coated items** into the egg and milk or alternate mixture (egg wash).

8. **Transfer the items** from the egg wash, allowing any excess liquid to run back into the egg wash container.

9. **Place the floured and egg-washed items into the bag** with the outer coating material. Seal and shake the bag to completely coat the items. If there is insufficient coating material to fully coat the items, add a bit more and shake again.

10. **The items are now fully coated** and ready to bake or fry. Remove the coated items from the bag, allowing any excess coating material to remain in the bag.

11. **Pan fry, deep fry, or bake** as you wish.

Yield: enough coating to cover about 1 lb (454 g) jumbo shrimp, or
about 2 lbs (908 g) chicken pieces

Nutritional Information
Due to the variations inherent in this recipe
nutritional calculations are not possible.

Variations:

In wheaty recipes the coating is usually just plain breadcrumbs because they are cheap and plentiful. Gluten-free breadcrumbs also work, but when you need to remove gluten from the recipe all sorts of other options present themselves. Here are just a few:

✓ **Flake Cereal Coating**
Crushed gluten-free flake type cereals make a tasty outer crust. They provide a great crunchy coating for chicken or veal cutlets.

✓ **Cornmeal Coating**
Try cornmeal as the outer crust. With a bit of Cajun seasoning this makes a fabulous coating for catfish.

✓ **Coconut Coating**
Unsweetened grated coconut is delicious as an outer crust. On jumbo shrimp this makes a terrific appetizer.

✓ **Crisp Flour Coating**
If you miss the crispy fried calamari found in most Greek restaurants, this is for you. Mix equal parts whole corn flour and corn starch to use as the outer crust material. With a little lemon and Tzatziki sauce you will be ready for ouzo!

✓ **Nut Meal Coating**
Almond, hazelnut or pecan meal (flour) as the outer crust will give a wonderful variety of crunchy nut flavours. On sole fillets, this will put your Sole Amandine way over the top, both in taste and texture.

Corn Batter

Sure to please on fish or seafood, the soft cake-like texture of this batter is almost like a fritter. Some of my testers think it makes a great corn dog; others say it is like a Cantonese-style chicken ball coating. I will leave that determination to you.

1 ¼ cups	whole corn flour	310 ml
2 tbsp	skim milk powder *or* non-dairy alternate	30 ml
1 tsp	salt	5 ml
½ tsp	xanthan gum	3 ml
1 ½ tsp	baking powder	8 ml
4	eggs	4
¾ cup	soda water	185 ml

Instructions:

1. **Mix dry ingredients together fully**, and then add eggs and soda water. Mix to form a smooth batter.
2. **Preheat deep fryer to 375ºF (190ºC).**
   Pro-tip: Any lower temperature will result in more of the oil being absorbed into the batter.
3. **Dip items to be battered** into the batter. Allow the excess to drip off, leaving a thin coating of batter behind.
   Pro-tip: For best results, be sure the pieces are no more than ¼ inch (6 mm) thick before battering.
4. **Very carefully place the battered items into the fryer** a few at a time, allowing room to fry between each.
5. **Turn each piece over** as the bottom becomes brown to allow the other side to cook. When the batter has become a light golden brown, the fish inside will be fully cooked and tasty.

Yield: enough batter to coat 4 - 6, 2 piece portions of fish fillets

Nutritional Information
Due to the variations inherent in this recipe, nutritional calculations are not possible.

Cajun Blackened Crust

The smoky, spicy flavour of blackened catfish and steak are back on the menu, without the gluten fillers found in many of the commercial brands.

2 tbsp	paprika	30 ml
1 tsp	ground dried oregano	5 ml
1 tsp	ground dried thyme	5 ml
½ tsp	cayenne pepper	3 ml
½ tsp	ground black pepper	3 ml
½ tsp	ground white pepper	3 ml
½ tsp	onion powder	3 ml
½ tsp	garlic powder	3 ml

Instructions:

1. **Mix together all ingredients fully**, and store in an airtight container.

Yield: about ¼ cup (60ml)

Variations:

This staple of Louisiana cooking is a great way to add a spicy crust to your favourite fish or meat. Just rub a liberal coating of the spice mix onto the surface of your choice of firm fleshed fish or meat. Place fish or meat in an extremely hot cast iron pan and cook until desired doneness. The outside surface will develop a slightly blackened appearance and create a bit of smoke if you're on the right track. In this case a little bit burnt is a good thing.

✓ **Blackened catfish**
  Catfish or any other firm fleshed fish such as halibut, salmon, or cod
  Blackened steaks
  Spicy, smoky steak, need I say more?
✓ **Blackened pork chops**
  Your pork chops will have a lot more zip with this than with just applesauce, but the two flavours together are fabulous.

Chinese Style Ginger Fried Coating

If you crave the taste of crispy fried ginger beef,
pork or chicken; this recipe will put that
take-out taste back on the menu.

	main	
1 lb	beef, pork, *or* chicken cut in thin matchstick size	450 g
1	celery stalk cut in thin slices	1
1	carrot cut in thin slices	1
½ -1 tsp	hot chilli flakes	3-5 ml

	marinade	
2 tbsp	gluten-free soy sauce, tamari	30 ml
2 tbsp	minced fresh ginger	30 ml
1 tbsp	dry sherry *or* Chinese cooking wine	15 ml
1 tsp	sugar	5 ml

	sauce	
2 tbsp	gluten-free soy sauce, tamari	30 ml
2 tbsp	water	30 ml
1 tbsp	dry sherry *or* Chinese cooking wine	15 ml
1 tbsp	vinegar	15 ml
¼ cup	sugar *or* honey	60 ml
1 tsp	sesame oil	5 ml
to taste	hot chilli oil	to taste

4 cups	*oil for deep frying*	1 litre

	coating	
1	egg white	30 ml
¼ cup	water	60 ml
½ cup	cornstarch	125 ml

Instructions:

1. **Prepare the first group of ingredients** and set aside.
2. **Mix marinade ingredients together fully,** then add to the meat in the first set of ingredients and set aside to marinate for 30 minutes. Reserve the vegetables for later.
3. **Mix together the sauce ingredients** and set aside.
4. **Preheat the oil in a wok for deep frying.**
5. **Beat the egg white** until foamy and then add the water and cornstarch. Mix thoroughly to form a batter.
6. **Pour the batter** onto the marinated meat and mix to coat.
7. **Deep fry the meat** in small batches of about ¼ of the battered meat at a time. Deep fry until golden brown, remove and set aside. Continue until all meat has been fried.
8. **Drain oil from wok** and wipe out any residue of batter, but do not wash the wok. Return it to the heat with the vegetables and stir fry. After a few moments add the sauce and just bring to a boil.
9. **Return the fried beef to the wok,** and toss to coat with sauce and briefly reheat the beef.
10. **Serve hot** with rice and other side dishes of your choice to bring back this take-out classic.

Nutritional Information
Due to the variations inherent in this recipe,
nutritional calculations are not possible.

Holidays

Living gluten-free can make the holidays some of the most challenging times of the year. It seems every family has its own set of special foods which help define the holidays. Unfortunately, most of these foods are traditionally loaded with gluten. As family gathers together and special, seasonal foods are prepared, it can be a recipe for disaster when cravings kick into high gear. It is only natural to miss Grandma's shortbread and the traditional turkey stuffing that always seems to disappear before the rest of the turkey leftovers. The items missed will vary from person to person, but the overall feeling of deprivation is something we all have in common.

The recipes in this chapter were all among the list of things my family could not do without. We serve the gluten-free versions provided here to all our guests, gluten-free and wheaty alike. I am pleased to write that several family members did not realize any difference, and some even liked the gluten-free versions better.

For many, the holiday foods that are most difficult to do without are special seasonal breads. Dressed up seasonal breads are common in many cultures, and frequently are simple variations on regular breads eaten year round. Try adding that secret family touch to a similar textured bread recipe from this book to make the old family recipes possible again. For example, the Stollen *(p. 258)* is a variation of the Almond Bread *(p. 128)*.

This chapter contains some North American holiday favourites and a few gluten-free versions of my special family recipes to make holidays a time of celebration, not deprivation. You may find that your old family favourites are just variations on the recipes in this chapter. Feel free to customize the recipes in this chapter to make them more like the special family recipes that define your tastes of the holidays.

Almond Crescents

A tray of Christmas cookies at my house would be incomplete without this classic almond delight.

1 cup	sweet rice flour	250 ml
¾ cup	almond flour	185 ml
²/₃ cup	corn starch	165 ml
¹/₃ cup	tapioca starch	85 ml
½ tsp	xanthan gum	3 ml
1 cup	butter *or* non-dairy alternate	250 ml
²/₃ cup	icing sugar	165 ml
1 tbsp	brown sugar	15 ml
1	egg	1
1 tsp	almond extract	5 ml

Instructions:

1. **Fully mix the first group of ingredients** and set aside.
2. **Cream together fully** the next group of ingredients in a mixer.
3. **Add in the reserved dry ingredients** and mix until fully incorporated. Be sure to stop the mixer and scrape down the sides of the bowl to allow the creamed ingredients to be completely combined.
4. **Forming the traditional crescent shape** of these cookies is relatively easy. First, roll the dough into 1 inch balls.
   Pro-tip: I use a 1 inch (2.5 cm) diameter thumb release ice cream scoop for this.
5. **Roll each ball between the wet palms of your hands.** Resist the idea of using extra flour to form the dough as it will leave the cookies with a starchy taste. Shape them into a cylindrical shape about 2 ½ inches (6.5 cm) long with both ends tapering to blunted points. The shape will resemble an aerial view of a canoe. Bend this shape into a crescent by draping it over one of your fingers.
6. **Place the formed cookies onto a baking sheet lined with baker's parchment** and bake about 12 minutes at 325ºF (165ºC).
7. **Remove from the oven** and do not handle until cooled.
8. **Dress them up further** by dipping one end into melted chocolate. Cool until set before serving.

Yield: about 3 dozen

Nutritional Information
Calculations based upon the basic recipe excluding
optional ingredients and variations.
Per cookie

energy	94 calories/393 kJ
protein	2 g
fat	6 g
carbohydrate	6 g
sodium	54 mg
potassium	47 mg
calcium	15 mg
iron	trace

This traditional German Christmas cookie is one of the quintessential tastes of
the holidays for my family. The cookie itself is very much like an almond
shortbread and the chocolate puts it over the top in appearance and taste. You
can prepare the cookie in any shape you wish, but the traditional shape does add
a lot of interest because the ends tend to be crisp and the middle a bit softer.

Cinnamon Sugared Almonds

This is a wonderful crunchy snack for the holidays, or any other time. The recipe makes a fairly large quantity, but don't worry, just set out a full dish and watch them disappear. Try some with an espresso or cappuccino for a great flavour combination.

2.2 lbs	unblanched almonds *(with the brown skin on)*	1 kg
3 cups	white sugar	750 ml
2 tbsp	ground cinnamon	30 ml
½ cup	water	125 ml
½ tsp	ground star anise *(optional)*	3 ml

Instructions:

1. **Spread the almonds out one layer deep** on baking sheets lined with parchment.

2. **Roast almonds in a 325°F (165°C) oven** until lightly browned and fragrant. Set aside.

   Pro-tip: Take care to not under-roast or over-roast the almonds. Under-roasted almonds have a starchy taste and over-roasted almonds become bitter.

3. **In a large pan or wok, cook the remaining ingredients** together to the hardball stage (a drop of the mixture will form a hard ball if dropped into ice water).
   Caution! Melted sugar can cause severe burns.

4. **Add the almonds to the melted cinnamon sugar mixture** and quickly mix to coat all the almonds. Do not be concerned if some of the cinnamon sugar does not stick to the almonds. Reserve it for use in desserts or in coffee.

Yield: about 10 cups (2.5 litres)

Nutritional Information

Calculations based upon the basic recipe excluding
optional ingredients and variations.
Per ½ cup (125 ml) serving

energy	412 calories/1724 kJ
protein	10 g
fat	26 g
carbohydrate	41 g
sodium	6 mg
potassium	370 mg
calcium	142 mg
iron	2 mg

Variations:

While the above recipe is by far my favourite, this concept works well with a variety of different nuts and spice combinations. Here are just a few for you to consider:

- ✓ **Spicy Cajun Sugared Pecans**
  Replace the almonds with pecans and the spices with a Cajun spice blend. This sweet and spicy combination is great after a spicy meal.
- ✓ **Maple Sugared Walnuts**
  Replace the almonds with walnuts, and replace half the sugar and all the water with 1 ½ cups (375 ml) maple syrup. This classic combination speaks for itself.
- ✓ **Vanilla Sugared Hazelnuts**
  Replace the almonds with hazelnuts, and replace the cinnamon with 3 tbsp (45 ml) vanilla extract. This combination reminds me of European hazelnut pastries without all the baking.
- ✓ **Chocolate Sugared Almonds**
  Replace the cinnamon with ¼ cup (60 ml) cocoa powder for a wonderful nutty chocolate flavour.
- ✓ **Aztec Sugared Almonds**
  Add ¼ cup (60 ml) cocoa and ¼ - ½ tsp (1 - 3 ml) cayenne pepper to the recipe as written for a sweet spicy chocolate flavour that Montezuma would have loved.

Whipped Shortbread

*These melt-in-your-mouth shortbread cookies
are sure to become a favourite. The cookie press method makes
them quick and attractive as well as delicious.*

1 cup	sweet rice flour	250 ml
2/3 cup	corn starch	185 ml
1/3 cup	tapioca flour	85 ml
1/2 cup	icing sugar	125 ml
1/2 tsp	xanthan gum	3 ml
1/4 tsp	salt	1 ml
1/2 lb	soft butter *(alternates not recommended)*	225 g
2 tbsp	brown sugar	30 ml
3/4 tsp	vanilla	4 ml
1	egg white	1

Instructions:

1. **Fully mix the first group of ingredients** and set aside.
2. **Cream together** the next group of ingredients in a mixer.
3. **Add in the reserved dry ingredients** a bit at a time, beating until the mixture resembles whipped cream. Be sure to stop the mixer and scrape down the sides of the bowl to allow the creamed ingredients to be fully combined.
4. **Use a cookie press or piping bag** to form smallish cookies on baking sheets lined with bakers' parchment.
5. **Bake at 300ºF (150ºC) for about 10 minutes** until lightly golden, but not browned. Depending on your oven, you may need to double up identical baking sheets or use air core baking sheets to prevent over-browning the bottom of the cookies.

Yield: about 5 dozen small cookie press formed cookies

Nutritional Information
Calculations based upon the basic recipe excluding
optional ingredients and variations.
Per cookie serving

energy	48 calories/201 kJ
protein	trace g
fat	3 g
carbohydrate	3 g
sodium	41 mg
potassium	4 mg
calcium	2 mg
iron	trace mg

Variations:

These shortbread cookies will fool all but the most finicky shortbread
aficionados. The brown sugar adds that little bit of colour required to take the
pallor out of the gluten-free flours. I do not recommend using alternates to butter
for this recipe because the dominant flavour in shortbread is butter. The recipe
will work with alternates, but without the dominant flavour of butter, what is the
point of making shortbread? This recipe also accepts some interesting variations
worth trying. Here are just a few:

- ✓ **Cinnamon Shortbread**
  Add 1 tbsp (15 ml) cinnamon to the dough to add a distinctive flavour
  and red/brown colour.
- ✓ **Chocolate Shortbread**
  Add ¼ cup (60 ml) cocoa powder to the dough to give your shortbread a
  great bittersweet chocolate taste.
- ✓ **Nut Shortbread**
  Add ½ cup (125 ml) of finely ground nuts such as almonds, pecans or
  hazelnuts.

Fruitcake

A commonly derided Christmas specialty, fruitcake is a great addition to holiday sweet trays. This moist and flavourful gluten-free version is much better than the wheaty commercially prepared "bricks" that have earned their reputation.

1 ½ lb	light sultanas	675 g
1 lb	glace cherries	450 g
1 lb	fruitcake glace mix	450 g
½ lb	candied mixed peel	225 g
¾ cup	slivered almonds	185 ml
¾ cup	pecans	185 ml
1 cup	corn starch	250 ml
¾ cup	brown rice flour	185 ml
½ cup	tapioca starch	125 ml
1 tsp	xanthan gum	5 ml
1 tsp	baking powder	5 ml
½ tsp	salt	3 ml
1 tsp	cinnamon	5 ml
1 cup	butter *or* non-dairy alternate	250 ml
1 cup	brown sugar	250 ml
1 cup	white sugar	250 ml
4	eggs	4
¼ cup	orange juice	60 ml
1 tsp	vanilla	5 ml
1 tbsp	instant coffee granules	15 ml
4 tbsp	rum *or* brandy (*optional*)	60 ml

Instructions:
1. **Mix together the first group of ingredients** (fruit) and set aside.
2. **Mix together the second group of ingredients** (dry) in a second bowl.

3. **Mix half of the dry ingredients into the fruit** taking care to separate any clumps of candied fruits. Reserve the other half of the dry ingredients.

4. **Beat together the third set of ingredients well** before adding the reserved dry ingredients. Fold this together with the fruit and dry mixture from step 3.

5. **Divide the batter** into two loaf pans 9 x 5 x 3 inch (23 x 13 x 7 cm) lined with bakers' parchment.

6. **Bake 2 ½ - 3 hours in a 325ᵒF (165ᵒC) oven** together with pan of water. This water pan adds steam to the oven and prevents premature browning.

7. **Allow to cool** fully before continuing. Like all fruitcakes, this cake has wonderful keeping qualities. I generally bake my Christmas fruitcake in September and wrap it first in a tea towel dampened with 2 tbsp (30 ml) rum, then in a plastic freezer bag. I add 1 tbsp (15 ml) rum or brandy per month for the first 2 months. When stored in the refrigerator the flavours within the cake combine and mature. Allowing time for the cake to mature makes a significant difference to its subtlety of taste. The rum or brandy is not necessary for the maturation process; it only adds another layer of flavour. Fruitcake can also be frozen, but this does slow the maturation process considerably.

Yield: 2, 9 x 5 x 3 inch (23 x 13 x 7 cm) loaves, about 48 slices

Nutritional Information
Calculations based upon the basic recipe excluding
optional ingredients and variations.
Per 60 g (2 oz) slice

energy	223 calories/933 kJ
protein	2 g
fat	7g
carbohydrate	42g
sodium	99mg
potassium	163 mg
calcium	26 mg
iron	1mg

Gingerbread

Whether for houses or people,
this gingerbread is sure to please.

1 ½ cups	sweet rice flour	375 ml
¾ cup	corn starch	185 ml
½ cup	tapioca starch	125 ml
½ tsp	xanthan gum	3 ml
½ tsp	salt	3 ml
1 tsp	powdered ginger	5 ml
¼ tsp	allspice	1 ml
½ tsp	baking soda	3 ml
½ tsp	baking powder	3 ml
¼ cup	butter *or* non-dairy alternate	60 ml
1	egg	1
¾ cup	brown sugar	185 ml
$^1/_3$ cup	molasses	85 ml
¼ cup	sour cream *or* soft tofu	60 ml

Instructions:
1. **Mix together** the first group of ingredients (dry) and set aside.
2. **Cream together** the next group of ingredients; then stir in sour cream and molasses.
3. **Mix in the dry ingredients** to form a firm dough.
4. **Roll out** to desired thickness.

Pro-tip: Use a bit of icing sugar to prevent sticking.

5. **Cut with cookie cutters** and place on baking sheets lined with bakers' parchment. This dough does not toughen much with re-rolling so feel free to let the kids play.
6. **Bake at 350ºF (180ºC)** for 7 - 10 minutes for an average-sized gingerbread person (**Note:** Baking time depends on thickness of dough).

Yield: about 2 dozen, 6 inch (15 cm) people

Nutritional Information

Calculations based upon the basic recipe excluding
optional ingredients and variations.

Per 6 inch (15 cm) gingerbread person

energy	106 calories/444 kJ
protein	1 g
fat	3 g
carbohydrate	14 g
sodium	108 mg
potassium	96 mg
calcium	24 mg
iron	trace

Variations:

✓ This crisp, firm gingerbread tastes great and it has the structure required to make a great **gingerbread house**.

✓ Make gingerbread people to hang as **decorations**. You probably won't need to remove them from the tree when it is time to take it down as they will likely have escaped and run away; at least that is what the story says. The crumbs tell a different story.

Hot Cross Buns

Without these, it isn't Easter!

1 cup	almond flour	250 ml
1 cup	brown rice flour	250 ml
1 cup	tapioca starch	250 ml
½ cup	corn flour	125 ml
3 tbsp	sugar	45 ml
1 tbsp	xanthan gum	15 ml
1 tbsp	rapid rise yeast	15 ml
1 tsp	gelatine	5 ml
¾ tsp	salt	3 ml
1 tsp	cinnamon	5 ml
¼ tsp	cloves	1 ml
¼ tsp	nutmeg	1 ml
2	eggs	2
¼ cup	vegetable oil	60 ml
1 ¼ cups	milk *or* non-dairy alternate	310 ml
¼ cup	glace fruitcake mix	60 ml
½ cup	raisins *or* currants	125 ml

Instructions:

1. **Mix all dry ingredients** in a heavy-duty mixer with a flat paddle installed.
2. **In a separate container beat the eggs until frothy.**

Pro-tip: An immersion blender works well for this.

3. **Combine eggs** with the other wet ingredients, fruitcake mix and raisins.
4. **Add the wet to the dry** and mix on low/medium for about three minutes. Soft, sticky dough will form.
5. **Separate the dough into 12 equal balls** about 2 inches (5 cm) round. Place the balls into a greased 9 x 13inch (23 x 33 cm) cake pan.

Pro-tip: Handle the dough with wet hands to prevent it from sticking.

6. **Score the top of each bun in a cross pattern** with a wet spatula.
7. **Allow the dough to rise** in a warm, draft free area until it is nearly double its original size.

8. **Bake at 375ºF (190ºC)** for about 20 - 25 minutes until golden brown. Serve as is, or frost in a cross pattern to complete this traditional Easter treat.

Nutritional Information
Calculations based upon the basic recipe excluding optional ingredients and variations.

Per bun

energy	274 calories/1146 kJ
protein	9 g
fat	8 g
carbohydrate	44 g
sodium	164 mg
potassium	345 mg
calcium	93 mg
iron	2 mg

Frosting

1 cup	icing sugar, *(Make sure yours is gluten-free)*	250 ml
1 tbsp	water	15 ml
½ tsp	vanilla	3 ml

Instructions:

1. **Combine all the ingredients** and mix into a smooth paste.
2. **Use a pastry bag** with a smooth ¼ inch (5 mm) tip or a heavy duty plastic bag with a small corner cut off to pipe the icing onto the hot cross buns in the characteristic cross shape.
3. **Allow the icing to dry** slightly before serving.

Mincemeat

This UK specialty is the quintessential taste of Christmas for some, but is often made with gluten-containing ingredients. This homemade version is gluten-free.

2 cups	grated apple	500 ml
1 cup	currants	250 ml
1 cup	raisins	250 ml
1 cup	fruit juice	250 ml
	(such as orange or apricot nectar)	
¾ cup	brown sugar	185 ml
½ cup	chopped glace citrus peel	125 ml
1/3 cup	chopped suet *or see below**	85 ml
	*(Be sure the suet you use is gluten-free as it is commonly processed with wheat flour. *If you cannot find 'clean' suet, replace with 1/3 cup lard or vegetable shortening and 1 tsp sweet rice flour.)*	
1 tbsp	grated lemon zest	15 ml
1 tsp	allspice	5 ml
1 tsp	cinnamon	5 ml
¼ tsp	cloves	1 ml
1 tsp	salt	5 ml

Instructions:

1. **Combine all the ingredients** in a saucepan and simmer 15 minutes.
2. **Allow to cool** before using.

Yield: about 4 cups (1 litre); will fill about 30 muffin cup sized tarts

Nutritional Information

Calculations based upon the basic recipe excluding
optional ingredients and variations.

Per 2 tbsp (30 ml) serving

energy	83 calories/347 kJ
protein	trace
fat	3 g
carbohydrate	14 g
sodium	70 mg
potassium	109 mg
calcium	12 mg
iron	trace

Variations:

This is a basic gluten-free version of a culinary cultural icon. The variations in spicing and ingredients vary by family in the UK, so feel free to alter the recipe to suit your tastes.

- ✓ Team this mincemeat with the flaky pastry *(p. 278)* to fill that craving for mincemeat pies or tarts around Christmas time.
- ✓ Some enjoy this filling year round as a spread on scones or toast.

Stollen

This classic German Christmas bread is great for those holiday sleep-in breakfasts, or for serving with coffee or tea to those inevitable drop-in guests.

1 cup	tapioca starch	250 ml
1 cup	brown rice flour	250 ml
1 cup	almond flour	250 ml
3/4 cup	potato starch	185 ml
1/4 cup	sugar	60 ml
1 tbsp	instant rise yeast	15 ml
1 tbsp	xanthan gum	15 ml
3/4 tsp	salt	3 ml
1/4 cup	raisins	60 ml
1/4 cup	currants	60 ml
1/2 cup	mixed candied fruit	125 ml
1/4 cup	candied cherries, cut in half	60 ml
1/4 cup	chopped hazelnuts	60 ml
1/4 cup	slivered almonds	60 ml
1/4 cup	rum	60 ml
3/4 tsp	cider vinegar	3 ml
1 cup	milk *or* non-dairy alternate at 110ºF (40ºC)	250 ml
2	eggs	2
1/2 cup	melted butter *or* non-dairy alternate	125 ml
1/4 cup	icing sugar	60 ml
1/4 cup	melted butter *or* non dairy alternate	60 ml

Instructions:

1. **Mix dry ingredients** in a heavy-duty mixer with a flat paddle installed.
2. **Combine the ingredients in the second group** in another bowl to allow the fruit to absorb the rum.
3. **Beat eggs until frothy** in a separate container.

Pro-tip: I use an immersion blender for this.

4. **Warm the milk** or alternate to about 120ºF (40ºC). This will feel very much like a warm bath, and combine it with the other wet ingredients.

5. **Add the wet to the dry** and mix on low/medium for about three minutes. A soft sticky dough will form.

6. **Add the reserved fruit and rum mixture,** and mix until fully incorporated.

7. **Divide the dough in half.** Dust the dough with icing sugar to prevent sticking.

8. **Form each part into a slightly rounded rectangle** about 8 x 12 inches (20 x 30 cm). Fold ²/₃ of the dough over the remaining ¹/₃ along its shorter side to yield a rectangular loaf that is higher along one side than the other. This fold will be a bit like the flap on an envelope with the addressed side facing up.

Pro-tip: See variations below for an idea on how to make use of this fold.

9. **Place the formed dough on baking sheets** lined with bakers' parchment and leave it to rise in a warm, draft free area until 1 ½ times the original size.

10. **Bake at 375ºF (190ºC)** for about 25 - 30 minutes until golden brown. Brush the loaves with the butter and then dust with the icing sugar to give them their traditional snowy look.

Yield: 2, low 12 x 7 x 2 inch (30 x 18 x 5 cm) oval shaped loaves; about 30 slices per recipe

Nutritional Information
Calculations based upon the basic recipe excluding optional ingredients and variations.
Per 1 slice serving, about 50 g (1 ¾ oz)

energy	223 calories/933kJ
protein	2 g
fat	7 g
carbohydrate	42 g
sodium	99 mg
potassium	163 mg
calcium	26 mg
iron	1 mg

Variations:
This traditional Christmas bread is great on its own.
- ✓ Dress it up even more by forming a 1 inch (2.5 cm) rope of **marzipan / almond paste** and placing it into the fold in step 8 above. It will provide a beautiful, decorative detail when cutting the loaf.

Sugar Cookies

Regardless of whether they are shaped like hearts, dinosaurs or snowmen; they have the taste and texture to bring back those childhood memories.

¾ cup	tapioca starch	185 ml
½ cup	sweet rice flour	125 ml
½ cup	whole corn flour	125 ml
½ tsp	xanthan gum	3 ml
½ tsp	baking powder	3 ml
1	egg	1
¼ cup	butter *or* non-dairy alternate	60 ml
2 tbsp	milk *or* non-dairy alternate	30 ml
½ tsp	vanilla extract	3 ml
½ cup	sugar	125 ml
1 tbsp	brown sugar	15 ml

Instructions:

1. **Measure and mix** the first group of ingredients and set aside.
2. **Cream together** the next group of ingredients fully before mixing in the reserved dry ingredients. Continue mixing until a smooth dough forms.
3. **Roll the dough out** to about ¹/₈ inch (3 mm) thickness using a little tapioca starch to prevent sticking.
4. **Use cookie cutters** to cut to any desired shape, and feel free to add sprinkles before baking.
5. **Bake at 375ºF (190ºC)** on a baking sheet lined with baker's parchment until lightly golden. This will take 8 - 10 minutes for average sized cookies. You may need to double the pan underneath to prevent the bottom from browning before the top is done.
6. **Allow to cool** slightly before handling. The cookies will be very soft when you remove them from the oven.
7. **Decorate** as you would any other sugar cookie.

Yield: about 2 ½ dozen average sized cookies

Nutritional Information
Calculations based upon the basic recipe excluding
optional ingredients and variations.
Per average sized cookie

energy	55 calories/230 kJ
protein	1 g
fat	2 g
carbohydrate	8 g
sodium	26 mg
potassium	13 mg
calcium	8 mg
iron	trace

Variations:

These are the quintessential cookies for decorating. They can be any shape that suits the season.

✓ **Valentines cookies**
Top with cinnamon hearts candies before baking heart shaped cookies. All your sweethearts will love them.

✓ **St. Patrick's Day**
Add a little green food colour to the dough or the icing, and cut into shamrock shapes. They will be tastier and safer than the green beer.

✓ **Easter**
Bunnies, eggs, baskets and the like are sure to make a tasty variation from 'just chocolate'.

✓ **Mothers Day**
Why not let the kids decorate special cookies for mom?

✓ **Anytime**
I am sure you can find uses for this recipe in just about every month of the year for a special holiday, but they are great anytime. Enjoy!

Tourtiere

*This French Canadian meat pie is
a welcome Christmas treat.*

1	small onion diced	1
1 clove	garlic chopped fine	1 clove
1	stalk celery	1
4	slices bacon cut into small strips	4
1 lb	ground pork	450 g
1	medium baking potato peeled and grated	1
1	medium apple grated	1
1 tsp	ground cinnamon	5 ml
¹/₈ tsp	ground nutmeg	0.5 ml
¹/₈ tsp	ground mace	0.5 ml
2	bay leaves	2
¹/₈ tsp	ground cloves	0.5 ml
¼ cup	maple syrup (*optional*)	60 ml
	salt and pepper to taste	
	flaky pastry (*p. 278*)	
1	egg yolk	1
1 tbsp	water	15 ml

Instructions:

1. **Place the first group of ingredients in a saucepan** and cook over medium heat until the onion has become soft and translucent.

2. **Stir in the next group of ingredients** and cook at a simmer for about 30 minutes, stirring occasionally. When most of the liquid has evaporated, remove the bay leaves and set aside while you prepare the dough.

3. **Prepare flaky pastry** (*p. 278*). This recipe will require a bit more than half of the dough recipe.

4. **Divide the dough** you will need in 60 / 40 proportions, with the larger portion becoming the bottom.

5. **Roll the dough** out and line a 9 inch (23 cm) pie plate.

6. **Place all the Tourtiere filling** into the dough-lined pie plate.

7. **Mix the egg yolk and water,** and brush the edge of the pastry before placing the top pastry over the filling.

8. **Press the edges together** to form a seal. Cut a small hole in the top to allow steam to escape. Brush the top with the egg yolk and water mixture.

9. **Bake 30 -45 minutes** at 375ºF (190ºC) until lightly browned.

Yield: 6 - 8 servings

Nutritional Information
Calculations based upon the basic recipe excluding
optional ingredients and variations.
Per ⅛ pie serving

energy	432 calories/1807 kJ
protein	14 g
fat	28 g
carbohydrate	20 g
sodium	113 mg
potassium	406 mg
calcium	50 mg
iron	2 mg

Variations:

This traditional French Canadian meat pie is a great holiday labour-saver. Make it ahead of time and pop into the freezer. During the holidays, you can thaw and bake it for an easy meal with a salad or variety of pickles.

✓ For a great holiday appetizer, try making Tourtiere in muffin tins. Use mini-muffin tins for a tasty two-bite version.

Bread Stuffing for Turkey

*The traditional holiday bird is back on the menu
with an apple sage dressing.*

8 cups	dry gluten-free bread cubes	2 litres
2	diced medium onions	2
1	diced medium apple	1
5	diced stalks celery	5
¾ cup	butter *or* non-dairy alternate	185 ml
1 ½ tbsp	sage *or* poultry seasoning	22 ml
1 tsp	salt	5 ml
¼ tsp	pepper	1 ml
¼ cup	milk *or* non-dairy alternate *or* stock	60 ml

Instructions:

1. **Cut dry, leftover gluten-free bread** into roughly ³/₈ inch (1 cm) cubes. Be sure the bread is quite dry or it will become soggy if you choose to stuff it into the turkey. This is important because gluten-free bread will not hold as much moisture as wheaty bread. If your bread isn't very dry, place it in a 225°F (105°C) oven until crisp. Place the cubes into a large bowl and set aside.

Pro-tip: I like to use a mixture of different types of breads; I tend to save the crusts from bread in a bag in the freezer for this purpose.

2. **Cut the onions, apple and celery, and sauté** with the butter or alternate until they become soft

3. **Add the next group of ingredients** and stir to combine.

4. **Add the assembled ingredients to the bowl of breadcrumbs** and mix until all the bread cubes are seasoned with the mixture.

Pro-tip: If the mixture seems drier than what you would expect based upon experience with wheaty stuffing do not be alarmed. The difference in the absorption of liquid of gluten-free breads will result in a nice moist, but not soggy stuffing. The stuffing will absorb some of the juices from inside the bird.

5. **Place the prepared stuffing inside the washed cavities** (neck and body) of your turkey and place in the oven immediately to begin roasting. Do not pre-stuff a turkey or you risk food poisoning.

Pro-tip: A mesh stuffing bag makes removing the stuffing from the cavity after roasting much easier.

Pro-tip: You can also bake the stuffing in a covered casserole dish if you prefer, but it will be necessary to add a little stock to make up for the moisture from the bird that will be missing.

Yield: about 8 cups (2 litres); enough to stuff a 10 - 12 lb (4.5 - 5.5 kg) turkey

Nutritional Information
Calculations based upon the basic recipe excluding optional ingredients and variations.
Per ½ cup (125 ml) serving

energy	104 calories/435 kJ
protein	1g
fat	9 g
carbohydrate	6g
sodium	244 mg
potassium	97 mg
calcium	24 mg
iron	trace

Variations:

This traditional bread stuffing is a very simple basic version. It can be made with as many variations as there are cooks. Feel free to use it for other poultry as well. Variations in the herbs and spices used, and the aromatic vegetables and fruits added, will give this recipe unlimited possibilities.

✓ Try replacing the apple with currants, pear, apricots, cranberries, or plums. In fact any flavourful fruit that is not overly moist will work.

✓ The traditional sage seasoning can be replaced with rosemary, tarragon, fennel, thyme, savory, bay leaf or marjoram to name just a few herbs.

✓ Spices such as nutmeg, allspice, cardamom, and cinnamon can create some less traditional and interesting variations.

✓ The addition of nuts and other flavourful seeds can also add another dimension to your stuffing.

Just play with what you have on hand you will undoubtedly come up with some tasty combinations.

Sweets

When removing gluten from our diet, one of the biggest changes we face is our severely limited options for feeding our sweet tooth. A trip to a bakery, with dozens of cakes and pastries, will usually leave us hungry and frustrated. Even if we find a bakery that prepares some gluten-free items such as nut-based cakes or meringues, cross contamination issues can make the risk too great. Restaurant dessert menus seem to dwindle to fresh fruit, cheese (without the crackers), and sometimes ice-cream, if a gluten-free variety is available.

While researching this book and talking with many people following a gluten-free diet, it became evident that the lack of desserts was the one area that was hardest to bear. During these conversations many people told me that they were most likely to 'fall off the gluten-free wagon' for sweets. In my experience as a chef I have witnessed countless patrons 'leave room' for dessert by skipping the entrees entirely. Most of us know what we should eat, but sometimes we would rather just eat what we want to eat. These cravings are made worse when what we want to eat is forbidden. This leaves us with three options: deprivation, illness or baking. As deprivation is the leading cause of cheating on all diets, and illness is no fun at all, there really is only one viable option. Do the baking and enjoy the sweet delights of your labour.

With the variety of sweets offered in this chapter, I hope your sweet tooth and your need for a gluten-free diet can come to a mutually beneficial arrangement. Years ago my ninety-eight year old grandmother taught me an important lesson I would like to share with you, "Eat your dessert first and enjoy it because you never know if you'll live until the end of your next meal." This was said in jest, but it resounded with a truth that shouldn't be ignored; great joy can be derived from indulging your sweet teeth. As a parent of young children, I don't condone this literally, but I do believe, as my grandmother did, that a few sweets now and then can do more good for the disposition than harm for the diet.

Almond Potato Cake

Decadently rich, this classic Portuguese dessert
never has had any flour in it.

2 cups	sugar	500 ml
½ cup	butter *or* non-dairy alternate	125 ml
10	large egg yolks	10
1 cup	cold, unseasoned mashed potato with nothing added, firmly packed	250 ml
½ lb	ground almonds	225 g
5	egg whites	5
¼ tsp	salt	2 ml
¼ cup	sugar	60 ml

Instructions:

1. **Cream together** sugar and butter.
2. **Beat in egg yolks** one at a time.
3. **Mix in mashed potato and almonds.**
4. **In a separate bowl** beat egg whites and salt until soft peaks have formed.
5. **Fold the two mixtures together** gently, but thoroughly.
6. **Pour** into a well greased 9 inch (23 cm) spring form pan.
7. **Bake at 325°F (165°C)** for 1 hour and 45 minutes, or until the cake begins to pull away from the sides of the pan.
8. **Cool 15 minutes** then loosen edges to remove the spring form, and turn the cake upside-down onto a cake plate. Cool thoroughly before cutting. Small portions are advised as this cake is very rich. Don't be alarmed if the cake falls slightly as it cools, this is normal.

Yield: 16 portions

Nutritional Information
Calculations based upon the basic recipe excluding
optional ingredients and variations.
Per 1 slice serving

energy	250 calories/1046 kJ
protein	5 g
fat	13 g
carbohydrate	32 g
sodium	141 mg
potassium	168 mg
calcium	42 mg
iron	1 mg

Serving suggestions:

This cake requires no frosting, but goes wonderfully with strawberries or pineapple, marinated in port wine.

Angel Food Cake

The old classic is back, this time without the gluten

½ cup	icing sugar	125 ml
¾ cup	potato starch	185 ml
¼ cup	tapioca starch	60 ml
1 ¼ cups (about 10 whites)	egg whites at room temperature *Ensure that no egg yolk has gotten by when separating the whites because it will prevent the whites from whipping up.*	310 ml (about 10 whites)
½ tsp	salt	3 ml
1 tsp	cream of tartar	5 ml
1 tsp	vanilla	5 ml
¾ cup	icing sugar	185 ml

Instructions:

1. **Sift together first group of ingredients** several times to ensure they are fully combined and set aside.
2. **Place next group of ingredients in a scrupulously clean glass or metal mixer bowl.** Plastic bowls have a nasty habit of retaining grease and the slightest trace of oil or grease will prevent the whites from whipping up fully.
3. **Beat whites until stiff,** but not dry looking peaks form.
4. **Add vanilla.**
5. **Gradually whip in ¾ cup (185 ml) of icing sugar** by adding about a 2 tbsp (30 ml) at a time until it is completely combined.
6. **Gently fold in first group of ingredients** about a ½ cup (125 ml) at a time until fully combined.
7. **Pour batter into an _ungreased_ 9 inch (23 cm) tube pan.**
8. **Bake about 45 minutes in a preheated 350ºF (180ºC) oven.**
9. **To cool, invert the pan** over a funnel or any other such object that can allow the cake to hang upside-down without the cake resting on the surface of your work table. Allow the cake to cool fully like this, about 1 ½ hours, to

allow the cake to fully set. Generally you will need to run a spatula between the cake and the pan to loosen it before it can be removed from the pan.

Pro-tip: **Cutting a fresh angel cake can be an exercise in frustration.** Try dividing it by using two forks held back to back in a prying motion or use the special comb-like cake dividers available at kitchenware stores

Yield: 1, 9 inch (23 cm) tube pan; about 12 portions

Nutritional Information
Calculations based upon the basic recipe excluding optional ingredients and variations.
Per $1/12$ of recipe

energy	101 calories/423 kJ
protein	3 g
fat	trace
carbohydrate	23 g
sodium	131 mg
potassium	78 mg
calcium	2 mg
iron	trace

Variations:

Variations to this classic cake need to be done with a very light touch. Any flavouring added must be folded in at the end of step 5, taking great care that the amount used will not affect the stability if this somewhat fussy cake. Customize this cake with frostings and fruit compotes or coulis to dress it up a bit.

Chocolate Cake

Whether you make this as cupcakes or as a layer cake, it has a very rich chocolaty taste and velvety texture.

6 oz	semisweet chocolate *(about 1 cup chips)*	180 g
1 cup	milk *or* non-dairy alternate	250 ml
½ cup	vegetable oil	125 ml
½ cup	cornstarch	125 ml
½ cup	potato starch	125 ml
¼ cup	tapioca starch	60 ml
¼ cup	cocoa powder	60 ml
1 ½ tbsp	baking powder	22 ml
1 tsp	xanthan gum	5 ml
½ tsp	salt	3 ml
4	beaten eggs	4
1 ½ cups	icing sugar	375 ml
1 tsp	vanilla	5 ml

Instructions:

1. **Melt** chocolate and butter in the milk.
2. **Set aside** to cool to no warmer than100ºF (40ºC), just warm to the touch.
3. **Sift together** next group of ingredients and set aside.
4. **Cream chocolate mixture** together with eggs, icing sugar and vanilla.
5. **Stir in flour mixture** and mix to a smooth batter.
6. **Separate batter** into 12 cupcakes or pour into a 9 inch (23 cm) spring form pan.
7. **Bake** about 25 minutes for cupcakes, or 35 - 40 minutes for 1 cake pan in a preheated 350ºF (180ºC) oven.

Yield: 12 cupcakes, or 1 spring form pan

Nutritional Information

Calculations based upon the basic recipe excluding
optional ingredients and variations.
Per $^1/_{12}$ of the cake, or 1 cupcake serving

energy	295 calories/1235 kJ
protein	3 g
fat	16 g
carbohydrate	39 g
sodium	181 mg
potassium	128 mg
calcium	73 mg
iron	1 mg

Variations:

This basic cake recipe can be host to a myriad of variations. Try different fruit
and mousse fillings, and frostings.

Choux Paste

Cream puffs, éclairs and profiteroles are all back on the menu. But don't stop there, the possible variations for this versatile dough are almost limitless.

½ cup	cornstarch	125 ml
⅓ cup	brown rice flour	85 ml
3 tbsp	tapioca starch	45 ml
1 tsp	xanthan gum	5 ml
1 cup	water	250 ml
¼ cup	butter *or* non-dairy alternate	60 ml
½ tsp	salt	3 ml
6	eggs	6

Instructions:

1. **Mix dry ingredients fully** and set aside.
2. **Bring next group of ingredients to a boil** on the stove.
3. **Remove from heat** and stir in reserved dry ingredients with a wooden spoon.
4. **Add eggs one by one** completely stirring in each before adding the next. Once all eggs are incorporated the dough is complete.
5. **Shape the dough** into whatever form you require, keeping in mind that the dough will expand by about double when baked. The simplest method is to simply spoon or scoop the dough onto baking sheets lined with bakers' parchment. For more finesse and control, the dough can be piped out of a pastry bag. Or in a pinch, dough can be squeezed out of a heavy duty plastic bag with a small hole cut in one corner. Regardless of the method of forming the dough, a variety of sizes can be achieved for different uses. *See variations below for a few options.*
6. **Bake at 350ºF (180ºC)** until golden.
7. **Turn the oven down** to 225ºF (105ºC) and continue baking to crisp them. The best way to check this is to give one a little squeeze. It should feel firm, not mushy, for most uses. It should feel very crisp for use as crackers. No matter what you do with this versatile dough I am sure you will enjoy it!

Yield: about 2 ½ dozen, 3 inch (7.5 cm) cream puff shells

Nutritional Information
Calculations based upon the basic recipe excluding
optional ingredients and variations.
Per 3 inch (7.5 cm) cream puff shell

energy	44 calories/185 kJ
protein	1
fat	2 g
carbohydrate	4 g
sodium	63 mg
potassium	16 mg
calcium	5 mg
iron	trace

Variations:

✓ If tiny balls the size of peas are made and baked until crisp they make wonderful crackers to float in soups.

✓ Made golf ball size they can be stuffed with whipped cream or even better, chocolate mousse for an elegant dessert.

✓ There are also the ever popular cream puff or éclair sizes.

✓ Savoury fillings such as creamed turkey, mushroom ragout, or beef stew can turn this recipe into a dressed up sort of pot pie without rolling any dough.

✓ Try mixing in any herb or spice which suits the intended use.

✓ Two-bite sized profiteroles can be stuffed with any hot or cold filling you can imagine for appetizers. Curried shrimp, egg salad, and mushroom ragout are only a few of the possible options.

Crustless Cheesecake

The best part of the cheesecake without the extra work of the crumby bottom. The cheesecake batter naturally forms a bottom crust while it bakes so the extra steps are unnecessary. The smaller portion size suggested is great for this very rich cake.

	cake batter	
6 – 8oz packages	light cream cheese (room temperature)	6 - 250g packages
10	eggs	10
2 cups	sugar	500 ml
1 tbsp	vanilla	15 ml

	topping	
1 cup	fat reduced sour cream	250 ml
1	zest of 1 lemon *Do not use if changing the flavour with the variations below.*	1
2 tbsp	sugar	30 ml

Instructions:

1. **Mix cream cheese** in a heavy-duty mixer (fairly slowly to prevent the beating in of air) with sugar and vanilla.
2. **Add eggs one at a time** allowing time for each one to be incorporated before adding the next.
3. **Periodically stop the mixer** and scrape the unmixed cream cheese off the sides of the bowl to give it a chance to mix into a smooth batter.
4. **Pour batter** into a foil lined 9 inch (23 cm) spring form pan.
5. **Place this pan on top of a baking sheet** to prevent premature browning on the bottom of the cake.
6. **Bake for 1½ - 2 hrs at 250ºF (120ºC).** Test for doneness by giving the pan a little shake. When it is done it will no longer move like a liquid.

Pro-tip: The standard cake tester method does not work for this recipe.

7. **Mix together topping ingredients** and reserve while the cake is baking.
8. **When the cake is done** remove it from the oven and spread the topping on

immediately. The heat of the cake will cause the topping to turn from a liquid into a solid glaze. Allow the cake to cool fully before attempting to remove from the pan.

Yield: 16 portions

Nutritional Information
Calculations based upon the basic recipe excluding optional ingredients and variations.
Per $^1/_{16}$ of cake

energy	347 calories/1452 kJ
protein	13 g
fat	18 g
carbohydrate	34 g
sodium	517 mg
potassium	136 mg
calcium	139 mg
iron	2 mg

Variations:

Here are just a few, try these or branch out on your own.

- ✓ **Any crumb crust** you like can be added to it, if you wish.
- ✓ **Chocolate Marble Cheesecake**
  Try separating out about $^1/_4$ of the batter and adding ¼ cup (60 ml) of cocoa powder to it. Swirl it into the rest of the batter in the pan with a gentle folding action.
- ✓ **Pumpkin Cheesecake**
  Add ¾ cup (185 ml) pumpkin puree and 2 tsp (10 ml) pumpkin pie spice and make a gingersnap crust for a great Thanksgiving variation.
- ✓ **Very Berry Cheesecake**
  Add ¾ cup (185 ml) crushed berries of your choice to the batter before baking. Be sure to drain off any excess liquid to prevent making the cake watery.
- ✓ **Orange Cheesecake**
  Add ½ cup (125 ml) orange juice concentrate to the batter and replace the lemon zest with orange zest.

Flaky Pie Pastry

This pastry is a bit more delicate to handle than its wheaty counterpart, but with the tips provided it yields a great pastry without hassles.

2 cups	sweet rice flour	500 ml
1 cup	tapioca starch	250 ml
½ cup	whole corn flour	125 ml
1 ½ tsp	xanthan gum	8 ml
2 tbsp	brown sugar	30 ml
½ tsp	baking powder	3 ml
1 cup	cold vegetable shortening *or* lard	250 ml
1 cup	milk *or* non-dairy alternate	250 ml
1 tsp	vinegar	5 ml
½ tsp	salt	3 ml
1	egg yolk	1
1 tbsp	milk *or* non-dairy alternate	15 ml

Instructions:

1. **Fully combine all dry ingredients.**
2. **Cut in shortening or lard** with a pastry cutter, or rub in shortening or lard with your hands until a crumbly meal with pea-sized pieces of shortening remains.
3. **Stir in milk or alternate and vinegar,** and work by hand until just combined into a dough.
4. **Roll pastry out.**

Pro-tip: Flexible silicone baking mats lightly dusted with sweet rice flour are great for rolling delicate gluten free pastry. They also don't slide around on counters while rolling making the whole process easier than the frequently suggested wax paper method. Roll up the mat and the pastry together to transfer it to the pie plate. Simply turn the roll over and unroll for trouble free pastry.

Alternately, if you are only making a bottom shell the dough can be pressed directly into the pan, eliminating the rolling step.

FYI: It is **not** necessary to allow gluten-free dough to rest for a while like wheaty dough. That resting step is required to minimize the effects of the gluten in the wheaty pastry; not a concern in gluten-free pastry.

5. **Fill dough shell as you wish** and prepare the top
6. **Mix together egg yolk and milk or alternate** to form an egg wash. Use this mixture as the 'glue' to attach the top and bottom crusts.
7. **Once top is in place pierce it** in a few places with a knife or fork to allow any steam to escape during baking.
8. **Brush surface** with remaining egg wash to yield a richly coloured shiny crust.

Yield: 2, 8 inch (20 cm) double crust pies or 2, 10 inch (25 cm) open top pies.

Nutritional Information
Calculations based upon the basic recipe excluding optional ingredients and variations.
Per ¹/₆ slice of an 8 inch (20 cm), double crust pie

energy	300 calories/1255 kJ
protein	3 g
fat	18 g
carbohydrate	15 g
sodium	123 mg
potassium	71 mg
calcium	43 mg
iron	1 mg

Variations:

An entire book could be filled with variations for pie pastry, but I will leave you with these few ideas. I am sure you can fill in the blanks from your personal, "I really miss …" list. Do not be concerned that the included sugar may make the pastry too sweet for savoury dishes; it is included only to aid in browning to a natural looking colour. More sugar can be added if desired to make sweet dough.

✓ **Pot pies**
✓ **Fruit or cream pies**
✓ **Quiche or tarts**

Meringue Shells

A great use for extra egg whites, and with a bit of fruit and custard, or whipped cream the basis of a great dessert.

4 or ½ cup	egg whites	4 or 125 ml
¼ tsp	salt	1 ml
¼ tsp	cream of tartar	1 ml
1 cup	sugar	250 ml
1 tsp	vanilla	5 ml

Instructions:

1. **Trace 2, 10 inch (25 cm) circles or 12, 3 inch (7.5 cm) individual sized circles** onto the underside of bakers' parchment, dark enough that it can bee seen through the paper. Place the parchment on baking sheets and set aside.
2. **Using an electric mixer beat egg whites, salt and cream of tartar** on medium low until very soft peaks form. Add sugar and vanilla, and beat on medium high until stiff peaks form.
3. **Divide meringue equally among the prepared circles** you have drawn on the parchment paper lined baking sheets. Spread meringue out to an even thickness at least ¾ inch (2 cm) thick using the outlines for even sizing.
4. **Bake 2 - 3 hours at 225ºF (105ºC)** until the meringues are dry.
5. **Allow to cool on a rack.**

Yield: 2, 10 inch (25 cm) round shells, or approx. 12, 3 inch (7.5 cm) round shells

Nutritional Information
Calculations based upon the basic recipe excluding optional ingredients and variations.
Per 3 inch (7.5 cm) shell

energy	71 calories/297 kJ
protein	1 g
fat	0 g
carbohydrate	17 g
sodium	61 mg
potassium	25 mg
calcium	1 mg
iron	trace

Variations:

Whether you make the vanilla, chocolate or nut version, meringue shells are best topped with cream fillings and fruit. Although many bakeries produce cookie sized meringues to eat out of hand, this very sweet and dry use of this recipe is not recommended. This old- fashioned dessert can be painfully sweet if not balanced with appropriate fillings. If using custards or crème Anglaise reduce the amount of sugar slightly and choose fruits that are slightly tart such as blackberries, cherries, kiwi, or citrus.

- ✓ **Pavlova**

    This classic meringue dessert is simply whipped cream and fresh fruit layered with the meringue shells. A delicious summer treat.

- ✓ **Chocolate Meringue shells**

    Add ¼ cup (60 ml) cocoa powder by mixing it into the sugar before proceeding with the recipe as written.

- ✓ **Nut Meringue shells**

    Add 2 more egg whites to the recipe and add 1 cup (250 ml) finely ground nuts such as hazelnuts to the mixture at the same time as the sugar. Bake slightly hotter at 275ºF (130ºC) to give the nuts a bit more of a toasted taste. Fill as you wish and enjoy this nutty version.

- ✓ **Black Forest Pavlova**

    Chocolate meringue shells layered with whipped cream, sour cherries and a touch of kirsch liqueur make a delicious twist on the traditional black forest cake.

Pound Cake

You can change the texture of this cake by either adding the eggs whole for a traditional dense pound cake, or beat the egg whites separately before adding them for a lighter texture.

1 ½ cups	potato starch	375 ml
½ cup	tapioca starch	125 ml
½ tsp	xanthan gum	3 ml
¹/₄ tsp	salt	2 ml
¹/₄ tsp	cream of tartar	2 ml
1 cup	butter or non-dairy alternate	250 ml
1 cup	sugar	250 ml
4	eggs	4
½ tsp	vanilla	3 ml
¹/₄ tsp	mace *(optional)*	2 ml
1 tbsp	brandy *or* Cointreau *(optional)*	15 ml
2 tbsp	orange *or* lemon juice	30 ml

Instructions:

1. **Measure and fully mix** ingredients in the first group and set aside.
2. **Cream butter and sugar** in an electric mixer; add eggs 1 at a time allowing time for each to incorporate before adding the next.
3. **Add remaining wet ingredients**.
4. **Mix in reserved dry ingredients** and beat on high for 1 minute.
5. **Bake about 55 - 60 minutes at 325°F (165°C)** in a greased 9 x 5 x 3 inch (23 x 13 x 8 cm) loaf pan. Double the recipe to make a 10 inch (25 cm) tube pan.
6. **Brush on a glaze,** if desired, before the cake cools. *See variations below.*

Yield: 1, 9 x 5 x 3 inch (23 x 13 x 8 cm) loaf pan

Nutritional Information

Calculations based upon the basic recipe excluding
optional ingredients and variations.

Per $^{1}/_{16}$ serving

energy	225 calories/941 kJ
protein	2 g
fat	13 g
carbohydrate	28 g
sodium	164 mg
potassium	29 mg
calcium	9 mg
iron	trace

Variations:

With changes to the liquids used, and the addition of candied fruits, nuts or seeds this basic recipe can be easily altered to suit your taste. Also, a variety of different flavours are possible with the addition of different glazes added when the cake is just removed from the oven. Here are just a few ideas to get you started.

- ✓ **Poppy Seed Pound Cake**
  Add ½ cup (125 ml) of poppy seed to the batter to give the cake a whole new character.
- ✓ **Chocolate Pound Cake**
  Add ¼ cup (60 ml) cocoa powder to the batter to give this cake a chocolaty character.
- ✓ **Spiced Pound Cake**
  Add your choice of sweet savoury spices. Try cinnamon, nutmeg, cloves, cardamom, allspice, ginger, or star anise.
- ✓ **'Half Pound' Cake**
  This isn't really a half pound cake; it just has a lighter texture. Try beating the egg whites separately and folding them in at step 4 above. The extra air added will make the cake much lighter, but still tastes like pound cake.

Glaze Variations:

The basic glaze for pound cake is ½ cup (125 ml) sugar and ¼ cup (60 ml) lemon juice. Brush the glaze onto the cake just as it is pulled from the oven and it will be completely absorbed by the cake. This is a great classic taste, but by changing the liquid other flavours are possible. Try using coffee or liqueurs in the same proportions, or try using ⅓ cup (85 ml) of any of the many frozen juice concentrates without any additional sugar. To liven up this old fashioned dessert try cranberry, apple, orange, lime, pineapple, or berry flavours.

Sour Cream Chocolate Cake

This moist dark chocolate cake is perfect for cupcakes or as a layer cake. This is the birthday cake of choice for my kids. This recipe is on the large side and will make a 3 layer cake, or 16 average sized cupcakes.

1 cup	potato starch	250 ml
½ cup	cornstarch	125 ml
½ cup	sweet rice flour	125 ml
⅔ cup	cocoa powder	165 ml
1 ½ tsp	baking powder	8 ml
1 ½ tsp	baking soda	8 ml
½ tsp	xanthan gum	3 ml
½ tsp	salt	3 ml
3	eggs	3
1 ½ cups	sugar	375 ml
¾ cup	vegetable oil	185 ml
1 tbsp	vanilla	15 ml
1 cup	sour cream *or* soft tofu	250 ml

Instructions:

1. **Measure and mix first group of ingredients** and set aside.
2. **Beat second set of ingredients in a mixer until fully combined.**
3. **Add dry ingredients** to wet and beat 1 minute on high.
4. **Separate batter** into 12 for large cupcakes or 16 for smaller cupcakes, or pour into a 9 inch (23 cm) spring form pan.
5. **Bake** about 25 minutes for cupcakes, or 45 - 55 for 1 cake pan in a preheated 350ºF (180ºC) oven.
6. **Allow the cake to cool** a few minutes before removing from the spring form pan to aid in removing it from the pan,, but do not allow it to cool completely in the pan or it will become mushy. A cake with a soft interior and a firm crust is easiest to work with, and the firm crust softens up under frostings.

Yield: 12 - 16 cupcakes; or 1, 9 inch (23 cm) spring form pan, or see variations below.

Nutritional Information

Calculations based upon the basic recipe excluding
optional ingredients and variations.

Per $^1/_{16}$ of recipe serving

energy	276 calories/1155 kJ
protein	2 g
fat	15 g
carbohydrate	33 g
sodium	250 mg
potassium	89 mg
calcium	52 mg
iron	1 mg

Variations:

This great chocolate cake couldn't be much easier to bake, and it has many uses and variations. This cake also freezes well so you may want to double the recipe and keep a plain cake on hand in the freezer for those unexpected guests. Simply cut and frost it when you need it. Professional bakers commonly use this method to save time and effort. Here are just a few ideas to get you started.

✓ **Any-Day Easy Cake**

   Pour the batter into a 13 x 9 x 2 inch (33 x 21 x 5 cm) pan for a great easy sheet cake. Top with your favourite frosting, or just serve with ice-cream or fruit for a treat easy enough that it can be made anytime.

✓ **Chocolate Jelly Roll**

   Bake the batter on a 12 x 16 inch (30 x 40 cm) jelly roll pan lined with bakers' parchment. If you take care to not over-bake the cake it rolls well and can be filled with fruit, cream fillings, frostings or jelly. Try whipped cream and some sour cherries for a black forest roll or hazelnut butter cream to make a Noel log.

✓ **Layer cake**

   This cake bakes up high enough to cut into 3 layers when baked in a 9 inch (23 cm) spring form pan. Fill it with whatever you like and frost it for special occasions.

Sweet Crumb Pie Crusts

Whether you begin with crumbs from bread, cookies, cake or cereal this recipe will make them into a great crust for pies.

1 ¾ cups	dry breadcrumbs, *or* crushed gluten free cereal, *or* cookie crumbs, *or* cake crumbs	440 ml
¼ - ⅓ cup	melted butter *or* non-dairy alternate *If the crumbs have little or no fat in them* *use the larger amount.*	60 - 85 ml
1 - 3 tbsp	sugar *(white or brown)* *If the crumbs have little or no sugar in them* *use the larger amount.*	15 - 45 ml
	spices *(optional)* *see variations below*	

Instructions:

1. **Ensure the crumbs are completely dry** by baking them in a 225ºF (105ºC) oven until crisp.
2. **Grind crumbs in a food processor** to a coarse powder.
3. **Add remaining ingredients** and mix to combine.
4. **Press mixture evenly** into a 10 inch (25 cm) spring form pan for use with cheesecakes and mousse tortes, or into an 8 inch (20 cm) pie plate for pies.
   - ✓ If the filling needs to be baked in the shell such as cheesecakes fill the shell before baking.
   - ✓ If the filling is already cooked for pies such as cream pies bake the shell at 375º F (190ºC) for 8 - 10 minutes. Allow to cool slightly before adding filling.

Yield: 1, 10 inch (25 cm) spring form pan or 1, 8 inch (20 cm) pie plate.

Nutritional Information
Due to the variations inherent in this recipe
nutritional calculations are not possible.

Variations:

This recipe is a great use for all those little leftover bits that might otherwise be wasted. Any recipe for pies, tortes or cheesecakes with crumb crusts can be done gluten-free with this recipe. Consider adding spices such as cinnamon, cardamom or nutmeg to any of the ideas below. Here are a few variations to get you started.

- ✓ **Gingersnap Crust**
  Crumble Ginger Snap cookies from *(p. 300)* and use the lesser amount of sugar and butter or alternate for a great spicy crust.

- ✓ **Chocolate Wafer Crust**
  Crumble Chocolate Wafers from *(p. 294)* and use the lesser amount of sugar and butter or alternate for a great chocolate crust. Grasshopper or chocolate cream pie is back.

- ✓ **Not-Graham Wafer Crust**
  Crumble Not-Graham Wafers from *(p. 306)* and use the lesser amount of sugar and butter or alternate to replace this staple of pie making.

- ✓ **Cereal Crust**
  When you don't have any crumbs of your own, or when you want an extra crunchy crust, crumble any gluten-free flake cereal and use the greater amount of both sugar and butter or alternate.

- ✓ **Cake Crumb Crust**
  Cakes don't usually have a chance to get dry in my home, but if it happens in your home, here is a use for it. Crumble dried out cake and use the lesser amount of both sugar and butter or alternate.

- ✓ **Nut Crust**
  Use ½ cup (125 ml) less dry breadcrumbs than called for in the recipe with ½ cup (125 ml) finely ground nuts such as pecans or hazelnuts for a flavourful variation. Use the greater amounts of both the sugar and the butter or alternate.

White Genoise Sponge Cake

This rich moist cake is the quintessential European cake. It is borrowed by pastry chefs the world over because of its versatility.

1 ¼ cups	potato starch	310 ml
¼ cup	tapioca starch	60 ml
½ tsp	xanthan gum	3 ml
⅔ cup	butter *or* non-dairy alternate	165 ml
3	eggs	3
⅔ cup	sugar	165 ml
1 tsp	vanilla	5 ml
1 tbsp	water	15 ml

Instructions:

1. **Measure and sift together first group of ingredients** and set aside.
2. **Melt butter or alternate** and set aside.
3. **Warm eggs to 95ºF (30ºC)** by allowing them to sit in hot tap water for a few minutes. This warming enables the eggs to whip up better.
4. **Beat eggs** 5 minutes on med/high with ½ the sugar until the mixture has reached a stage where it falls in a smooth ribbon like stream from a spoon.
5. **Add the rest of the sugar** and beat on high a further 2 minutes.
6. **Mix in vanilla, water and melted butter until fully combined.**
7. **Fold in dry ingredients** gently until fully combined.
8. **Bake** in a 9 inch (23 cm) greased spring form pan for 35 - 40 minutes at 325ºF (165ºC).
9. **Cool in pan for about 5 minutes,** then turn out onto a cooling rack. Allow to cool fully before cutting or icing.

Yield: 1, 9 inch (23 cm) spring form pan

Nutritional Information

Calculations based upon the basic recipe excluding
optional ingredients and variations.
Per $^1/_{12}$ of cake

energy	209 calories/875 kJ
protein	1 g
fat	11 g
carbohydrate	27 g
sodium	118 mg
potassium	17 mg
calcium	9 mg
iron	trace

Variations:

The variations available for this recipe are almost unlimited. Any sort of filling or frosting you can imagine for a cake will work.

- ✓ It can be baked in a flat sheet and used to make jelly or cream rolls if care is taken to not over bake it.
- ✓ It is also the cake of choice for any type of filled layer cake.

Chocolate Brownies

Rich, moist, chocolaty, yet requiring no frosting .... These brownies will amaze you with their richness and light texture.

2 cups	semi-sweet chocolate chips	500 ml
1 cup	butter *or* non-dairy alternate	250 ml
1 cup	brown sugar	250 ml
2 tsp	vanilla	10 ml
1 cup	cornstarch	250 ml
⅔ cup	sweet rice flour	165 ml
⅓ cup	tapioca starch	80 ml
1 ½ tsp	baking powder	7 ml
½ tsp	xanthan gum	3 ml
½ cup	chopped nuts *(optional)*	125 ml
4	eggs, lightly beaten	4

Instructions:

1. **Place first group of ingredients** in a double boiler to melt. Meanwhile, mix together the second group of ingredients. When the chocolate mixture has completely melted, stir in dry ingredients and eggs.

2. **Choose the form for baking the batter.** Although it takes a bit more time to portion out, I prefer to use mini-muffin tins that yield mini, bite-sized brownies. The consistent crisp outside and soft interior of each piece is worth the effort.

3. **Fill the greased mini-muffin tins** approximately half full.

   Pro Tip: I use a small 1 inch (2.5 cm) diameter ice cream-type scoop because uniform size results in uniform baking time and texture. For brownies of this size, bake at 375ºF (190ºC) for about 12 minutes.

4. **If you choose to bake in one pan,** use a 9 x 13 inch (23 x 33 cm) baking pan and bake for about 30 minutes. The brownies will be very soft when you remove them from the oven.

5. **Allow to cool** before handling.

Yield: about 5 dozen mini bite-size brownies; or 1, 9 x 13 inch (23 x 33 cm) pan

Nutritional Information
Calculations based upon the basic recipe excluding
optional ingredients and variations.
Per mini bite-size brownie

energy	83 calories/347 kJ
protein	1 g
fat	5 g
carbohydrate	9 g
sodium	49 mg
potassium	34 mg
calcium	13 mg
iron	trace

Chocolate Chip Cookies

Expert testers (kids and the young at heart) can't tell these from the originals. The big batch size makes keeping some dough on hand a bit easier.

1 cup	butter *or* non-dairy alternate	250 ml
1 ½ cup	brown sugar	375 ml
2	eggs	2
1 tbsp	vanilla	15 ml
1 ¼ cup	sweet rice flour	310 ml
²/₃ cup	corn starch	165 ml
¹/₃ cup	tapioca starch	85 ml
¼ tsp	xanthan gum	1 ml
1 tsp	salt	5 ml
1 ½ tsp	baking soda	8 ml
2 ½ cups	chocolate chips	625 ml
	be sure to check that yours are gluten-free	

Instructions:

1. **Cream first four ingredients** in mixer.
2. **Fully mix next group of ingredients** before adding to the first group.
3. **Fold in chocolate chips last** and mix until fully combined.
4. **Spoon dough** into approximately 1 inch (2.5 cm) round balls onto cookie sheet lined with bakers' parchment, allowing room for the cookies to spread.

Pro tip: I use a small 1 inch (2.5 cm) diameter ice cream-type scoop, because uniform size results in uniform baking time and texture.

5. **Bake at 375ºF (190ºC)** for 8 - 9 minutes. The cookies will be very soft when you remove them from the oven. Allow to cool slightly before handling.

To enjoy fresh baked cookies anytime, portion out cookie dough as above, flatten slightly and freeze. You can pull a few out of the freezer and bake them in minutes. Allow frozen dough to warm up at room temperature while your oven heats.

Yield: approximately 60, 2 inch (5 cm) cookies

Nutritional Information

Calculations based upon the basic recipe excluding
optional ingredients and variations.

Per 1 cookie serving

energy	105 calories/440 kJ
protein	1 g
fat	6 g
carbohydrate	11 g
sodium	103 mg
potassium	51 mg
calcium	8 mg
iron	trace

Chocolate Wafer Cookies

Enjoy as they are, crumble them into crusts,
or make your own ice cream sandwiches

½ cup	tapioca starch	125 ml
½ cup	sweet rice flour	125 ml
¾ cup	whole corn flour	185 ml
¼ cup	cocoa powder	60 ml
½ tsp	xanthan gum	3 ml
½ tsp	salt	3 ml
½ tsp	baking powder	3 ml
1 cup	sugar	250 ml
¼ cup	butter *or* non-dairy alternate	60 ml
⅔ cup	water	165 ml

Instructions:

1. **Measure and mix** dry ingredients and set aside.
2. **Cream wet ingredients** in a mixer until fluffy. Add reserved dry ingredients and mix into dough.
3. **Form dough** into approximately 1 inch (2.5 cm) round balls and place on cookie sheet lined with bakers' parchment. You can simply press the balls of the dough flat to about ⅛ inch (3 mm) thickness between two sheets of bakers' parchment with a second baking sheet. Take off the top baking sheet and peel off the top sheet of bakers' parchment before baking. This will yield the familiar round shape and it certainly is faster than the roll and cut method.

Alternately you can roll the dough using a little icing sugar to prevent sticking, to about ⅛ inch (3 mm) thickness and use cookie cutters to form any shape you wish.

Pro tip: I use a small 1 inch (2.5 cm) diameter ice cream-type scoop, because uniform size results in uniform baking time and texture.

4. **Bake at 375ºF (190ºC)** for 8 - 10 minutes.

Yield: about 3 dozen wafers

Nutritional Information
Calculations based upon the basic recipe excluding
optional ingredients and variations.
Per wafer serving

energy	55 calories/230 kJ
protein	Trace
fat	1 g
carbohydrate	9 g
sodium	50 mg
potassium	19 mg
calcium	6 mg
iron	trace

Date Squares/Matrimonial Squares

*No matter what you call these, they are back on
the allowed list and as delicious as always.*

	base	
½ cup	cornstarch	125 ml
⅓ cup	brown rice flour	85 ml
3 tbsp	tapioca starch	45 ml
1 cup	brown sugar	250 ml
2 cups	rolled soybeans *or* oats*	500 ml
½ tsp	baking soda	3 ml
¼ tsp	salt	2 ml
½ tsp	xanthan gum	3 ml
1 cup	butter *or* non-dairy alternate *(melted)*	250 ml
	filling	
½ lb	chopped, pitted dates	225 g
½ cup	water	125 ml

Instructions:

1. **Mix together** the first group of ingredients fully; then stir in melted butter gently to minimize breaking the flakes. Set aside.
2. **Cook dates and water** in a pot on the stovetop or in the microwave, mixing periodically until a gooey paste is formed.
3. **Press half of base mixture** into an even layer in a greased 8 inch (20 cm) square baking dish.
4. **Spread filling** mixture evenly over the base layer.
5. **Top with remaining base mixture** spreading it out evenly.
6. **Bake at 350ºF (180ºC)** for 30 - 40 minutes until golden brown.
7. **Allow to cool** fully before cutting for best results. My testers think it tastes even better the next day, if you can wait that long.

Yield: 1, 8 inch (20 cm) square pan

Nutritional Information

Calculations based upon the basic recipe excluding
optional ingredients and variations.

Per 2 inch (5 cm) square serving

energy	253 calories/1058 kJ
protein	4 g
fat	14 g
carbohydrate	30 g
sodium	196 mg
potassium	404 mg
calcium	38 mg
iron	1 mg

No-Bake Disappearing Squares

The name of these squares says it all. After just a taste, the rest of the batch seems to disappear. By choosing different cookies as the base many different variations are possible.

7 oz	crumbled gluten-free cookies *see variations below*	200 g
½ cup	pecans, hazelnuts *or* other nuts of your choice.	125 ml
¾ cup	brown sugar	185 ml
¼ cup	butter *or* non-dairy alternate	60 ml
2 tbsp	cocoa powder	30 ml
1 ½ tsp	vanilla	8 ml
1	egg	1
	frosting *(optional)*	

Instructions:

1. **Measure and crush cookies / wafers and nuts** to about pea size and set aside.
2. **Measure and mix** next group of ingredients in a saucepan.
3. **Bring mixture to a boil** and allow it to boil for 1 minute.
4. **Stir in reserved cookie / wafer and nut mixture** until fully combined.
5. **Place mixture in a greased 8 inch (20 cm) square baking pan**. Spread the mixture out flat and allow to cool in the fridge.

Yield: 1, 8 inch (20 cm) square baking pan

Nutritional Information
Due to the variations inherent in this recipe
nutritional calculations are not possible.

Variations:

This is an old family recipe which fills the need for a summertime sweet when it is too hot to bake. This basic no-bake square has many options for variations. Any gluten free cookie or wafer can be used to give this super easy treat a different character.

- ✓ Try Not-Graham Wafers *(p. 306)*, Ladyfingers *(p. 304)*, Ginger Snaps *(p. 300)* or Chocolate Wafers *(p. 294)* to name just a few.
- ✓ Store bought gluten-free cookies can also be used in this recipe.
- ✓ Even the lowly rice cake can get a boost from this recipe; just break up about 5 or 6 full size plain rice cakes and use them in place of the cookies.
- ✓ This recipe stands alone without frosting, but if you do want to add your favourite frosting it will dress it up a bit.

Ginger Snaps

Whether eaten as is, or crumbled into crusts or squares, these cookies have the old fashioned taste we love.

½ cup	tapioca starch	125 ml
½ cup	sweet rice flour	125 ml
¾ cup	whole corn flour	185 ml
½ tsp	baking powder	3 ml
½ tsp	xanthan gum	3 ml
½ tsp	salt	3 ml
1 tsp	ginger	5 ml
¼ tsp	cinnamon	1 ml
¼ tsp	cloves	1 ml
½ cup	sugar	125 ml
½ cup	butter *or* non-dairy alternate	125 ml
½ cup	molasses	125 ml
¼ cup	boiling water	60 ml

Instructions:

1. **Measure and mix** dry ingredients and set aside.
2. **Cream wet ingredients** in a mixer until fluffy. Add reserved dry ingredients and mix into dough.
3. **Form dough** into approximately 1 inch (2.5 cm) round balls and place on cookie sheet lined with bakers' parchment, allowing room for the cookies to spread.

Pro tip: I use a small 1 inch (2.5 cm) diameter ice cream-type scoop because uniform size results in uniform baking time and texture.

4. **Bake at 375ºF (190ºC)** for 8 - 10 minutes.

Yield: about 2 ½ dozen cookies

Nutritional Information
Calculations based upon the basic recipe excluding
optional ingredients and variations.
Per cookie

energy	76 calories/318 kJ
protein	trace
fat	3 g
carbohydrate	10 g
sodium	77 mg
potassium	90 mg
calcium	18 mg
iron	trace

Variations:

These classic cookies have many possible uses:
- ✓ Enjoy them as is with tea or coffee
- ✓ Crumble them into crumb crusts
- ✓ Make them into sandwich cookies with ice cream or your favourite jam.

Hermits

These raisin spice cookies are a gluten-free version of a treasured childhood memory, but are often enjoyed even more by adults.

¾ cup	cornstarch	185 ml
½ cup	sweet rice flour	125 ml
¼ cup	tapioca starch	60 ml
½ tsp	baking soda	3 ml
¼ tsp	salt	2 ml
½ tsp	cinnamon	3 ml
¼ tsp	nutmeg	2 ml
¼ tsp	cloves	2 ml
½ tsp	xanthan gum	3 ml
½ cup	butter *or* non-dairy alternate	125 ml
1 cup	brown sugar	250 ml
1	egg	1
2 tbsp	water	30 ml
1 tbsp	instant coffee	15 ml
¾ cup	raisins	185 ml
½ cup	chopped nuts (*optional*)	125 ml

Instructions:

1. **Mix dry ingredients** fully and reserve.
2. **Cream next group of ingredients** before adding the dry ingredients mixture.
3. **Mix to incorporate** and then fold in the raisins and nuts (if used).
4. **Spoon out the dough** into approximately 1 inch round balls onto bakers' parchment lined baking sheets allowing room for the cookies to spread.
Pro tip: I use a small ice cream type scoop for this because uniform size allows for uniform baking time and texture.
5. **Bake at 375ºF (190ºC)** for 8 - 9 minutes for cookies of this size. The cookies will be very soft when you remove them from the oven.
6. **Allow to cool** slightly before handling. To enjoy fresh baked cookies anytime, portion out the cookie dough as above, flatten them slightly and freeze. You can pull a few out of the freezer and bake them whenever you

wish, and they will be ready in only a few minutes. Allow the dough to thaw at room temperature while your oven heats up.

Yield: about 3 dozen

Nutritional Information
Calculations based upon the basic recipe excluding optional ingredients and variations.
Per 1 cookie serving

energy	68 calories/285 kJ
protein	trace
fat	3 g
carbohydrate	10 g
sodium	62 mg
potassium	41 mg
calcium	7 mg
iron	trace

Lady Fingers

These crisp little cookies can be used in many ways as a base for desserts, not the least of which is Tiramisu. These don't rise quite as much as their wheaty cousins, but they taste great.

½ cup	cornstarch	125 ml
½ cup	potato starch	125 ml
¾ tsp	baking powder	4 ml
½ tsp	xanthan gum	3 ml
3	egg yolks	3
½ cup	sugar	125 ml
½ tsp	vanilla	3 ml
2 tsp	water	10 ml
3	egg whites	3
¼ tsp	salt	1 ml
¼ tsp	cream of tartar	1 ml

Instructions:

1. **Measure and mix the first group of ingredients** and set aside.
2. **Beat yolks, sugar, vanilla and water** until smooth ribbons form when dropped from a spoon.
3. **Whip the whites** with salt and cream of tartar to form soft peaks.
4. **Fold reserved dry ingredients** into yolk mixture fully, and then fold in whites until fully combined.
5. **Use a pastry bag** with a ¼ inch (6 mm) plain tube to pipe out the mixture onto bakers' parchment lined baking sheets.
Alternately, a heavy duty freezer bag with ¼ inch (6 mm) cut off of the corner diagonally makes a great stand-in for a piping bag.
6. **Pipe out 3 inch (7 cm) long finger shapes** onto the lined baking sheets, allowing room for them to spread slightly.
7. **Bake 6 - 8 minutes** or until golden at 375ºF (190ºC).
8. **Allow to cool** slightly before transferring them to a cooling rack to cool completely.

Yield: about 5 dozen

Nutritional Information
Calculations based upon the basic recipe excluding
optional ingredients and variations.
Per ladyfinger

energy	18 calories/75 kJ
protein	trace
fat	trace
carbohydrate	4 g
sodium	18 mg
potassium	5 mg
calcium	5 mg
iron	trace

Variations:

This versatile little cookie can be enjoyed as is, served as a crisp accompaniment to ice creams and custards, or included in more elaborate desserts such as tiramisu or mousse tortes. Bake up a batch and they will likely disappear before you need to worry about what to do with them.

Not-Graham Wafers

These wafers are great for munching or can be used in a myriad of ways for baking.

1 ¼ cup	brown rice flour	310 ml
1 cup	yellow corn flour	250 ml
¼ cup	coarsely milled flax seed *(Pro-tip: You can mill this yourself in a small electric coffee mill.)*	60 ml
½ tsp	xanthan gum	3 ml
1 tsp	baking powder	5 ml
½ tsp	salt	3 ml
¼ cup	butter *or* non-dairy alternate	60 ml
1	egg	1
½ cup	brown sugar	125 ml
2 tbsp	milk *or* non-dairy alternate	30 ml
½ tsp	vanilla	3 ml

Instructions:

1. **Measure and mix** the first group of ingredients and set aside.
2. **Cut in butter** or alternate with a pastry cutter, or rub in with your hands until a coarse meal is formed. Add the remaining ingredients and continue mixing until a smooth dough forms.
3. **Using a little corn flour to prevent sticking, roll dough** to about ⅛ inch (3 mm) thickness.

Alternately, you can simply press small balls of the dough flat between two sheets of bakers' parchment on a baking sheet with a second baking sheet. This will not yield the familiar square shape, but it certainly is faster if you just intend to crumble them anyway.

4. **Cut dough** into the familiar square shape and poke holes in the surface with a fork to prevent large air pockets from forming during baking.
5. **Bake at 375ºF (190ºC)** on a baking sheet lined with bakers' parchment until lightly golden. This will take 10 - 12 minutes for average-sized wafers. You may need to double the pan underneath to prevent the bottom from browning before the top is done. The wafers will be very soft when you remove them from the oven.

6. Allow to cool slightly before handling.

Yield: 2 ½ dozen standard sized wafers

Nutritional Information
Calculations based upon the basic recipe excluding
optional ingredients and variations.
Per average sized wafer

energy	70 calories/293 kJ
protein	1 g
fat	2 g
carbohydrate	11 g
sodium	72 mg
potassium	52 mg
calcium	17 mg
iron	trace

Not Oatmeal Coconut Crisps

No oatmeal, just great cookies

½ cup	cornstarch	125 ml
⅓ cup	sweet rice flour	85 ml
3 tbsp	tapioca starch	45 ml
½ tsp	baking powder	3 ml
¼ tsp	salt	2 ml
¼ tsp	xanthan gum	2 ml
½ cup	butter *or* non-dairy alternate	125 ml
1 cup	brown sugar	250 ml
1	egg	1
1 cup	rolled soybeans *or* make them back into oatmeal cookies with gluten-free oats.	250 ml
½ cup	shredded unsweetened coconut	125 ml

Instructions:

1. **Mix together first group of ingredients** and set aside.
2. **Cream together next group** of ingredients before blending in first set of ingredients.
3. **Gently fold in** coconut and rolled soybeans until fully combined.
4. **Spoon out the dough** into approximately 1 inch (2.5 cm) round balls onto bakers' parchment lined baking sheets allowing lots of room for the cookies to spread.

Pro tip: I use a small ice cream type scoop for this because uniform size allows for uniform baking time and texture.

5. **Bake** at 375ºF (190ºC) for 8 - 9 minutes for cookies of this size. The cookies will be very soft when you remove them from the oven. If the cookies have run together while baking separate them with a knife while they are still warm.
6. **Allow to cool** slightly before handling. To enjoy fresh baked cookies anytime, portion out the cookie dough as above, just flatten them slightly and freeze. You can pull a few out of the freezer and bake them whenever you wish and they will be ready in only a few minutes. Allow the dough to thaw at room temperature while your oven heats up.

Yield: about 3 dozen cookies

Nutritional Information

Calculations based upon the basic recipe excluding
optional ingredients and variations.

Per 1 cookie serving

energy	69 calories/289 kJ
protein	1 g
fat	4 g
carbohydrate	8 g
sodium	55 mg
potassium	81 mg
calcium	14 mg
iron	trace

Peanut Butter Cookies

Rich and chewy with lots of peanut flavour!

¾ cup	cornstarch	185 ml
½ cup	sweet rice flour	125 ml
¼ cup	tapioca starch	60 ml
½ tsp	xanthan gum	3 ml
½ tsp	baking soda	3 ml
1 ½ cups	peanut butter (crunchy or smooth) *be sure yours is gluten free*	375 ml
1 cup	sugar	250 ml
1	egg	1
amount varies	water	amount varies

Instructions:

1. **Measure and mix** dry ingredients and set aside.
2. **Cream together next set of ingredients** in a mixer until fluffy. Add reserved dry ingredients and mix into a crumbly dough.
3. **Add water 1 tablespoon (15 ml) at a time,** allowing the water to be fully incorporated before adding any more until dough comes together to form a ball.

Pro-tip: This step is required to account for variations in the texture of different brands of peanut butter.

4. **Form dough into 1 inch (2.5 cm) balls** or use a small ice cream-type scoop. Press dough flat with the tines of a fork for traditional looking cookies.
5. **Bake at 375ºF (190ºC)** for 10 - 12 minutes or until lightly golden. Allow to cool before handling.

Yield: about 3 dozen cookies

Nutritional Information

Calculations based upon the basic recipe excluding
optional ingredients and variations.
Per cookie

energy	106 calories/444 kJ
protein	3 g
fat	6 g
carbohydrate	11 g
sodium	70 mg
potassium	75 mg
calcium	5 mg
iron	trace

Variations:

These cookies bring to mind the fresh baking at my grandma's house when I was a child. This recipe has more peanut butter than the average peanut butter cookie recipe to provide a really robust flavour. None of my testers could believe that the cookies were gluten-free.

I personally don't think the recipe needs anything, but some of my testers like them with chocolate chips or raisins. They also bake up well with other nut butters such as almond or cashew.

For those allergic to nuts, they bake up beautifully when made with the brown pea butter available in many health food stores.

Photo Negative Chip Cookies

A dark chocolate cookie with white chocolate chips.
The large batch size is no mistake; keep some of the dough in
your freezer to always have fresh baked cookies available.

1 cup	butter *or* non-dairy alternate	250 ml
1 ¾ cup	brown sugar	435 ml
2	eggs	2
1 tbsp	vanilla	15 ml
¼ cup	water	60 ml
1 ¼ cup	sweet rice flour	310 ml
⅔ cup	potato starch	165 ml
⅓ cup	tapioca starch	85 ml
⅔ cup	cocoa powder	165 ml
¼ tsp	xanthan gum	1 ml
1 tsp	salt	5 ml
1 ½ tsp	baking soda	8 ml
2 ½ cups	white chocolate chips *(be sure to check that these are gluten-free, and dairy-free if required)*	625 ml

Instructions:

1. **Cream first four ingredients** in mixer.
2. **Fully mix next group of ingredients** before adding to the first group.
3. **Fold in chocolate chips last** and mix until fully combined.
4. **Spoon dough** into approximately 1 inch (2.5 cm) round balls onto a cookie sheet lined with bakers' parchment, allowing room for the cookies to spread.
Pro tip: I use a small 1 inch (2.5 cm) diameter ice cream-type scoop because uniform size results in uniform baking time and texture.
5. **Bake at 375ºF (190ºC)** for 8 - 9 minutes. The cookies will be very soft when you remove them from the oven. Allow to cool slightly before handling.

To enjoy fresh baked cookies anytime, portion out cookie dough as above, flatten slightly and freeze. You can pull a few out of the freezer and bake them in minutes. Allow frozen dough to warm up at room temperature while your oven heats.

Yield: approximately 60, 2 inch (5 cm) cookies

Nutritional Information

Calculations based upon the basic recipe excluding
optional ingredients and variations.
Per 1 cookie serving

energy	118 calories/494 kJ
protein	1 g
fat	6 g
carbohydrate	13 g
sodium	115 mg
potassium	34 mg
calcium	7 mg
iron	trace

Almond Hazelnut Macaroons
A nut lovers dream!

1 ½ cups	ground almonds *Buy them ground or use a food processor to grind your own*	375 ml
1 ½ cups	ground hazelnuts *as above*	375 ml
1 cup + 1 tbsp	icing sugar *be sure yours is gluten-free*	265 ml
2	egg whites	2
½ tsp	salt	3 ml

Instructions:

1. **Mix together nuts** and 1 cup (250 ml) sugar and reserve.
2. **Beat egg whites** with 1 tbsp (15 ml) sugar until stiff but not dry; then fold into nut mixture gently until fully incorporated.
3. **Form into small evenly sized macaroons** with a pastry bag, spoon or scoop.
4. **Bake at 275ºF (130ºC)** on baking sheet lined with bakers' parchment for about 35 - 40 minutes or until lightly browned.
5. **Allow to cool** before removing from the baking tray.

Yield: about 2 dozen macaroons

Nutritional Information
Calculations based upon the basic recipe excluding optional ingredients and variations.
Per macaroon

energy	100 calories/418 kJ
protein	3 g
fat	7 g
carbohydrate	8 g
sodium	50 mg
potassium	93 mg
calcium	32 mg
iron	trace

Coconut Macaroons

Even though many commercially prepared macaroons contain gluten, this old classic recipe never had gluten

⅔ cup	sweetened condensed milk	165 ml
1	egg	1
1 tsp	vanilla	5 ml
1 pinch	salt	1 ml
3 ¾ cups	sweetened, shredded *or* flaked coconut	935 ml

Instructions:

1. **Mix first group of ingredients** together fully; then add coconut and mix to fully combine.

2. **Form into small evenly-sized macaroons** using a pastry bag, spoon or small scoop.

3. **Bake at 325°F (165°C)** on baking sheets lined with bakers' parchment for about 20 - 25 minutes or until lightly browned. Allow to cool before removing from the baking sheet.

Yield: about 2 dozen, 2 inch (5 cm) macaroons

Nutritional Information
Calculations based upon the basic recipe excluding optional ingredients and variations.
Per macaroon

energy	85 calories/356 kJ
protein	1 g
fat	5 g
carbohydrate	10 g
sodium	48 mg
potassium	70 mg
calcium	27 mg
iron	trace

Apple Crisp

This perennial favourite is back on the menu,
with a few variations available to update it

5 cups	chopped / sliced tart crisp apples	1.25 litre
½ cup	brown sugar	125 ml
2 tbsp	water	30 ml
1 tsp	cinnamon	5 ml
½ tsp	either cardamom, cloves *or* nutmeg *(optional)*	3 ml
½ cup	raisins *or* alternates, *see below*	125 ml
½ cup	brown sugar	125 ml
¼ cup	melted butter *or* non-dairy alternate	60 ml
3 tbsp	cornstarch	45 ml
2 tbsp	sweet rice flour	30 ml
1 tbsp	tapioca starch	15 ml
1 cup	rolled soybeans *or* gluten-free rolled oats	250 ml

Instructions:

1. **Peel (or don't)** core and chop or slice the apples into a 2 quart (2 litre) casserole dish.
2. **Add remaining ingredients from the first group** and mix together. Set aside.
3. **Cream butter and sugar** before blending in next group of ingredients.
4. **Fold in rolled soybeans / oats** last to prevent breaking them up too much.
5. **Spread the mixture** evenly over apple mixture and bake at 375ºF (190ºC) for 45 - 50 minutes.

Yield: 8 portions

Nutritional Information
Calculations based upon the basic recipe excluding
optional ingredients and variations.
Per 1 cup (250 ml) serving

energy	261 calories/1092 kJ
protein	4 g
fat	8 g
carbohydrate	44 g
sodium	69 mg
potassium	493 mg
calcium	53 mg
iron	2 mg

Variations:

This classic 'easier than pie' dessert is a quick and easy way to turn some fruit into a great, warm treat. It is even better when topped with some vanilla ice-cream.

- ✓ Try adding one (or a mixture) of the following: raisins, currants, dried cranberries, dried blueberries or nuts. Just play with the varieties and find what you like.
- ✓ Replace the apples with pears for an interesting variation.
- ✓ Replace all, or a portion, of the apples with rhubarb for a tarter version of this classic recipe.
- ✓ Replace 1 cup (250 ml) of the apples with seasonal berries to add some colour.

Beignets

This French cousin of the doughnut is easier to make because it requires none of the tedious forming. If you miss doughnuts, this recipe will fill the need with a lot less work.

¼ cup	cornstarch	60 ml
3 tbsp	brown rice flour	45 ml
1 ½ tbsp	tapioca starch	22 ml
½ tsp	xanthan gum	3 ml
1 tbsp	sugar	15 ml
½ cup	water	125 ml
¼ cup	butter *or* non-dairy alternate	60 ml
¼ tsp	salt	2 ml
2 tsp	vanilla	10 ml
4	eggs	4
	gluten-free powdered sugar to dust *(optional)*	

Instructions:

1. **Mix dry ingredients** fully and set aside.
2. **Bring next group of ingredients to a boil** on the stove, remove from heat and stir in the dry ingredients with a wooden spoon.
3. **Add eggs one by one** completely stirring in each before adding the next. Once all eggs are incorporated the dough is complete.
4. **Drop dough a tablespoon at a time into a deep fryer** heated to 365°F (185°C). Fry as many beignets at once as can comfortably fit with room between them. Fry until golden brown and puffy on both sides (you will need to turn them over).
5. **Drain well** on paper towels and dust with powdered sugar, if desired.

Yield: about 15 beignets

Nutritional Information

Calculations based upon the basic recipe excluding
optional ingredients and variations.
Per 1 beignet serving

energy	122 calories/511 kJ
protein	2 g
fat	10 g
carbohydrate	5 g
sodium	82 mg
potassium	21 mg
calcium	7 mg
iron	Trace

Variations:

Any of the many variations of icings and sprinkles available on doughnuts can
be used with this recipe. Here are a couple of suggestions to get you started.

✓ **Chocolate Beignets**

Add ¼ cup (60 ml) cocoa powder and 2 tsp (10 ml) sugar for a chocolate
version.

✓ **Dutch Spice Beignets**

Add ½ tsp (3 ml) cinnamon, a ¼ tsp (2 ml) nutmeg and ¼ cup (60 ml)
raisins for a classic variation.

Dark Chocolate Mousse

A 3-D dessert; dark, dangerous and delicious!
No gelatine, chemistry sets or fluff here; just the good stuff.

11 oz	high quality semi-sweet dark chocolate *(I use Belgian)*	300 g
2 cups	whipping cream *or* dairy-free whipped topping	500 ml
2	egg whites	2
1 tbsp	sugar	15 ml
1 oz	liqueur of your choice (Cointreau, Kirsch, Kahlua, …) *or* fruit juice *(optional)*	25 ml

Instructions:

1. **Melt chocolate** slowly in a double boiler.
2. **While it is melting, whip egg whites and sugar** to stiff, but not dry peaks. Remove this from your mixer bowl and reserve.
3. **Place whip cream or alternate in mixer bowl and beat** on medium only until firm, but not fully stiff.
4. **Fold egg whites and cream together with the liqueur** gently, but thoroughly.
5. **When chocolate has just melted,** but not become any hotter than required to just finish melting, fold chocolate into the egg white and cream mixture with a rubber spatula. Work quickly to prevent chocolate from setting into lumps in the cream mixture. Keep folding the mixture together until a uniform color and texture is achieved.
6. **Transfer the mousse** to a fairly shallow container with an air tight lid and chill for at least 2 hours. The mousse will keep up to a week in the refrigerator, but it never stays that long at my house.
7. **To serve, many options are open**. *See variations below*

Yield: about 7cups (1.75 litres)

Nutritional Information
Calculations based upon the basic recipe excluding
optional ingredients and variations.
Per ½ cup (125 ml) serving

energy	229 calories/958 kJ
protein	2 g
fat	19 g
carbohydrate	16 g
sodium	23 mg
potassium	114 mg
calcium	29 mg
iron	1 mg

Variations:

This decadently rich dessert can easily seduce you into attacking it in its container with a spoon, but if you can resist it long enough here are a few ideas to dress it up a bit.

- ✓ Shave curls off of the surface with the side of a dinner spoon that has been warmed in hot water. The curls will be formed into shapes sort of like hollowed balls. Garnish with fresh fruit of your choice and a dessert sauce to create an elegant dessert.
- ✓ Place some mousse between two of your favourite gluten-free cookies for an 'over the top' cookie sandwich.
- ✓ Roll some into a gluten-free crepe *(p. 56)* and drizzle with a fruit compote or coulis *(p. 329)*.

White Chocolate Mousse

You can't get much more decadent than this.
The technique is a bit of work, but it really is worth it;
after all, it was the dessert at my own wedding.

12 oz	high quality white chocolate *(I use Belgian)*	350 g
2 cups	whipping cream *or* dairy-free whipped topping	500 ml
4	egg whites	4
1 tbsp	sugar	15 ml
1 oz	liqueur of your choice (Cointreau, Kirsch, …) *or* fruit juice *(optional)*	25 ml

Instructions:

1. **Melt chocolate** slowly in a double boiler.
2. **While it is melting, whip egg whites and sugar** to stiff, but not dry peaks. Remove this from your mixer bowl and reserve.
3. **Place whip cream or alternate in mixer bowl and beat** on medium only until firm, but not fully stiff.
4. **Fold egg whites and cream together with the liqueur** gently, but thoroughly.
5. **When chocolate has just melted,** but not become any hotter than required to just finish melting, fold chocolate into egg white and cream mixture with a rubber spatula. Work quickly to prevent the chocolate from setting into lumps in the cream mixture. Keep folding mixture together until a uniform color and texture is achieved.
6. **Transfer the mousse** to a fairly shallow container with an air tight lid and chill for at least 2 hours. The mousse will keep up to a week in the refrigerator, but it never stays that long at my house.
7. **To serve, many options are open**. *See variations below*

Yield: 7cups (1.75 litres)

Nutritional Information
Calculations based upon the basic recipe excluding
optional ingredients and variations.
Per ½ cup (125 ml) serving

energy	241 calories/1008 kJ
protein	3 g
fat	13 g
carbohydrate	16 g
sodium	32 mg
potassium	110 mg
calcium	28 mg
iron	1 mg

Variations:

This decadently rich dessert can easily seduce you into attacking it in its container with a spoon, but if you can resist it long enough here are a few ideas to dress it up a bit.

- ✓ Shave curls off of the surface with the side of a dinner spoon that has been warmed in hot water. The curls will be formed into shapes sort of like hollowed balls. Garnish with fresh fruit of your choice and a dessert sauce to create an elegant dessert.
- ✓ Place some mousse between two of your favourite gluten-free cookies for an 'over the top' cookie sandwich.
- ✓ Roll some into a gluten-free Crepe *(p. 56)* and drizzle with a fruit compote or coulis *(p. 329)*.
- ✓ Consider adding some toasted chopped nuts to add a little flavour and texture.
- ✓ Serve it on or stuffed inside poached pears or peaches for a truly decadent dessert. For my own wedding the dessert was pears poached in hazelnut liqueur syrup, and stuffed with white chocolate mousse with toasted hazelnuts in it. A drizzle of raspberry coulis and a tuille fan finished it off. Friends and relatives still talk about it 20 years later.

Tiramisu

This Italian classic dessert was high on the list to convert to a gluten-free version. The wait is over; enjoy.

3	eggs separated	3
⅓ cup	sugar	85 ml
6 oz	mascarpone cheese	175 g
about 40 pieces	gluten-free lady fingers (p. 304)	about 40 pieces
¼ cup	chocolate *or* coffee liqueur	60 ml
¾ cup	espresso coffee	185 ml
3 oz (squares)	grated bitter sweet chocolate	85 g
¼ cup	unsweetened cocoa powder	60 ml

Instructions:

1. **Separate eggs** before combining egg yolks and sugar in a medium sized bowl, and beat well.
2. **In a separate bowl, beat egg whites** to stiff peaks.
3. **Combine egg yolk mixture with the mascarpone**, then fold in the egg whites to produce a creamy mixture.
4. **Arrange a tight layer of ladyfingers** in a 8 inch (20 cm) square serving dish.
5. **Mix liqueur and espresso, and drizzle** about half of it over the ladyfingers.
6. **Cover ladyfingers with mascarpone mixture** and grated chocolate, and dust it with about half of the cocoa powder.
7. **Cover the filling with a second layer of ladyfingers** and drizzle with remaining liqueur and espresso.
8. **Cover the dish with plastic wrap and refrigerate** for at least 4 hours before serving. The tiramisu can be made up to 24 hours in advance.
9. **Top with remaining cocoa powder** just before serving.

Yield: about 12 portions

Nutritional Information

Calculations based upon the basic recipe excluding
optional ingredients and variations.

Per portion

energy	222 calories/929 kJ
protein	3 g
fat	12 g
carbohydrate	25 g
sodium	86 mg
potassium	135 mg
calcium	30 mg
iron	1 mg

Variations:

This classic Italian dessert has lots of variations possible, but the egg and
mascarpone cheese mixture is the constant. Many purists would not approve of
the variations below, but they are just missing out on some great flavours. Here
are just a few variations if you want to change the original recipe.

- ✓ Change the liqueur used to alter the flavour. Try nut, orange, sambuca or grappa liqueurs.
- ✓ Replace the ladyfingers with slices of dry cake to dress up your leftovers.
- ✓ Replace the grated chocolate with ground toasted nuts to give your variation a rich nutty taste.
- ✓ Replace the espresso with fruit juice and layer in 1 ½ cups (375 ml) of soft fruits or berries such as peaches, plums, strawberries, or raspberries. With a fruity liqueur or dessert wine in place of the coffee liqueur this makes a fresh summer version. If this seems vaguely familiar it really is just a variation on the classic English trifle.

Dessert Soufflés

This dessert is full of hot air and loved for it.
While some will say that soufflés are out of fashion they
are still a wonderful warm dessert on a cold evening.
They are very unforgiving of waiting to be served, so be sure
to pay due respect by waiting fork in hand.

2 cups	milk *or* non-dairy alternate	500 ml
½ cup	tapioca starch	125 ml
⅓ cup	brown rice flour	85 ml
½ cup	sugar	125 ml
¼ cup	corn starch	60 ml
½ tsp	xanthan gum	3 ml
	see variations below	
4	eggs *(separated)*	4
½ tsp	salt *(if desired)*	3 ml

Instructions:

1. **Combine all the ingredients in the first group cold** in a saucepan; then bring to a simmer for 5 minutes to allow the flavours to develop. Stir frequently to prevent burning.

Alternately, this can be made over a double boiler to prevent burning.

2. **Remove from the heat and allow to cool slightly** while separating the eggs.
3. **Whip the whites and the salt** to firm, but not dry looking peaks.
4. **Stir the yolks into the cooked mixture.**
5. **Fold the beaten egg whites into the cooked mixture** until fully combined.
6. **Transfer the soufflé batter** into greased soufflé cups or a straight-sided 2 quart (2 litre) oven-proof casserole dish.
7. **Place the soufflé into a preheated 375ºF (190ºC) oven** until puffed to about double the size, is nicely browned on top and golden brown on the exposed sides. This will be about 45 - 50 minutes for the 2 quart (2 litre) size, less for smaller sizes.

Serve immediately for best results because the soufflé will begin to fall within a few minutes. It will still taste great, but the presentation will suffer.

Yield: 6 portions

Nutritional Information
Calculations based upon the basic recipe excluding
optional ingredients and variations.
Per 1 cup (250 ml) serving

energy	228 calories/1079 kJ
protein	7 g
fat	4 g
carbohydrate	41 g
sodium	257 mg
potassium	188 mg
calcium	117 mg
iron	1 mg

Variations:

I originally attempted this dish as a challenge from a friend who thought it would be impossible to make gluten-free. Fortunately, to the surprise of both of us, it worked very well. Soufflés aren't nearly as finicky as they are made out to be, and they make a great dessert.

✓ **Chocolate Soufflé**
Add ¼ cup (60 ml) cocoa powder to the mix above for a dark chocolate treat. Serve with lightly whipped cream and a few berries on the side to really dress it up.

✓ **Nut Soufflé**
Add ¼ cup (60 ml) finely chopped nuts such as hazelnuts to the mix for a nutty flavour. Serve with lightly whipped cream and a cranberry, or apricot compote for a wonderful European taste sensation.

✓ **Orange Liqueur Soufflé**
Early in my career I made, to order, as many as 50 individual dessert soufflés each night, and this was by far the most popular variation. Add the zest of an orange to the mix for a great citrus flavour. Serve with lightly whipped cream laced with your favourite orange liqueur. When the cream melts into the hot soufflé the aroma won't be the only thing that is intoxicating.

Butterscotch Sauce

Whether you drizzle this over ice-cream, or use it to decorate the plate for more elegant dessert it is sure to become a sweet favourite.

½ cup	light corn syrup	125 ml
½ cup	brown sugar	125 ml
2 tbsp	butter *or* non-dairy alternate	30 ml
1 pinch	salt	1 ml
⅓ cup	evaporated milk, heavy cream, *or* non-dairy alternate	85 ml

Instructions:

1. **Combine first group of ingredients** and boil to reduce to heavy syrup.
2. **Cool** fully before continuing.
3. **Stir in** the evaporated milk, cream, or alternate.

Serve hot or cold.

Yield: about 1 ¼ cup (310 ml)

Nutritional Information

Calculations based upon the basic recipe excluding optional ingredients and variations.

Per 1 tbsp (15 ml) serving

energy	50 calories/209 kJ
protein	trace
fat	1 g
carbohydrate	10 g
sodium	33 mg
potassium	25 mg
calcium	14 mg
iron	trace

Fruit Coulis

This fruit sauce is the quintessential boost needed to dress up desserts with color and flavour. Fruits that are becoming over-ripe, but not yet spoiled are especially good for this.

2 cups	fruit with inedible portions removed (stones, pits, hulls, *or* stems) *see variations below*	500 ml
1 - 2 tsp	fresh squeezed lemon juice	5 - 10 ml
2 - 3 tbsp	sugar	30 - 45 ml
1 tsp	tapioca starch	5 ml

Instructions:

1. **Prepare the fruit** you have chosen by removing any inedible portions. Coarsely chop larger fruits like peaches.
2. **Mix in remaining ingredients** taking care to stir out the starch lumps. You will need to vary the amount of lemon juice and sugar depending on the sweetness or tartness of the fruit you have chosen.
3. **Bring to a boil** and immediately remove from heat.
4. **Puree the mixture** in a blender and strain if it contains seeds or skin fragments which will detract from the finished sauce.
5. **Allow to cool.**

This sauce will keep about a week in the refrigerator or can be frozen.
Yield: about 1 ¼ cups (310 ml)

Nutritional Information
Due to the variations inherent in this recipe,
nutritional calculations are not possible.

Variations:

Try any berry or soft tree fruit with vibrant colours. **Strawberries, raspberries, blueberries, blackberries** and **kiwi** all give great results. **Peaches, apricots,** and yellow or purple fleshed **plums** are also great fruits for this recipe. Really, any combination of fruits can be tried. This recipe is a great way of turning fresh or frozen fruits into an elegant garnish for desserts, or just as a topping on a simple dish of ice-cream. If you place the coulis into a squeeze bottle with a small opening you can use it to paint designs on dessert plates just like pastry chefs do.

Crème Anglaise
The classic vanilla crème filling used in so many pastries

6	egg yolks	6
½ cup	sugar	125 ml
1 tbsp	vanilla	15 ml
2 tbsp	rum *or* brandy *(optional)*	30 ml
3 tbsp	butter *or* non-dairy alternate	45 ml
1 ½ cups	milk *or* non-dairy alternate	375 ml

Instructions:

1. **Mix together** the first group of ingredients with a whisk and set aside.
2. **Heat milk and butter** in a double boiler to a simmer and whisk ½ cup (125 ml) of the hot milk mixture into reserved ingredients. This will prevent the eggs from cooking into lumps before they can be mixed in.
3. **Mix the two mixtures together** and return it all to the double boiler.
4. **Whisk continually over the heat** until mixture thickens.
5. **Remove from heat** and place in an air tight container with a greased plastic wrap cover directly on the surface of the sauce. Take care to fully cover the surface of the sauce. This will prevent a skin from forming on the surface while it is cooling which will make lumps in the finished sauce / filling. Once the sauce / filling has cooled this plastic wrap can be removed.
6. **Allow to cool** before using. Use as prepared as a filling for cakes and pastries, or whisk in some milk to thin it enough to use it as a sauce.

Yield: 2 cups (500 ml)

Nutritional Information

Calculations based upon the basic recipe excluding
optional ingredients and variations.

Per 2 tbsp (30 ml) serving

energy	82 calories/343 kJ
protein	2 g
fat	5 g
carbohydrate	8 g
sodium	36mg
potassium	41mg
calcium	37 mg
iron	trace

Variations:

Crème Anglaise, a staple of pastry chefs, shows up in all sorts of creations such as éclairs, tarts and as a sauce for berries. Here are just a few ideas to make Crème Anglaise a useful part of your repertoire.

✓ **Tarts**

Paint melted chocolate into the inside of gluten-free tart shells (this prevents the pastry from becoming soggy) and fill with Crème Anglaise. Top with fresh fruit for a tasty pastry.

✓ **Éclairs**

Fill Choux Paste (p. 274) pastries with Crème Anglaise to recreate the classic éclair.

✓ **Vanilla Sauce garnish**

Thin out the Crème Anglaise with some milk or non-dairy alternate to make it a desirable consistency, and use it as a sauce over or under cake, fruit or whatever you like.

✓ **Berry Broil**

Fold ½ as much whipped cream or non-dairy alternate as Crème Anglaise together to make a mousse-like sauce. Sparsely cover fresh berries, such as strawberries or raspberries, with the sauce in single portion oven-proof dishes. Place under a very hot broiler just until the top starts to brown slightly. Serve warm. The heat seems to intensify the flavour of the berries and the creamy sauce makes it a decadent dessert.

✓ **Dessert crepes**

Fill some gluten-free crepes (p. 56) with your favourite fruit and Crème Anglaise. Top with some fruit coulis (p. 329) for a very elegant dessert.

Dulce de Leche

This South American milk based caramel sauce has no rival for its rich decadent flavour. The very long cooking time is worth the effort, and with only one ingredient it couldn't be simpler. This sauce began as a way to preserve excess milk in areas where refrigeration was scarce and sugar was plentiful. The sweetened condensed milk available in North American supermarkets has the right balance of sugar and milk; it just needs to be slowly caramelized to bring out the flavour.

---

canned sweetened condensed milk
***(Pro tip:** I make several cans at once because the finished sauce will keep indefinitely in the refrigerator.)*

Instructions:

1. **Open a small hole in the can(s)** with a can opener or by just lifting the pull-tab until the seal is broken.

Note: Do **not** attempt to heat the can without breaking the seal first, because doing so could cause the can to explode. Do **not** open the can(s) further at this point.

2. **Place the can(s) in a pot or slow cooker** and fill with water up to approximately ½ inch (1 cm) under the rim of the can(s).

3. **Bring the water to a low simmer** and keep simmering for 4- 5 hours (No, this is **not** a typo!) If you like your caramel lighter in colour, use the shorter time. Be sure to periodically top-up the water to prevent boiling dry.

Pro tip: I like to use a slow cooker for this with the lid on because it requires less attention.

4. **Remove the Dulce de Leche from the can(s)** when the cooking time is complete.

5. **Allow to cool** fully before continuing because it only takes on its finished consistency when cool.

6. **Whirl the cooled mixture in a blender** for a smooth texture. If you intend to use the Dulce de Leche as a sauce you may wish to thin it slightly with water. For use as a spread or filling use as is.

Yield: as much as you choose to make.

Nutritional Information
Calculations based upon the basic recipe excluding
optional ingredients and variations.
Per 1 tbsp (15 ml) serving

energy	62 calories/260 kJ
protein	2g
fat	2g
carbohydrate	11 g
sodium	25 mg
potassium	72 mg
calcium	55 mg
iron	trace

Uses:
- ✓ Use as a sauce to dribble over ice-cream, cakes or other desserts.
- ✓ To add an elegant touch to plated deserts, put it in a squeeze bottle with a small tip and use it to paint designs on the plate.
- ✓ Use as a filling for profiteroles, cakes or pastries.
- ✓ Enjoy it Brazilian style as a spread on toast for breakfast.

Sabayon Sauce

This quick egg based dessert sauce has many variations and spellings depending on the European country claiming it as their own, but all of them are delicious. The technique is the same everywhere, but the liquid used and amount of sugar varies greatly offering a huge range of flavour possibilities

2	egg yolks	2
¼ cup +/-	sugar	60 ml +/-
½ cup	liquid	125 ml
	(Marsala, Cointreau, Kirsch, white wine, red wine, ice wine, fruit juice, ...)	

Instructions:

1. **Mix all ingredients together** in a round bottomed stainless steel bowl with a balloon type wire whisk.

2. **Place the bowl over a pot of boiling water** so that the steam heats the bowl, but the bowl does not touch the water. If the diameter of the bowl is larger than the pot of water this is easier to accomplish. It also leaves the rim of the bowl free to handle it.

3. **Beat it vigorously** in a pattern where the whisk sweeps across the surface of the bowl which contacts with the sabayon mixture. Whisk back and forth to contact the entire surface of the bowl almost like you are attempting to color in a piece of paper with a crayon. This prevents any spots on the bottom of the bowl from cooking the eggs before they are fully mixed.

4. **Continue this technique until the mixture becomes a frothy foam** with no more liquid left at the bottom. This will take only a minute or so to accomplish.

Yield: about 1 ½ cups (375 ml)

Nutritional Information
Due to the variations inherent in this recipe,
nutritional calculations are not possible.

Variations:

Sabayon can be made as a sauce for cake, fruit, berries, or made with slightly less liquid and enjoyed as a warm mousse dessert. With this basic recipe you can make a tasty dessert sauce in just a few minutes.

- ✓ **Marsala Zabaglione**
  Use Marsala wine for the classic Italian version. It is served warm as a mousse dessert. Add a few Ladyfingers *(p. 304)* for that authentic touch.
- ✓ **Citrus Sabayon**
  Use orange lemon or lime juice as the liquid for a lively citrus flavour.
- ✓ **Dessert Wine Sabayon**
  Use port, ice-wine or sherry as the liquid for a sauce which can turn any fresh fruit or basic cake into a special dessert.

Index

A

Acknowledgements 6
Alfredo Sauce 213
Almond Bread 128
Almond Crescent Cookies 244
Almond Hazelnut Macaroons 314
Almond Potato Cake 268
Amaranth 36
Angel Food Cake 270
Apple Cinnamon Pancakes 53
Apple Crisp 316
Apple Crisp Muffins 80
Arrowroot 37
Asian Egg Drop Soup 205
Asian Sweet and Sour Sauce 210
Avgolemono Soup 188
Aztec Sugared Almonds 247

B

Bacon Corn Muffins 89
Bagels 102
Baked Potato Melts 76
Baking Gluten-Free 29
Banana Muffins 82
Banana Pancakes 53
Basic Muffin Batter 84
Batters and Coatings 230
  Batters, Corn 238
  Batters, Fish n' Chip 232
  Batters, Parmesan Egg 234
  Batters, Superlight Tempura 233
Bean and Bacon Soup 207
Bean Flour 37
Béchamel Sauce 218
Beef Stew 220
Beef Stock 172
Beignets 318
Berries and Cream Biscuits 61
Berry Muffins 85
Berry Pancakes 53
Berry Scones 63
Beurre Blanc Sauce 216
Biscuit Breakfast Sandwiches 61
Biscuit Cases 61
Biscuit French Toast 61
Biscuit Topped Stew 61
Biscuits with Berries and Cream 61
Biscuits, Buttermilk 60
Black Forest Pavlova 281
Bread Machines 31
Bread Stuffing 264
Breads and Flat-Breads 100
  Breads, Almond 128
  Breads, Bagels 102
  Breads, B. Rice Sorghum 132
  Breads, Brown Stovetop Bread 120
  Breads, Canapé Bases 117
  Breads, Cheese Crust Pizza 113
  Breads, Cheese Rolls 107
  Breads, Cinnamon Raisin Rolls 106
  Breads, Corn Tortillas 108
  Breads, Cranberry Ginger Rolls 107
  Breads, Dairy Free Sorghum/Corn 134
  Breads, Dessert Pizza 113
  Breads, Dried Fruit Naan 111
  Breads, Egg/Dairy Free French 122
  Breads, French 124
  Breads, Herb Crust Pizza 113
  Breads, Honey Brown 130
  Breads, Hot Cross Buns 254
  Breads, JAW Stovetop bread 118
  Breads, Low Allergen Stovetop 118
  Breads, Mock Multigrain Rye 126
  Breads, Multigrain Mock Rye 126
  Breads, Naan 111
  Breads, Nutty Rolls 107
  Breads, Oversized Burger 117
  Breads, Panini Sandwiches 117
  Breads, Pizza Dough 112
  Breads, Savoury Naan 111
  Breads, Stollen 258
  Breads, Stuffing 264
  Breads, Yeast-Free Stovetop 116
Breakfast and Brunch 50
Breakfast Sandwich, English Muffin 65
Breakfast Sandwiches, Biscuit 61

336

Breakfast Sandwiches, Pancake 53
Brown Poultry Stock 174
Brown Rice Flour 40
Brown Rice Sorghum Bread 132
Brown Sauce, Basic 220
Brown Wine and Herb Sauce 220
Brown Yeast Free Stovetop Bread 120
Brownies, Chocolate 290
Buckwheat 38
Buckwheat Crepes 58
Buckwheat Kasha 138
Burger, Oversized 117
Buttermilk Biscuits 60
Buttermilk Pancakes 52
Butterscotch Sauce 328

C

Cajun Blackened Crust 239
Cajun Sugared Pecans 247
Cake, Almond Potato 268
Cake
  Cake, Angel Food 270
  Cake, Cheesecake, Crustless 276
  Cake, Chocolate 272
  Cake, Chocolate Brownies 290
  Cake, Holiday Fruitcake 250
  Cake, Pound 282
  Cake, Sour Cream Chocolate 284
  Cake, White Genoise Sponge 288
Calzones 104
Can't Eat It-Says Who? 11
Canapé Bases 117
Carrot Raisin Muffins 86
Cases, Biscuit 61
Chana Flour 37
Cheating 12
Cheese Crackers 115
Cheese Crust Pizza 113
Cheese Rolls 107
Cheese Sauce 219
Cheese Soufflé 68
Cheesecake, Crustless 276
Chick Pea Flour 37

Chicken Stock 176
Chinese Style Ginger Fried Coating 240
Chocolate Brownies 290
Chocolate Cake 272
Chocolate Chip Cookies 292
Chocolate Chip Muffins 85
Chocolate Crepes 57
Chocolate Meringue Shells 281
Chocolate Mousse 320
Chocolate Shortbread 249
Chocolate Sugared Almonds 247
Chocolate Wafer Cookies 294
Chocolate, White mousse 322
Choux Paste 274
Cider Reduction Sauce 227
Cinnamon Raisin Rolls 106
Cinnamon Shortbread 249
Cinnamon Sugared Almonds 246
Citrus Butter Sauce 217
Coatings
  Coatings, Cajun Blackened Crust 239
  Coatings, Chinese Style Ginger 240
  Coatings, Coconut 237
  Coatings, Cornmeal 237
  Coatings, Crisp Flour 237
  Coatings, Flake Cereal 237
  Coatings, Nut Meal 237
  Coatings, Three Part 236
Coconut Coating 237
Coconut Curry, Easy 222
Coconut Macaroons 315
Conversions, Recipe 47
Cookies
  Cookies, Almond Crescent 244
  Cookies, Almond Hazelnut Mac. 314
  Cookies, Chocolate Chip 292
  Cookies, Chocolate Shortbread 249
  Cookies, Chocolate Wafer 294
  Cookies, Cinnamon Shortbread 249
  Cookies, Coconut Macaroons 315
  Cookies, Ginger Snaps 300
  Cookies, Gingerbread 252
  Cookies, Hermits 302
  Cookies, Lady Fingers 304
  Cookies, Not Oatmeal Coconut 308
  Cookies, Not-graham Wafers 306

Cookies, Nut Shortbread 249
Cookies, Peanut Butter 310
Cookies, Photo Negative Chip 312
Cookies, Shortbread 248
Cookies, Sugar 260
Copyright 2
Corn Batter 238
Corn Chowder 195
Corn Flour 38
Corn Muffins 88
Corn Tortillas 108
Cornmeal 38
Cornmeal Coating 237
Cornstarch 38
Couscous, Rice 162
Crackers, Cheese 115
Crackers, Garlic and Herb 115
Crackers, Hazelnut 115
Crackers, Multigrain 115
Crackers, Sesame 115
Crackers, Soda 114
Cranberry Butter Sauce 217
Cranberry Ginger Rolls 107
Cream Puffs 275
Cream Sauce, Basic 212
Cream Soup, Basic 190
Crème Anglaise Sauce 330
Crepe Crisps 57
Crepes 56
Crepes Buckwheat 58
Crepes, Chocolate 57
Crepes, Herb or Spice 57
Crepes, Layered Dessert 57
Crepes, Sandwich Wrap 57
Crepes, Stuffed 57
Crisp Flour Coating 237
Crisps, Crepe 57
Curried Squash Soup 203

D

Dairy Free Sorghum and Corn Bread 134
Dark Chocolate Mousse 320
Date Squares 296
Dealing With the Urge to Cheat 12
Demi Glace Sauce 220

Dessert Pizza 113
Dessert Soufflés 326
Dijon Sauce 219
Directions 33
Double Corn Muffins 89
Doughnuts, Beignets 318
Dried Fruit Naan 111
Dried Fruit Scones 63
Drop Noodles 166
Dulce de Leche Sauce 332

E

Easy Hot Lunches 76
Eating Out Gluten-Free 19
Éclairs 275
Egg Noodle Dough 150
Egg/Dairy Free French Bread 122
Egg-Free Pancakes 54
Egg-Free Pasta 153
Eggs Benedict 65
Empanadas 104
English Muffin Breakfast Sandwich 65
English Muffin Mini Pizza 65
English Muffins 64

F

Finding Hidden Gluten 14
Fish n' Chip Batter 232
Fish Stock 178
Flake Cereal Coating 237
Flaky Pie Pastry 278
Florentine Sauce 219
Flour
  Flour Soy Flour 37
  Flour, Bean 37
  Flour, Brown Rice 40
  Flour, Buckwheat 38
  Flour, Chana 37
  Flour, Chick Pea 37
  Flour, Corn 38
  Flour, Garbanzo 37
  Flour, Garfava 37
  Flour, Glutinous Rice 41
  Flour, Nut 39

Flour, Oat 39
Flour, Potato 40
Flour, Quinoa 40
Flour, Rice 40
Flour, Romano/Cranberry Bean 37
Flour, Sorghum 41
Flour, Sweet Rice41
Flour, Teff 41
Flour, White Rice 40
Following the Directions 33
French Bread 124
French Onion Soup 198
French toast, Biscuit 61
Fruit Coulis Sauce 329
Fruitcake 250
Fruity Hollandaise Sauce 225

G

Garbanzo Flour 37
Garfava Flour 37
Garlic and Herb Crackers 115
Gf-Ola 66
Ginger Fried Coating, Chinese Style 240
Ginger Snaps 300
Gingerbread 252
Gluten-Free Flour Mix 35
Gluten-Free in a Wheaty Home 15
Gluten-Free Label 17
Gluten-Free Pantry 36
Glutinous Rice Flour 41
Gnocchi 156
Graham, Not Wafers 306
Grains,
  Grains, Basic Pilaf 170
  Grains, Buckwheat Kasha 138
  Grains, Millet 140
  Grains, Pastas and Side Dishes 136
  Grains, Polenta 158
  Grains, Quinoa 142
  Grains, Rice Couscous 168
  Grains, Risotto 144
  Grains, Teff Basic 146
  Grains, Wild Rice 148
Granola 66
Greek Egg Drop Soup 205

Guar Gum 38
Gum, Guar 38
Gum, Xanthan 41

H

Ham Stock 180
Hazelnut Crackers 115
Hazelnut Spaetzle 167
Helpful Hints 42
Herb Cream Sauce 213
Herb Crust Pizza 113
Herb Gnocchi 157
Herb Sauce 219
Herb Spaetzle 167
Herb Velouté Sauce 215
Herbed Corn Muffins 89
Herbed Hollandaise Sauce 225
Hermits Cookies 302
Hidden Gluten 14
Hints, Helpful 42
Holidays 242
  Holidays, Almond Cres. Cookies 244
  Holidays, Aztec Sugared Almonds 247
  Holidays, Bread Stuffing 264
  Holidays, Cajun Sugared Pecans 247
  Holidays, Choc. Sugared Almonds 247
  Holidays, Chocolate Shortbread 249
  Holidays, Cinnamon Almonds 246
  Holidays, Cinnamon Shortbread 249
  Holidays, Fruitcake 250
  Holidays, Gingerbread 252
  Holidays, Hot Cross Buns 254
  Holidays, Maple Sugared Walnuts 247
  Holidays, Mincemeat 256
  Holidays, Nut Shortbread 249
  Holidays, Stollen Bread 258
  Holidays, Sugar Cookies 260
  Holidays, Tourtiere 262
  Holidays, Van. Sugared Hazelnuts 247
  Holidays, Whipped Shortbread 248
Hollandaise Sauce, Lazy 224
Honey Brown Bread 130
Hot Cross Buns 254
Hot Pepper Corn Muffins 89

I

Information, Nutritional 49
Introduction 8

J

Japanese Rice 154
Java Date Muffins 90
JAW Stovetop Bread 118

K

Kasha, Buckwheat 138

L

Labelling 17
Lady Fingers 304
Latkes, Potato 160
Layered Crepe Desserts 57
Lazy Gnocchi 156
Leafy Vegetable Cream Soup 191
Leafy Vegetable Cream Soup 197
Leek and Potato Soup 206
Legume Cream Soup 191
Lemon Poppy Seed Muffins 85
Low Allergen Stovetop Bread 118
Lower Fat Alfredo Sauce 219
Lower Fat Mushroom Sauce 219
Lower Fat Seafood Sauce 219
Lunch Options 70

M

Maple Sugared Walnuts 247
Marmalade Muffins 85
Matrimonial Squares 296
Mexican Egg Drop Soup 205
Millet 39
Millet, Basic 140
Mincemeat 256
Mixed Peel Scones 63
Mock Multigrain Rye 126

Mousse, Dark Chocolate 320
Mousse, White Chocolate 322
Muffins 78
Muffins, Apple Crisp 80
Muffins, Bacon Corn 89
Muffins, Banana 82
Muffins, Basic Batter 84
Muffins, Berry 85
Muffins, Carrot Raisin 86
Muffins, Chocolate Chip 85
Muffins, Corn 88
Muffins, Double Corn 89
Muffins, English 64
Muffins, Herbed Corn 89
Muffins, Hot Pepper Corn 89
Muffins, Java Date 90
Muffins, Lemon Poppy Seed 85
Muffins, Marmalade 85
Muffins, Pumpkin Spice 92
Muffins, Raisin Bran 94
Muffins, Spice 85
Muffins, Sweet Pepper Corn 89
Muffins, Veggie 85
Muffins, Zucchini Coconut 96
Muffins, Zucchini Raisin 98
Mulligatawny Soup 200
Multigrain Crackers 115
Multigrain Mock Rye Bread 126
Mushroom Cream Sauce 213
Mushroom Cream Soup 191
Mushroom Velouté Sauce 215
My Journey 9

N

Naan Bread 110
No-Bake Disappearing Squares 298
Not Oatmeal Coconut Crisp Cookies 308
Not-Graham Wafers 306
Nut Flour 39
Nut Meal 39
Nut Meal Coating 237
Nut Meringue Shells 281
Nut Shortbread 249
Nutritional Information 49
Nutty Rolls 107

O

Oat Flour 39
Oats 39
Omelettes 76
Orange Hollandaise Sauce 225
Oversized Burger 117

P

Pancake Breakfast Sandwiches 53
Pancakes, Apple Cinnamon 53
Pancakes, Banana 53
Pancakes, Berry 53
Pancakes, Buttermilk 52
Pancakes, Crepes 56
Pancakes, Egg-Free 54
Panini Sandwiches 117
Pantry, Gluten-Free 36
Paprika Spaetzle 167
Parmesan Egg Batter 234
Pasta
  Pasta Cream Soup 191
  Pasta, Drop Noodles 166
  Pasta, Egg Noodle Dough 150
  Pasta, Egg-Free 153
  Pasta, Gnocchi 156
  Pasta, Hazelnut Spaetzle 167
  Pasta, Herb Gnocchi 157
  Pasta, Herb Spaetzle 167
  Pasta, Paprika Spaetzle 167
  Pasta, Perogies 151
  Pasta, Polenta 158
  Pasta, Poppy Seed Spaetzle 167
  Pasta, Ravioli 151
  Pasta, Rice Couscous 168
  Pasta, Soba Noodles 164
  Pasta, Spaetzle 166
  Pasta, Spinach Gnocchi 157
  Pasta, Tomato Gnocchi 157
  Pasta, Tortellini 158
Pastry
  Pastry, Black Forest Pavlova 281
  Pastry, Chocolate Meringue Shells 281
  Pastry, Choux Paste 274

Pastry, Cream Puffs 275
Pastry, Éclairs 275
Pastry, Flaky Pie 278
Pastry, Nut Meringue Shells 281
Pastry, Pavlova 281
Pastry, Profiteroles 275
  Pastry, Sweet Crumb Pie Crust 286
Peanut Butter Cookies 310
Perogies 151
Photo Negative Chip Cookies 312
Pilaf, Basic 170
Pizza Dough 112
Pizza Pockets 104
Pizza, Mini English Muffin 65
Polenta 158
Poppy Seed Spaetzle 167
Pot Pies 215
Pot Pies 220
Potato Flour 40
Potato Latkes 160
Potato Starch 39
Poultry Cream Soup 191
Pound Cake 282
Profiteroles 275
Pumpkin Spice Muffins 92

Q

Quesadillas 76
Quinoa 40
Quinoa Flour 40
Quinoa, Basic 142

R

Raisin Bran Muffins 94
Ravioli 152
Recipe Conversions 47
Red Chowder Soup 192
Red Clam Chowder 193
Red Poultry Chowder 193
Red Seafood Chowder 193
Red Spicy Sausage Chowder 193
Red Wine Butter Sauce 217
Reduction Sauces 226
Restaurant Card 23

Rice Couscous 168
Rice Cream Soup 191
Rice Flour 40
Rice Paper Rolls 74
Rice, Japanese 154
Risotto, Basic 144
Roasted Pepper Chowder 193
Roasted Squash Soup 202
Roasted Vegetable Stock 182
Roasted Yam Soup 203
Romano/Cranberry Bean Flour 37
Root Vegetable Cream Soup 191

S

Sabayon Sauce 334
Sandwich Wraps 57
  Sauce, Basic Brown 220
  Sauce, Basic Velouté 214
  Sauce, Béchamel 218
  Sauce, Beurre Blanc 216
  Sauce, Citrus Butter 217
  Sauce, Cranberry Butter 217
  Sauce, Red Wine Butter 217
  Sauce, Wine Butter 216
Sauces
  Sauces 208
  Sauces, Alfredo 213
  Sauces, Asian Sweet and Sour 210
  Sauces, Basic Cream 212
  Sauces, Basic Veloute 214
  Sauces, Beef Stew 220
  Sauces, Brown Wine, Herb Sauce 220
  Sauces, Butterscotch Sauce 328
  Sauces, Cheese 219
  Sauces, Cider Reduction 227
  Sauces, Coconut Curry 222
  Sauces, Crème Anglaise 330
  Sauces, Demi Glace Sauce 220
  Sauces, Dijon 219
  Sauces, Dulce de Leche 332
  Sauces, Florentine 219
  Sauces, Fruit Coulis Sauce 329
  Sauces, Fruity Hollandaise 225
  Sauces, Herb 219
  Sauces, Herb Cream 213

Sauces, Herb Velouté Sauce 215
Sauces, Herbed Hollandaise 225
Sauces, Lazy Hollandaise 224
Sauces, Lower Fat Alfredo 219
Sauces, Lower Fat Mushroom 219
Sauces, Lower Fat Seafood 219
Sauces, Mushroom Cream 213
Sauces, Mushroom Velouté sauce 215
Sauces, Orange Hollandaise 225
Sauces, Pot Pies 220
Sauces, Reduction 226
Sauces, Sabayon 334
Sauces, Seafood Cream 213
Sauces, Seafood Velouté sauce 215
Sauces, Stir Fry 228
Sauces, Stock Reduction 227
Sauces, Vinegar Reduction 227
Sauces, White Wine 219
Sauces, Wine Reduction 227
Savoury Naan 111
Savoury Squash Soup 203
Scones 62
Scones, Berry 63
Scones, Dried Fruit 63
Scones, Mixed Peel 63
Seafood Cream Sauce 213
Seafood Cream Soup 191
Seafood Velouté Sauce 215
Sesame Crackers 115
Shortbread Cookies 248
Soba Noodles 164
Soda Crackers 114
Sorghum Flour 41
Soufflé, Cheese 68
Soufflés, Dessert 326
Soups 186
  Soups and Stocks 171
  Soups, Asian Egg Drop 205
  Soups, Avgolemono 188
  Soups, Basic Cream 190
  Soups, Bean and Bacon 207
  Soups, Corn Chowder 195
  Soups, Curried Squash 203
  Soups, French Onion 198
  Soups, Greek Egg Drop 205
  Soups, Leafy Veg. Cream Soup 191

Soups, Leek and Potato 206
Soups, Legume Cream 191
Soups, Mexican Egg Drop 205
Soups, Mulligatawny 200
Soups, Mushroom Cream 191
Soups, Pasta Cream 191
Soups, Poultry Chowder 193
Soups, Poultry Cream 191
Soups, Red Chowder 192
Soups, Red Clam Chowder 193
Soups, Red Seafood Chowder 193
Soups, Rice Cream 191
Soups, Roasted Pepper Chowder 193
Soups, Roasted Squash 202
Soups, Roasted Yam 203
Soups, Root Vegetable Cream 191
Soups, Savoury Squash 203
Soups, Seafood Cream 191
Soups, South-Western Squash 203
Soups, Spicy Sausage Chowder 193
Soups, Stalk Vegetable Cream Soup 191
Soups, Stracciatella 204
Soups, Tomato Leafy Vegetable Cr. 197
Soups, Tomato Legume Cream 197
Soups, Tomato Mushroom Cream 197
Soups, Tomato Pasta Cream 197
Soups, Tomato Poultry Cream 197
Soups, Tomato Rice Cream 197
Soups, Tomato Root Vegetable Cr. 197
Soups, Tomato Seafood Cream 197
Soups, Tomato Stalk Vegetable Cr. 197
Soups, Vichyssoise 206
Soups, White Chowder 194
Soups, White Clam Chowder 195
Soups, White Poultry Chowder 195
Soups, White Sausage Chowder 195
Soups, White Seafood Chowder 195
Sour Cream Chocolate Cake 284
South-Western Squash Soup 203
Soy Flour 37
Spaetzle 166
Spice Muffins 85
Spinach Gnocchi 157
Stalk Vegetable Cream Soup 191
Starch, Corn 38
Starch, Potato 39

Stew, Biscuit Topped 61
Stir Fry Sauce 228
Stock Reduction Sauce 227
Stocks and Soups 171
Stocks 171
Stocks, Beef 172
Stocks, Brown Poultry 174
Stocks, Chicken 176
Stocks, Fish 178
Stocks, Ham 180
Stocks, Roasted Vegetable 182
Stocks, Vegetable 184
Stollen Bread 258
Stracciatella Soup 204
Stuffed Crepes 57
Sugar Cookies 260
Superlight Tempura Batter 233
Sushi 72
Sweet and Sour Sauce 210
Sweet Crumb Pie Crust 286
Sweet Pepper Corn Muffins 89
Sweet Rice Flour 41
Sweets 266

T

Table of Contents 4
Teff 41
Teff Basic 146
Teff Flour 41
Three Part Coatings 236
Tiramisu 324
Tomato Cream Soup 196
Tomato Gnocchi 157
Tomato Legume Cream Soup 197
Tomato Mushroom Cream Soup 197
Tomato Pasta Cream Soup 197
Tomato Poultry Cream Soup 197
Tomato Rice Cream Soup 197
Tomato Root Vegetable Cream Soup 197
Tomato Seafood Cream Soup 197
Tomato Stalk Vegetable Cream Soup 197
Tortellini 152
Tortilla Pie 76
Tortillas, Corn 108
Tourtiere 262

Travelling Gluten-Free 25

V

Vanilla Sugared Hazelnuts 247
Vegetable Sock 184
Veggie Muffins 85
Veloute Sauce, Basic 214
Vichyssoise 206
Vinegar Reduction Sauce 227

W

Wafer Cookies, Chocolate 294
Waffles 53
Where is the Gluten-Free Flour Mix 35
Whipped Shortbread 248
White Chocolate Mousse 322
White Chowder 194
White Clam Chowder 195
White Genoise Sponge Cake 288
White Poultry Chowder 195
White Rice Flour 40
White Seafood Chowder 195
White Spicy Sausage Chowder 195
White Wine Sauce 219
Why Gluten-Free 10
Wild Rice 148
Wine Butter Sauce 216
Wine Reduction Sauce 227
Working With Bread Machines 31

X

Xanthan Gum 41

Y

Yeast Free Brown Stovetop Bread 120
Yeast-Free Stovetop Bread 116
Yorkshire Pudding 168
You Are Invited 28

Z

Zucchini Coconut Muffins 96
Zucchini Raisin Muffins 98